The Mockingbird Next Door

The Mockingbird Next Door

LIFE WITH HARPER LEE

MARJA MILLS

THE PENGUIN PRESS

New York

2014

THE PENGUIN PRESS
Published by the Penguin Group
Penguin Group (USA) LLC
375 Hudson Street
New York, New York 10014

USA · Canada · UK · Ireland · Australia
New Zealand · India · South Africa · China

penguin.com
A Penguin Random House Company

First published by The Penguin Press, a member of Penguin Group (USA) LLC, 2014

Copyright © 2014 by Marja Mills

Photograph Credits
Insert pages 1 (top), 3 (bottom): Carla Mills (Collection of Marja Mills)
1 (bottom), 2 (bottom, top): Chicago Tribune, September 13th, 2002. © 2002 Chicago Tribune.
3 (top), 5 (bottom): Collection of Thomas Lane Butts 4 (top, bottom), 5 (top): Marja
Mills 6 (top), 7: Donald Uhrbrock / The Life Images Collection / Getty Images
6 (bottom): Courtesy of Preston B. Barnett 8 (top): © Bettmann/Corbis
8 (bottom): Courtesy of Alice Finch Lee on behalf of the Estate of A. C. Lee

LIBRARY OF CONGRESS CATALOGING-IN-PUBLICATION DATA

Mills, Marja.
The Mockingbird Next Door : Life with Harper Lee / Marja Mills.
pages cm
ISBN 978-1-59420-519-4
1. Lee, Harper.   2. Mills, Marja.   3. Authors, American—20th century—Biography.
4. Alabama—Biography.   I. Title.
PS3562.E353Z75   2014
813'.54--dc23
[B]
2013039938

Printed in the United States of America
1   3   5   7   9   10   8   6   4   2
Designed by Gretchen Achilles

For my parents, Dave and Carla Mills

Author's Note

This is a work of nonfiction. It is based upon notes, tapes, transcripts, interviews, and conversations from my time in Monroeville. Events and conversations are rendered as I remember them and verified to the best of my ability.

The Mockingbird Next Door

Prologue

In the summer of 2005, I was having coffee at Burger King with Harper Lee.

By that time, we were friends and next-door neighbors in her hometown of Monroeville, Alabama. We'd first met in 2001, when I was on assignment for the *Chicago Tribune*. I had developed a rapport with Nelle, as her friends call her, and her sister Alice. Over time, the idea of my writing a book about the Lee sisters, with their guidance, had taken root in our conversations. With their blessing, I had rented the house next door.

At the time of our Burger King visit, Nelle was growing increasingly resentful and anxious about a coming unauthorized biography and two Truman Capote movies in the works. I think the combination of those events encouraged her to open up to me even more. I wasn't an unknown quantity but someone she knew and trusted, sitting across the table from her.

I wouldn't have been sitting there if I had included anything she had said was off the record in my newspaper article, or if I had pushed her to divulge things she felt were no one's business. Even the fact that I'd never asked her to autograph a copy of *To Kill a Mockingbird* for me factored in. I didn't feel I was entitled to more from her than she wanted to share. I wanted to hear as much as she was willing to share, of course. But I didn't push it. That patience seemed to ease Nelle's mind.

"I know what you can call your book," she told me, leaning in and stabbing her finger in the air, as she liked to do when making a point.

"*Having Their Say.* I know they used it with the Delaney sisters but titles aren't copyrightable." Nelle beamed.

Having Our Say: The Delaney Sisters' First 100 Years was a bestselling book about two African American sisters, one sweet and one salty, looking back on their lives.

In this scenario, Alice, her elder sister by fifteen years—sharp and still practicing law in her nineties—was the sweet one. Nelle was the saltier one. I smiled. I didn't take it as a mandate for the title but rather as a measure of Nelle's enthusiasm.

I was delighted they were ready to have their say, in any measure, and to look back on their lives. It has been a privilege to get to know the sisters, their family, their friends, their hometown, and their passions. With the Lees as my teachers, I learned more about literature, family, history, faith, friendship, and fun than I did in any classroom.

This book is my attempt to tell the story of my time with the Lees and to honor all that they shared with me. I could not have done it without the trust, support, and encouragement of Nelle and Alice Lee and their closest friends.

To the best of my ability, I have let them have their say. All humor and erudition should be credited to the Lees. Any errors are my own.

Chapter One

D o you want to take a trip? You can say no."

Tim Bannon, my editor at the *Chicago Tribune,* stood at my cubicle. He ran the daily features section on the fifth floor of the Gothic Tribune Tower in downtown Chicago and was pleasantly low-key by newspaper standards. Tim knew I liked to travel for stories, and that if the story took me to an unusual part of the country, so much the better. I had loved spending time at a monastery in rural Missouri for one story and at The Citadel, the military college in South Carolina, for another. Tim also knew I had been out sick a lot that year, 2001. In 1995, I had been diagnosed with lupus, an autoimmune condition that frequently left me fatigued. I wanted him to know I was still able to do my job. I purposely accepted before finding out more.

"Sure. Where to?"

"Monroeville, Alabama."

Tim saw my quizzical look and smiled.

"It's Harper Lee's hometown. We know she doesn't give interviews. But I think it's worth going there anyway."

Enough said.

A couple of weeks earlier, the Chicago Public Library had chosen the elusive author's *To Kill a Mockingbird* as the first selection in its One Book, One Chicago program. The idea was to get Chicagoans in every corner of the city reading and discussing the same book. It didn't hurt that *To Kill a Mockingbird* happened to be the favorite of Chicago Mayor Richard M. Daley, as he told me a couple of months earlier for a story I wrote about his reading habits. That he was a reader at all surprised some folks. His press conferences were hard to follow. He didn't necessarily exit the same sentences he entered. But he loved books, and he especially loved *To Kill a Mockingbird*. In that, he was part of a phenomenon that began in 1960 and continues to this day.

When the novel was published in July of that year, Harper Lee was a few months past her thirty-fourth birthday. From the beginning, Lee was a collection of contradictions. She was an Alabama native whose love of the state's back roads was matched only by her love of New York City streets. Her public shyness masked a wicked wit. During the publicity engagements for the novel's publication, when she wasn't averting her gaze, her dark eyes could alternate between a penetrating stare and a mischievous gleam. She was a distinctive blend of engaging and elusive.

Lee labored for several years to produce the novel. She coaxed the story out of a Royal manual typewriter in her small Manhattan cold-water flat and on visits home. Atticus Finch is a principled attorney and the widowed father of two children. As the novel begins, his tomboy daughter, Scout, is about to turn six. Her older brother, Jem, is almost ten. With their father, they endure the suspicion and outright hatred directed at Atticus when he defends Tom Robinson, a black man falsely accused of raping a white woman, Mayella Ewell, in their segregated town. In the novel's climactic scene, Bob Ewell, father of Mayella, comes after the children. Boo Radley, the neighborhood recluse who has frightened and fascinated the children in equal measure, saves them.

Through the experiences of Scout, Jem, and their best friend, Dill, Lee paints a vivid picture of small-town childhood in the segregated South. She also explores complex themes in the lives of her characters, from mental illness to addiction, racism, and the limitations society imposed on women.

The story of small-town childhood and racial injustice in Depression-era Alabama garnered glowing reviews and stayed on the best-seller list for nearly two years. In 1961, Lee won the Pulitzer Prize for fiction. The Academy Award–winning 1962 film version of the novel, starring Gregory Peck, became a classic in its own right.

It was a stunning debut. With time, Lee's novel became something more: a national touchstone in a culture becoming ever more fragmented. In a 1991 survey, the Library of Congress asked readers which book most influenced their lives. Only the Bible outranked *To Kill a Mockingbird*. It has sold an estimated forty million copies or more and been translated into three dozen languages, from Swedish to Urdu. It is required reading for at least 70 percent of U.S. high school students.

The novel became a classic at the same time as it defied Mark Twain's definition of one: "a book people praise and don't read." References to the work appear in movies, on television, in countless other books, and in comic strips, cartoons, and lyrics. People cite the novel as the reason they became writers or lawyers. The characters' unusual names have a comfortable familiarity even to those who haven't read the novel in years, or perhaps never did. Atticus Finch. Scout. Boo Radley. The unusual names from Depression-era Alabama now populate the glossy pages of *People* and *Us Weekly,* as celebrities, as well as plenty of regular folks, name their children Harper, Atticus, or Scout.

As the novel's cultural influence grew, so did Lee's mystique. A few years after the book was published, she essentially stopped giving interviews. The second novel she had once discussed never appeared. Her rare public appearances made headlines. Her speeches, when she did accept an occasional award, usually consisted of two words: "Thank you." When she was loquacious, she went on twice as long. "Thank you very much."

Given her long public silence, in fact, plenty of people assumed Harper Lee was dead. At age sixty-six in 1993, she made dry reference to that fact in the foreword to yet another printing of the novel. Lee told her readers that she was "still alive, although very quiet."

By the time I was given my assignment in 2001, she was seventy-five. In the modern world, she was as beloved and unknown as a person can be. She divided her time between Manhattan and her Alabama hometown. That much was known. Her full name was Nelle Harper Lee but she was simply Nelle to the tight circle of friends who protected her privacy. Periodic "In Search of Harper Lee" articles over the years offered glimpses into the author's life, if only from afar. One newspaper story described the log cabin exterior and linoleum floors of David's Catfish House, on the outskirts of Monroeville, and passed along intelligence gleaned from a waitress. The author and her older sister, attorney Alice Lee, always sat at a back table. They were quite hard of hearing, both of them. The waitress could report, firsthand, that they squabbled about who got to pay for the other. Not much else seemed to be known about her life after writing one of the most cherished novels of the twentieth century.

Lee's responses to the never-ending requests for interviews ranged from "no" to "hell, no." Usually, her literary agency and publisher declined on her behalf. In Monroeville, Alice practiced law with their father's old firm, Barnett, Bugg & Lee, and also served as gatekeeper for her sought-after sister.

I expected that I would be turned away as so many reporters had been before. If nothing else, I could write about the small town that produced the author and inspired her fictional Maycomb. But first, I had to find it on a map. I pulled out my atlas.

Like Maycomb, Monroeville is a southern Alabama county seat located well inland. It is an out-of-the-way place, near no major airport or even the interstate. Nonetheless, the town of sixty-five hundred draws literary pilgrims from around the world. People want to visit the courthouse replicated in the movie. They want to run their hands along the polished banister of the balcony where a young Harper Lee watched her father try cases just as Scout does in the novel and the film. They want to walk past the spot where Lee climbed a chinaberry tree with her childhood friend and next-door neighbor Truman Capote. Devoted fans of the novel, the ones who can recite favorite lines by heart, want details. Do the tree's poisonous yellow berries still fall to the earth along Alabama Avenue? Is the tree even still there, or those two childhood homes? Does the feeling Lee captured of a small-town, Southern childhood still exist?

For this hastily planned trip, I'd submit, meekly, the standard request for an interview, knowing that was as likely as a blizzard in August. Then I'd fly down and try to give Chicago readers a sense of the town that produced Harper Lee and annually sells out the two-act play adapted from the novel.

For One Book, One Chicago, the library system was gearing up for an onslaught of interest in the book. The city's seventy-eight libraries were stocking their shelves with nearly two thousand additional copies of the novel, including some Spanish and Polish translations. Lee declined the city's invitation to speak, but sent a rare statement in support of the program. She wrote, "When the people of Chicago assemble in various parts of the city to read and discuss *To Kill a Mockingbird*, there is no greater honor the novel could receive. People of all backgrounds and cultures coming together to put their critical skills to work—nothing could be more exciting!"

Like millions of others, I had read the book in school, as a shy fourteen-year-old who loved English, feared math, and ran on my high school cross-country team in Madison, Wisconsin. From the first pages, I was transported on a snowy afternoon to the red clay streets of an Alabama county seat during the Depression.

Now I had an assignment, a plane ticket, and a colleague, photographer Terrence James, also assigned to the story. I hadn't worked with Terrence before but I'd seen him around the paper. He was African American, wore black jeans and boots, and had cornrows to his shoulders. He seemed enthusiastic about this assignment, as I was.

Terrence and I got better acquainted on the flight to Atlanta. We mapped out our assignment, where we wanted to go, and whom we wanted to see. In Atlanta, we rented a car for what turned out to be a nearly six-hour drive to Monroe County. Atlanta was a rookie mistake: I could have booked a flight into Montgomery, Mobile, or Florida's coastal Pensacola. All were closer. But the Atlanta flight was cheaper. It didn't look as far on the map as it turned out to be. The drive, however, gave us a chance to put Monroeville in a geographic context we could picture. Parachuting in, as journalists often do, you miss something.

We got off the interstate about a half hour from Monroeville. Along Highway 84, the foliage gets thicker. Elsewhere, in fact, kudzu drapes over hundred-year-old oak trees. It crawls up ravines. It creeps across the caved-in tin roofs of abandoned country shacks. It forms an intricate web of green so dense it seems to be hiding something.

We drove up hills, wound around curves. Trucks with bundles of freshly cut lumber thundered past. Terrence gripped the steering wheel tighter. We saw the "patchwork sea of cotton fields and timberlands" Lee describes in the novel. Large machinery now does the picking. It's faster and cheaper. In *To Kill a Mockingbird* times, rows of men, women, and children did the picking. It was oppressively hot, back-breaking, finger-stinging work, plucking the tufts of cotton off the plant and putting them into burlap sacks.

We passed the occasional gas station and general store with "Coca-Cola" in fading white script on peeling red paint. We stopped at one of them. It was the kind of place that looked like it might still have Coke in those little six-and-a-half-ounce green bottles, the kind my grandfather used to have at his one-man Coca-Cola bottling operation in Black River Falls, Wisconsin. I checked. No, even here it was cans and plastic bottles only. Next to the cash register and the March of Dimes box was a giant plastic jar of hard-boiled eggs in vinegar. Beside that was another big jar with something vaguely pink floating in the brine. Pickled pig's feet. I'd never tasted either. I'd stick to Diet Coke for now.

As we got closer to Monroeville, NPR faded. Now the choices were country music, conservative commentary, or fiery preaching on a couple of stations. Around every other bend was a redbrick church or a tiny white one with a steeple stabbing blue sky and a cemetery out back. Most of the churches were Baptist, but we also saw ones that were Methodist, First Assembly, and Pentecostal.

In a clearing between a redbrick school and woods dripping in kudzu, we spotted a basketball court. Young men playing. Young women watching.

Terrence slowed the car and looked at me.

"Yes, let's," I said.

We pulled into the area of trampled grass where other cars were parked, our rental conspicuously shiny and new among the old wide-bodied Chevrolets held together with spare parts and ingenuity. People stared openly at Terrence and me as we walked to the sidelines. Terrence carried a large camera around his neck. He is fairly tall. I stand fully five feet three and a half inches, with blue eyes, blond hair, and what's charitably called alabaster skin, a whiter shade of pale. Mine was the only white face in the crowd.

We explained why we were there. We were just chatting, mostly. This was our first chance to get acquainted with the area, see what people had to say about life in this part of the country. Had they been assigned *To Kill a Mockingbird* in school? A few had. Most had not. This also was the first of many times I was glad we had our bases covered between the two of us: male and female, black and white. Of course, once we opened our mouths and spoke, our accents lumped us together in one important way. We were Yankees.

As we spoke with the young men and women, the harshness of the sun gradually faded. I glanced at my watch. It was 6:35 P.M. This was what photographers call the golden hour, the magical interlude when everything is bathed in a soft light and, in the words of the painter James Whistler, "common things are touched with mystery and transfigured with beauty."

Terrence crouched down to photograph a couple of the pickup ballplayers from that vantage point.

A light rain began to fall. In the muggy August air, it was gentle relief. As it picked up, Terrence returned the lens cap to his camera. I closed my notebook against the falling drops. One of the young men waved at us. "Come back anytime."

Terrence and I made our way back onto the two-lane highway to Monroeville. We'd have to find our way in the dark to the Best Western on the outskirts of town and then be up early to cram as many interviews as possible into our first day there.

Nearing the city, the feeling of a place out of time ends abruptly. Familiar chains pop up. At the Best Western, our rooms had an uninspiring view of parking lot and fence. Across a large field, the lights from David's Catfish House glowed softly.

For dinner, I fed quarters into the outdoor vending machines. I retrieved peanut butter crackers from the well of the snack machine, and held a blessedly cold can of Diet Coke to my forehead. I smelled an odor I could not place. It wasn't coming from the big garbage can in the alcove; it was carried on the faint breeze blowing over the field. It smelled like paper mill with a sour finish, like boiling cabbage. It was fertilizer, I later learned.

This was a poor county in a poor state. Where were the jobs now that the Vanity Fair plant had scaled way back? The apparel manufacturer set up shop here in 1937, and it became the town's economic engine, propelling it out of the worst of the Depression. There were a lot of jobs for men and, for the first time at these wages, women. But most of the manufacturing work had gone elsewhere in recent years. The money tourists spent on meals and motels didn't begin to make up for the jobs lost to cutbacks and closings. Monroeville suffered an unemployment rate of 18 percent.

Terrence rapped on my door. Monroe County was dry, going back to Prohibition. Conecuh County was not. Terrence suggested we get libations back across the county line. We had passed Lee's Package Goods, no relation to the sisters, and doubled back to stop in. The place was a cross between forlorn and forbidding. It had peeling paint and bars on the windows. Other than the WELCOME TO MONROE

COUNTY sign and the store, there was nothing much around here except fields.

The jangle of the bell on the door announced our arrival. A heavyset young white woman behind the counter looked our way. So did a middle-aged Asian woman who appeared from a back room. They didn't smile at us. They just looked at us without expression. Under harsh lights they sized up their customers. We must not have looked like too much trouble.

After we returned to the motel, we shared a quick drink in this dry county.

"Half a glass is good, thanks." I wanted to go over my notes before tomorrow.

"Half a glass."

Terrence poured my wine into a water glass from the bathroom counter, which faced out into this standard-issue motel room.

He offered a toast.

"To Monroeville."

"To Monroeville."

We clinked glasses. Not rotgut. Not great.

In my room, I pulled out my paperback copy of the novel and climbed under the covers. I was tired from our trip, but before I made my acquaintance with Lee's hometown, I wanted to get lost again in the rhythm of her language. I wouldn't be able to go to sleep right away anyway.

This edition, published by Warner Books, had a simple illustration on the cover: the silhouette of a bird flying away from a tree. In the knothole of the tree, someone had stashed a ball of yarn and a pocket watch.

Just a few weeks earlier, it had been shiny and new, its spine unbroken, its 281 pages crisp and untouched. Now pages were turned down at the corners. Passages were highlighted in yellow and sentences underlined in black ink with scribbled notations in the margins.

On page 5, I had underlined one of the novel's most-quoted passages.

"Maycomb was an old town, but it was a tired old town when I first knew it. In rainy weather the streets turn to red slop; grass grew on the sidewalks, the courthouse sagged in the square. . . . Men's stiff collars wilted by nine in the morning. Ladies bathed before noon, after their three-o'clock naps, and by nightfall were like soft teacakes with frostings of sweat and sweet talcum."

The grown Scout is looking back at the world of her childhood. She is in no hurry to tell the story. Right away, we hear her warmth, her wit, and a subtle wistful quality. She invites us to the events that changed everything one summer when she was a young girl, events set in motion, her brother reckons, long before either of them was born.

Horton Foote selected the passage to begin the film adaptation of the book. He grew up in a small town in Texas, not Alabama, but he said Lee had captured a place that he knew intimately from his own childhood. Lee called Foote's film one of the best adaptations ever made. Gregory Peck won an Academy Award for what he called the role of a lifetime. Horton Foote also won an Oscar, for his screenplay. Lee had not wanted to write the screenplay. She trusted Foote. As he put it, "It was just like we were cousins. I just felt I knew this town. It could have been a replica of my own." So began a decades-long friendship, not only with Foote but with Peck, who met her father in Monroeville to prepare for his role.

Robert Duvall made his debut as a young film actor playing the reclusive Boo Radley, seen only at the end of the film. Elmer Bernstein's haunting score is recognizable from the first notes. They evoke a child's simple tinkering on a piano. As the title sequence begins, we see a young girl's hands opening an old cigar box. She sings to herself as she pokes around the box of treasures. There are a few Buffalo nickels, a set of jacks, some marbles, a harmonica, a whistle, and a pocket watch. It's a childhood of roaming free, of unbridled imaginations using those simple props to conjure up stories of high drama and death-defying feats.

When the film came out in 1962, Monroeville had a downtown movie theater. A young Harper Lee, her dark hair cropped short, smiled broadly for a photo below the marquee advertising *To Kill a Mockingbird*. Not long after, the theater burned. It was not rebuilt.

The next morning, I stepped out of my motel room and into the furnace of Monroeville in August. The Best Western is on Highway 21, which becomes Alabama Avenue. To reach the courthouse, according to the clerk at the motel, all we had to do was follow the road about five miles. It ended right at the town square. We passed an unremarkable stretch of auto parts places and assorted businesses. Next we came upon the Monroe County Hospital, up a short, steep hill to our left, then a strip mall with a Winn-Dixie supermarket, a Rite Aid, and a dollar store. We passed Radley's Deli, a weathered gray building, named for Boo Radley. We drove the generic stretch you find anyplace in America—McDonald's, Burger King, KFC—before we spotted the low-slung Vanity Fair building. Pete's Texaco, a classic, cluttered old gas station, looked like it hadn't changed much over the decades. On the corner where Alabama Avenue crosses Claiborne Street was Lee Motor Company, also no relation to the author. I had read she didn't like the mural of a giant mockingbird painted on the side of the brick building. Across the street, on another mural, Scout and Jem stand by the neighborhood tree. The snug 1930s post office anchors the southeast side of the town square. We parked in one of the diagonal parking spaces across the street, in front of the Old Court-house. Adjacent to it is what everyone calls the new courthouse. It was built in 1963.

Seen from the north, Lee wrote, the Maycomb County courthouse was early Victorian and looked all right. "From the other side, how-ever, Greek revival columns clashed with a big nineteenth-century clock tower housing a rusty unreliable instrument, a view indicating a people determined to preserve every physical scrap of the past." Mon-roeville once had such an unreliable instrument, a problem addressed with a modern solution. Now when the bell tolls the hours, it is a re-cording that rings out from the clock tower.

We made our way up a short flight of steps and through the pair of tall, heavy doors that welcome *Mockingbird* tourists. The courthouse is a magnet for people from around the country looking for a connection to the novel and the movie, those seeking a glimpse of the real world that inspired that fictional one. A small gift shop sold *To Kill a Mocking-bird* T-shirts and key chains, and posters of the town's annual produc-tion of the play.

Terrence and I ducked our heads into the large courtroom that served as the basis for the one in the movie. It was large, with a curv-ing balcony, painted white, along the second floor, and tall windows overlooking the square. Terrence began taking pictures and I climbed slightly uneven wooden steps to the stuffy second floor.

I heard Kathy McCoy, the director of the museum and its annual *To Kill a Mockingbird* production, before I saw her. Behind a closed door, she was having a loud, animated phone conversation. Her accent was Southern but not the same kind you heard around here. She was from Kentucky.

I wanted to know what McCoy could tell me about the community, the play she directed each year here at the courthouse, the Lees' role around town, and who might remember the old Monroeville and be willing to speak with me. I asked her about the tourism here, and what she could tell me about Harper Lee, knowing that tension has simmered for years between the Lee sisters and those looking to capitalize on the book's fame.

"Harper Lee doesn't want us to commercialize the book," McCoy told me, "but we feel what we're doing is a service to the community and to the rest of the world." She and her staff put together a guidebook titled *Monroeville: The Search for Harper Lee's Maycomb* and published a guide for tours of the town. On the town square, fans of the novel can peer at the redbrick building where Lee's father maintained his law office and where Harper Lee wrote part of the novel. On Alabama Avenue, they can see the spot where Lee's childhood home once stood, the spot that now is home to Mel's Dairy Dream, a white shack with a walk-up window for ordering ice cream cones and burgers. Gone, too, is the home next door, where a young Truman Capote lived for a time with his aunts. A plaque and a little bit of an old stone fence mark the spot.

That day, several people from out of town were looking around the centerpiece of the courthouse, the wood-floored courtroom, where a young Harper Lee had seen her attorney father in action, the one replicated in the movie. Visitors sit in the "colored" balcony, just as Scout did during Tom Robinson's trial. The bolder ones approach the judge's bench and lift the gavel, letting it drop with an authoritative rap. Simple props, such as a period calendar, hang on the wall to re-create the Maycomb of the novel for playgoers.

Once you step outside, though, finding the contours and flavor of the Monroeville of that era is harder. Even when the book came out in 1960, Monroeville had changed drastically from its Depression-era days. The size of it, the look of it, the feel of it, all were dramatically different.

When producer Alan Pakula and director Robert Mulligan set about bringing the novel to the movie screen, they considered filming on location in Monroeville. But they decided against it. It didn't look enough like the town of the 1930s they were trying to re-create. The town still had some of its charm, but it was too modern to stand in for 1930s Maycomb.

Instead, they replicated the courtroom in which a young Nelle had watched her father argue cases, and went to work creating Maycomb on set in Hollywood. For exterior shots, they incorporated some old California bungalows that could be made to look like homes in Nelle's Maycomb.

The film's art director, Henry Bumstead, wrote producer Alan Pakula from Monroeville. He abbreviated Monroeville as "Mv" and *To Kill a Mockingbird* as "TM." The letter is dated November 1961.

Dear Alan,

I arrived here in Mv this afternoon after a very interesting and beautiful drive from Montgomery. . . . During my drive, I was very much impressed by the lack of traffic, the beautiful countryside and the character of the Negro shacks that dot the terrain.

Harper Lee was here to meet me and she is a most charming person. She insisted I call her Nelle—feel like I've known her for years. Little wonder she was able to write such a warm and successful novel.

Mv is a beautiful little town of about 2,500 inhabitants. It's small in size but large in Southern character. I'm so happy you made possible for me to research the area before designing TM.

Most of the houses are of wood, one story and set up on brick piles. Almost every house had a porch and a swing hanging from the porch rafters. Believe me, it's a much more relaxed life than we live in Hollywood.

I also visited the old courthouse square and the interior of the courtroom Nelle wrote about. I can't tell you how thrilled I am by the architecture and the little touches which will add to our sets. Old pot-bellied stoves still heat the courtroom. Beside each one stands a tub filled with coal. Nelle says we should have a block of ice on the exterior of the courthouse steps when we shoot this sequence. It seems that people chip off a piece of ice to take into the courthouse with them to munch on to try to keep cool. It reminded me of my "youth," when I used to follow the ice wagon to get the ice chips. Nelle is really amused at my picture taking and also my taking measurements so that I can duplicate the things I see. She said she didn't know we worked so hard. This morning she greeted me with "I lost five pounds yesterday following you around taking pictures of doorknobs, houses, wagons, collards, etc—can we take time for lunch today?" Nelle says the exterior of Mrs. DuBose's house should have paint that is peeling. Also the interior should have dark woodwork, Victorian furniture and be grim. Her house would be wired for electricity, but she would still be using oil lamps—to save money, so Nelle says. Boo Radley's should look like it had never been painted—almost haunted.

Warmest regards,

Henry Bumstead

When readers of *To Kill a Mockingbird* first come to Monroeville, they want it to be just like the town they know from the novel and the movie. They want to see the place where the characters they love—

Scout and Atticus, Jem and Dill and Boo—live and play, work and dream.

"People moved slowly then. They ambled across the square, shuffled in and out of the stores around it, took their time about everything. A day was twenty-four hours long but seemed longer. There was no hurry, for there was nowhere to go, nothing to buy and no money to buy it with, nothing to see outside the boundaries of Maycomb County. But it was a time of vague optimism for some of the people: Maycomb County had recently been told that it had nothing to fear but fear itself."

So visitors in search of Maycomb just assume they're not looking hard enough or in the right places. Maycomb must be here somewhere. It must exist.

"The form of a town changes, alas, more quickly than the human heart," Charles Baudelaire once wrote. Monroeville, like any town, has been altered in manifold and important ways since the 1930s. Those who love the novel, however, haven't budged. Their expectations are steadfast. Two decades ago, McCoy told me, Monroe County drew about two thousand visitors a year. Now the annual tally was closer to twenty thousand and climbing, and a good four-fifths of those folks say that the novel is what brought them.

The museum's annual spring production of the play *To Kill a Mockingbird* draws visitors to a stage only Monroeville can offer. The first act unfolds on the lawn of the Old Courthouse Museum, where the breeze carries the scent of pink azaleas and mockingbirds sometimes alight on tree branches. The second act, the infamous trial, takes place inside, in the old-fashioned courtroom familiar to anyone who has watched the movie. Every year, the performances sell out.

McCoy directed me to walk out the door of the Old Courthouse and across a bit of lawn to the new one to interview Otha Lee Biggs, the county probate judge. Biggs was a powerful figure here who was involved with the annual play and *Mockingbird* matters generally.

Judge Biggs operated out of an office piled to the rafters with books and papers. He was an older, dark-haired man and he played his part with a certain theatricality. His official duties had to do with running the county. His unofficial duties included gleaning information from journalists who thought they were the ones interviewing him. We spoke very generally about the town, the book, and the Lees, whom he had known for a long time.

I would come to learn that Biggs was one of the ways the Lees often knew who was in town and why. It was an early warning detection system. When they especially wanted to avoid someone likely to come knocking on their door, they occasionally would hit the road for their sister Louise's home in Eufaula or, closer to home, a motel over in Evergreen, the neighboring Conecuh County seat.

My next visit, per McCoy's directions, would be to Charlie McCorvey, an educator and county commissioner who played the role of Tom Robinson every spring. At Monroeville Middle School, McCorvey greeted me warmly and asked who I had been to see so far. McCorvey was a large man with silver-rimmed glasses. Once a year, to play Tom Robinson, he would trade his button-down shirt and tie for worn overalls.

Local people constitute the cast every year: lawyers and doctors, preachers and plumbers, businessmen and shop owners. And educators. In one particularly difficult scene, Bob Ewell berates Tom Robinson, spitting out the *n* word in his stream of racist vitriol. Hard to be the white actor saying it. Hard to be the black actor hearing it. Occasionally, African American friends would ask McCorvey if it made sense to depict the humiliation and violent end that his character suffered. But McCorvey's instincts as an educator told him this was another form of teaching. "Some of these kids think the days of segregation and 'yessuh,' 'nossuh' are ancient history but they are not. This makes it more real to them."

Kathy McCoy also suggested I speak with a retired businessman named A. B. Blass. He went to school with Nelle, caddied for her father at the local golf course built by Vanity Fair, and now often spoke to the reporters who cycled through town.

In his living room, Blass told me of the time in the early 1960s when A. C. Lee put a reassuring hand on Blass's shoulder and said simply, "You did right, son." Blass had stood up, in his way, to the Ku Klux Klan, which was threatening violence against band members the first year the parade was to be integrated. Blass canceled the parade rather than put the marching bands in harm's way or allow the tradition of the segregated parade to continue.

Blass had recounted a collection of Lee stories many times to many journalists, until they were stones rubbed smooth by time and the telling. His voice was almost hypnotic, low and slow. I had the sense from Kathy McCoy that the Lee sisters did not appreciate what A. B. Blass had to share about their family, though McCoy didn't explain exactly what their objections were.

As he spoke, I gathered that the reason might be that he described Nelle's mother as an emotionally disturbed woman.

"She was touched," Blass said. "I remember as a little boy walking to school, I'd see her there on their front porch, talking to herself. I'd walk back the same way after school and she'd still be there sometimes, just talking to herself like that."

I'd learn later that the Lees took issue with this characterization, to say the least. I'd hear how they remembered Frances Lee as a "gentle soul," a woman who played the piano and sang, loved crossword puzzles, and enthusiastically traded books back and forth with Truman Capote's mother when she lived next door. Frances Lee did suffer a nervous breakdown at one point, after a harrowing experience, one the Lees had not discussed publicly. Her second child, Louise, cried in distress around the clock for months and couldn't properly digest anything her desperate parents gave her. The baby recovered when a pediatrician found a special formula she could digest. As I came to know the Lees, the way their mother was depicted over the years was high on the list of things they wanted to set straight.

Nelle, according to Blass, was a scrappy girl unafraid to cuss and use her fists, every bit as feisty as the fictional Scout Finch. Blass remembered A. C. Lee as a quiet man with an even temperament. His sense of propriety and civility was steadfast. Even when the heat and humidity bore down, Mr. Lee wore his business suit on the golf course. Blass thought it was a shame Nelle Harper no longer socialized with some of the people she had grown up with, himself among them. He suspected she didn't appreciate his willingness to talk to the press about the Lee family. He was correct, I learned later.

I had most of what I needed for my newspaper story after a few days, within the constraints of the Lees and their close friends not granting interviews. Terrence and I would head home soon. But first, I had to at least request an interview with Harper Lee or her sister Alice in person. If anyone answered the door, I would be polite, and then I would be gone.

Terrence drove our rental car to the older neighborhood of red-brick houses across from the big, rambling junior high that used to be the high school; Harper Lee studied there when it was newly built.

Alice Lee's home wasn't listed in the local phone book. A researcher in the *Tribune*'s reference room—the morgue, to old-timers—easily pulled the number from online records. One thing I hadn't found in my file full of articles and background materials was a photo of the Lee home. In one of the most frequently reproduced photos of Lee as a young woman, she is in a rocking chair next to her father. The photos accompanied a 1961 *Life* magazine feature about Lee at home. The interior of the white screened porch, on the side of the house, is visible but you can't tell what the house looks like from the street. According to the articles I read, even the location of the house was kept secret, at least by some of the residents who declined to disclose its whereabouts to various tourists and journalists.

I felt uneasy about knocking on their door. But I needed to be able to tell my editors I at least tried.

Chapter Two

Terrence didn't pull into the Lees' driveway. He idled the car along their quiet street.

"Well," I told him, "I'll probably be right back."

It was early evening, and still light out. The air was warm and still. We knew Alice Lee probably would be home after her day at the law office. I walked up a few wooden steps and knocked on a white wooden door. Its old brass knocker had "Alice F. Lee" engraved in feminine script. I took a step back. Nothing.

I pressed the doorbell, stepped back again, and waited. Nothing. All right then. At least I tried. I'd wait another minute, then join Terrence in the air-conditioned car and call it a day.

Just before I turned around to go back to the car, a tiny woman using a walker came to the door. She had large glasses and wore a tailored light blue skirt and matching suit jacket. Her gray hair, parted on the side, was clipped neatly in place with a single bobby pin. I introduced myself. She leaned in to hear better. I raised my voice and repeated who I was and why I was there.

"Yes, Miss Mills. I received the materials you sent. And the letter."

Her voice was a raspy croak. She had read what I sent about Chicago's library system picking *To Kill a Mockingbird* for One Book, One Chicago. From her sources, she knew I had been making the rounds. I had read about Alice Lee, Harper Lee's much older sister. She was eighty-nine years old and still a practicing attorney. From the clips I'd seen, I knew she often ran interference for her sister, politely but firmly declining interviews. I was surprised when she invited me in.

Across the threshold, a musty smell greeted me. A large oak bookcase, shoulder-high and to my right, dominated the small entryway. Just beyond a short hallway was a small telephone nook. A little white chair was pulled up to a waist-high ledge with the telephone.

"Please come in," she said.

I followed Alice Lee into the living room. Books were everywhere. They filled one bookshelf after another, stood in piles by her reading chair, and were stacked on the coffee table and most available surfaces, for that matter.

She saw me taking all this in. "This is mostly a place to warehouse books." She smiled and her eyes crinkled at the corners. I strained to catch what she was saying. It wasn't just the raspy voice that made that difficult. I was still learning to decipher the local accent, more pronounced in the older people I met. Of course, around here, I was the one with the accent. "When I hear a consonant," Harper Lee once said, "I look around."

"Pull up that chair, won't you?" With her hands still resting on her walker, she nodded at a low wooden rocker by the piano on the far wall. The living room was compact. I carried the chair four or five feet and set it near hers. She stood by a gray upholstered recliner and a side table piled with papers.

I was thrilled to be invited in, but I felt a rush of regret, too, for bothering her, especially now that I saw for myself how petite and vulnerable and, well, ancient, she appeared to be, with so little hearing and the gray metal walker. "For balance," she told me.

The interior of the house was as modest as the exterior. An old plaid couch with skinny wooden arms was pushed against one wall. A floor lamp and another side table piled with books and papers were between the couch and the recliner. Along the far wall was an old brown piano. Above it hung a painting of the sea that was more angular, more modern, than the rest of the living room. Another wall had a fireplace flanked by two upholstered chairs. Glass and porcelain knick-knacks formed a silent sentry atop the white, wooden mantel.

She slowly lowered herself into the chair, then let go and dropped the last few inches. She managed a dignified plop into her seat. As we spoke, I heard someone rustling around in the back. The kitchen was just off the square dining room, which, in turn, was just around the corner from where I sat with Miss Alice. No room was very far from another.

Some of the bookshelves in the dining room were waist high, others a bit lower. Pushed against any wall that had room for them, they had the haphazard zigzag of a city skyline. But the window above one of them looked out on a deep, dark backyard with towering trees.

Alice answered my questions about the book, the town, their family, her famous sister. I scribbled in my reporter's notebook, putting a star by quotations I thought I might include in my story.

Big homes or expensive clothing didn't interest her sister, Alice told me. "Those things have no meaning for Nelle Harper," Alice Lee said. "All she needs is a good bed, a bathroom, and a typewriter. . . . Books are the things she cares about."

Her sister teased Alice about the time she began storing books and newspapers in the oven. She didn't cook and had run out of bookshelf space.

A pleasant aroma was coming from the back of the house. I couldn't place it. It was the scent of baking bread, only fainter.

Could that be Harper Lee in the kitchen? The possibility was electrifying. Was she listening to our conversation? Would she make an appearance? I thought it better not to ask.

Meantime, I could feel a sheen of sweat on my face. No air-conditioning on here. Alice easily got cold but not hot, she told me. She had grown up without air-conditioning and rarely felt the need for it.

"I hope it's not too warm for you," she said. Her voice was almost a croak.

"No, not at all. Thank you."

I waited until she glanced away to quickly swipe my hand across my forehead and wipe it on my pants.

I had stepped into another era without AC, computers, or cell phones. The Lees had only recently purchased a television. A manual typewriter rested on a chair in the dining room. Nelle used it to answer some of the correspondence that still poured into their post office box.

"She doesn't even have an electric typewriter," Alice said. "We do not belong in the twenty-first century as far as electrical things are concerned." She paused. "Hardly even the twentieth."

I mentioned that in *To Kill a Mockingbird*, the word *scuppernongs* had sent me to the dictionary.

She got a gleam in her eye.

"Follow me."

She led me to the kitchen. It looked unchanged from the fifties. The floor was black-and-white-checked tile. The cabinets were painted white. Stacks of papers, bowls, and cracker boxes and various piles of just stuff crowded the counters.

My unspoken question about who was doing the cooking there was answered. A tall black woman with wisps of graying hair stood at the stove. She poked at the frying pan with a spatula. She was making fried green tomatoes.

Alice made the introductions. When her sister—Nelle Harper—was in New York, Alice explained, Julia Munnerlyn was her live-in help. She looked after Alice, stayed overnight, drove her to and from work, and fixed the simple meals Alice preferred. And her favorite food, fried green tomatoes.

I would come to learn that one of Julia's sons, Rudolph Munner-lyn, was Monroeville's police chief, the first African American to hold that position.

"She wanted to know about scuppernongs," Alice told her. Julia slipped the breaded green tomatoes out of the pan and onto a plate with a paper towel to absorb the grease. She worked with the deft hand of someone who has done that a hundred times before. She had kind eyes, watchful eyes, and a warm smile for the stranger in the kitchen. She reached into the small, white refrigerator and retrieved a big bowl.

Julia put the bowl on the counter to my left and set out a paper towel.

"For the seeds."

She and Alice beamed at me.

"Try one," Alice said.

Both women were amused that this local fruit was exotic to me.

"A friend brought these by the other day," Alice said.

The scuppernongs did indeed look like big grapes. They were red-dish purple, plump, and sweet with just a bit of tartness as well. As I slipped the seeds into the paper towel, I was trying to take it all in: the scuppernongs; the two women; the considerably cluttered, somehow comfortably dated interior of this house. Chances were I'd never see it again.

They told me that scuppernongs grow on vines, and were plentiful around here. Both were in good humor. The affection between the two women was obvious.

Poor Terrence was still out in the rental car. But I knew he knew the longer I stayed, the better.

"Would you care for a little tour of the house?"

"Well, sure. Thank you."

Julia dipped a second batch of slices in breading and, with a practiced hand, slid them into the frying pan.

Despite the walker, Alice was light on her feet. She stepped carefully but quickly. Her walk across the fairly narrow kitchen was almost a skitter.

I realized I was still holding the crumpled paper towel.

"Is there a . . ."

"I'll take that," Julia said. She threw away the paper towel and returned to the stove.

Julia soon finished making the fried green tomatoes and covered the plate with a paper towel.

I nodded at Julia. "Very nice to meet you."

She gave me a warm smile, still looking amused. "Nice to meet you, too."

I followed Alice into the rather dark hallway, with wooden floors, on the other side of the kitchen. It led to the home's three bedrooms. First, immediately on the left, was a small bathroom with pink tiles. A pair of women's stockings hung to dry. Above the sink, a dental appointment reminder was tucked into the side of the mirror.

Across the hallway was a compact room with a spare bed. This was the only bedroom with a window on West Avenue and the blinds were drawn. The room held additional bookshelves and, on a small table, the fax machine that was Alice's lifeline to friends and family now that her severely limited hearing made phone calls impossible. It was Alice's quickest link to her sister in New York and even her friends just down the street.

Every week, she told me, Nelle faxed her the Sunday *New York Times* crossword puzzle. The puzzles were a shared pleasure, one they had in common with their mother.

Alice began to tell me about their family. Frances Lee had died in 1951. Nelle was only twenty-five then and still adjusting to life in New York City. She worked as an airline reservations clerk and wrote on the side. *To Kill a Mockingbird* wouldn't be published for another nine years. Only six weeks after Frances Lee died unexpectedly that summer, following a surprise diagnosis of advanced cancer, Alice, Nelle, and their middle sister, Louise, lost their only brother, Ed. He was found lifeless in his bunk one morning at Maxwell Air Force Base in Montgomery. Only thirty years old, he'd had a brain aneurysm and left a wife and two small children.

The sorrow of those events still flickered across Alice's face as she recounted them a half century later. When she spoke of the shock of the two deaths, Alice dropped her gaze, and her already raspy voice grew scratchier.

"Daddy was a trouper," she said. "He lost his wife and his son in a short period but he kept going." And so did Alice. At work at their firm, the two of them took refuge in the purpose and routine of their shared law practice.

The following year, Alice and A.C. moved to this house from the family's longtime home on Alabama Avenue where Frances Lee gave birth to Nelle in an upstairs bedroom, where Nelle and Ed climbed the chinaberry tree in the yard, where A.C. pored over the *Mobile Register* and *Montgomery Advertiser* every day and indulged his fascination with the crimes detailed in magazines such as *True Detective*.

But Alabama Avenue was growing more commercial, and the tranquillity of West Avenue appealed to father and daughter. A.C. had suggested the move to West Avenue before the events of that terrible summer, but Frances wasn't interested. She didn't want to leave the street where she had friends for a wooded area being newly developed. She'd been out there, to visit a friend who had just had a baby. The memory prompted an affectionate chuckle from Alice. "She said she didn't want to move out there with all the owls and bats."

On her extended visits home from New York, Nelle had a new place to call home. As a girl, she liked to watch her father in action at the courthouse. As a woman, she still accompanied him to the law office some days to work on her manuscript about the character he inspired, Atticus Finch.

Alice and her house held a wealth of Lee family stories. In this spare room with the fax, we lingered in front of a bookcase. I asked Alice about their favorite authors. High on her sister's list, she told me, were William Faulkner and Eudora Welty, Jane Austen and Thomas Macaulay. The first three are familiar names to most people who've taken high school English, whether or not they remember what they read. Nowadays, *Home Alone* actor Macaulay Culkin has far greater name recognition than Thomas Babington Macaulay, the British writer, historian, and Whig politician. Thomas Macaulay died in 1859. More than a century later, Culkin's parents named him in honor of the original Macaulay. Fame is a strange beast.

Alice preferred nonfiction, especially British and American histories, and Nelle devoured those, too. I spotted a shelf lined with many such histories. Judging by the jackets, some were recent, but many were published decades ago.

"Have you spent time in England?" I asked.

She ran her deeply lined hand across the spines of a row of books. It was a tender gesture. Loving, even. "This," she said, "is how I've traveled."

Alice's room, down the hallway a bit and on the left, had a bed with a bright pink coverlet, an old dresser, and, naturally, a crammed bookcase. Other books were in piles on a chair and on the floor. Still more books and rafts of papers were scattered across half the bed.

Like her father, I would later learn, Alice had a peculiar reading habit at bedtime. She would lie flat on her back and hold the open book above her face to read it. Seems like an uncomfortable position but it worked for A. C. Lee and it worked for his daughter. If Alice couldn't fall asleep, she had her own version of counting sheep. She silently ran through the names of Alabama's counties. Or American vice presidents. Chronologically. But in reverse order.

At the end of the hallway, she showed me Nelle's bedroom. This originally was their father's quarters. It was as modest as the rest of the house. When Nelle was in New York, Julia occupied the room. The walls were blue. Built-in bookshelves lined the wall to the left of the door. A small figurine of a cat perched on a shelf at eye level. A trunk sat under one window. A small door led to the private bath.

As fascinated as I was by this unexpected house tour, I didn't want to overstay my welcome. But Alice brushed aside my concern about that and continued the conversation.

My thoughts turned to Terrence again. I told Alice that he was out in the car. Would it be okay if he came in to take her photograph?

"Well, yes. All right. Invite him in."

I hurried out through the darkness to the rental car. It was still a warm night but not nearly as warm and close as in the house.

Terrence lowered his window. He grinned.

"Sorry, sorry, sorry." I said it so fast it came out as one word. "I had no idea I'd be in there so long. That is Miss Alice. She's wonderful, Terrence. Come on in. She said it's okay to bring your camera."

"Oh, fantastic." Terrence followed me up the wooden steps to the front door.

Already I was looking forward to telling him about my conversations on our drive back to the Best Western.

"I hope you have enjoyed your visit to Monroeville," Alice told Terrence.

"Very much."

We chatted some more in the living room, and then Terrence, tentatively, got down to business. "Is this good here?" he asked. Alice had resumed her spot in the recliner.

"Yes." Alice smiled at Terrence but also looked a touch wistful. "I never did like photographs of myself. The problem is they look like me."

Terrence spoke to her gently, put her at ease as much as he could.

"I just hope I don't crack your camera," Alice told him. She said this with the wry delivery I came to know well. The real life "Atticus in a Skirt," as Nelle called her, had that in common with the novel's quiet attorney. Just as a neighbor in the novel observes of Atticus, Alice could be "right dry."

Alice had one request for me. Could I stay on long enough to interview the Methodist minister who was a good friend to both Lees? I said I'd like to and I'd ask my editors if I could extend my visit.

I inquired if I might ask her some more questions the following day, either here or at her law office. I expected she might decline, reasonably enough. Already she had been generous with her time. To my delight, she invited me to stop by her office.

Terrence and I bid her good night and slid into the rental car. We drove back to the motel, excited by this unexpected development.

The next morning, I called my editors. We agreed it made sense to stay on. Alice speaking on the record, particularly about their parents and her sister's experience with fame, was unusual.

We had another long interview that day, in the suite of offices above the Monroe County Bank. Barnett, Bugg & Lee was a two-lawyer firm consisting of Alice and a young male attorney she had taken under her wing. Another attorney was of counsel. A receptionist sat at a desk near the front door and relayed callers' messages to Alice. She could no longer hear well enough to use the telephone. As with Atticus Finch and many other small-town lawyers, real estate transactions, tax returns, and wills were at the heart of Alice's practice.

At one point I asked her about her sister's long public silence. "I don't think any first-time author could be prepared for what happened. It all fell in on her," Alice said, "and her way of handling it was not to let it get too close to her."

And what about the first question everyone had about her sister: Why didn't she write another book?

Alice leaned forward in her office chair. "I'll put it this way . . . When you have hit the pinnacle, how would you feel about writing more? Would you feel like you're competing with yourself?"

Chapter Three

The following day, my phone rang at the Best Western.

"Hello?"

"Miss Mills?"

"Yes, this is Marja."

"This is Harper Lee. You've made quite an impression on Miss Alice. I wonder if we might meet."

It was as if I had answered the phone and heard "Hello. This is the Wizard of Oz." I felt my adrenaline spike. With effort, I kept my speaking voice from going up a couple of octaves.

"That would be wonderful."

The voice on the other end was slightly husky and almost musical, her Alabama accent undiminished by the years in New York City. She didn't sound the least bit shy.

This was not to be an interview for my newspaper story, she said, but a chance to visit. "Would eleven A.M. be all right? At the Best Western?"

"That would be great. Whatever works best for you."

"All right, then. I'll see you at eleven."

I hung up the phone and collected myself.

I called Terrence's room, then Tim in Chicago. Who would have guessed? It was exciting and a little nerve-wracking.

Tim reacted as Terrence had. "What? Really?"

That night, in bed, I opened the novel again. I slipped under the covers and into the cadence of her prose and the pace of life in 1930s Maycomb.

No matter what the parameters were, I was intrigued by the opportunity to meet with this mysterious literary legend, this woman whose book had meant the world to so many millions of people for so many years. And I never expected to actually be able to speak with her, anyway; so many reporters, year after year, had come to Monroeville before me and left with nothing to write except more stories about hunting for Harper Lee.

The next morning, I went over my notes. I imagined she might want to know who had spoken with me.

The knock came at the appointed time.

I opened the door to my motel room. The light was harsh compared with the dark room. I blinked. Everything about the woman before me looked solid and practical: the short white hair, the large glasses, the black sneakers fastened with wide Velcro straps. Her bangs were cut high and straight across her forehead. She was solidly built and on the tall side. She wore a simple white cotton blouse over casual tan pants. She had on a bit of lipstick but otherwise no makeup or jewelry.

"Hello," I said. "Please come in."

"Miss Mills." She smiled and stepped into the coolness of the room. I closed the door.

"I'm so glad to meet you," I said. "Would you like to have a seat here?" I motioned to the small table. Not that there was much alternative. Other than a chair pulled up to the desk against the wall opposite the beds, the table offered the only place to sit. It was a bit cramped, shoved up against the window immediately to the left of the front door as you entered the room. I took the chair by the window and she sat to my left, facing the window. "I can open this if you'd like more light," I said with a shrug. I wondered if she would prefer the privacy of closed curtains.

"No, this is just fine. Thank you."

Based on what I'd read, I expected either someone of great reserve or perhaps someone angry about my being in town and unafraid to express her displeasure.

She was neither. Her voice had a pleasant lilt, and although she was reserved while we exchanged greetings, as soon as we began talking she came across as down-to-earth and self-assured. She repeated nearly word for word what she had said on the phone. "Well, you've made quite an impression on Miss Alice."

"She was wonderful."

"I understand you had quite a conversation."

"We did. I just wrote her a note." I nodded toward the desk. "I've been making the rounds and told her I'd keep her up to date on that. She told me I should talk to Dale Welch and Reverend Butts."

She scowled and leaned in a bit closer.

Was that the wrong thing to say?

"Pardon me. I didn't hear you."

I raised my voice. "Your sister told me I should talk to Dale Welch and Reverend Butts."

The scowl deepened. She cupped her hand to her right ear. "What?"

The air-conditioning unit just to my right and under the window seemed to have two settings: noisy and off. I switched it to off. The loud rumble and blowing abruptly ceased. It was a reckless move in summertime southern Alabama but it worked.

"Is this better?" I asked. "I can turn it back on if it gets too warm."

Her face relaxed and she smiled. "No, that's better."

Alice had filled her in on our conversations.

Before we began talking in earnest, she was very clear: This would not be an interview. "Just a visit."

I agreed, and filled her in on the One Book, One Chicago happenings.

I mentioned the movie showings. I'd enjoyed Gregory Peck's remarks in a documentary about meeting Lee and filming *To Kill a Mockingbird*.

At the mention of Peck, she leaned forward. Her eyes danced.

"Isn't he delicious?"

She had as many questions for me as I had for her. She wanted to know more about the One Book, One Chicago program, and she also asked about the director of the program, Mary Dempsey, with whom she had spoken. She also asked about the specifics of my stay, including where I had gone, who had spoken with me, and what they had said. I didn't feel I was being grilled; her tone was conversational.

I did want to know what she thought of Monroeville today.

"I read that when they were going to film the movie, they decided Monroeville had changed too much from the thirties for them to film here."

She made a face, as if she had tasted something sour. There was something childlike in her expressions, not childish but animated, spontaneous in an appealing way. At the same time she spoke with an almost formal grammar.

"This is not the Monroeville in which I grew up. I don't like it one bit."

She was not one to equivocate, clearly.

We spoke at some length about how the character of the town had

changed. She also echoed Alice's comments about the continual attention she received and the toll it took on both of them. As she put it,
"Forty years of this gets to be a bit much."

She was a woman of formidable intellect. I would have loved to
hear her expound on any number of topics. But I trod carefully that
first day. I was concerned about her famously private nature. Yet here
she was, putting me at ease. I came to realize later that she set the tone
of any conversation.

"Alice told me a little about your parents, and Finchburg. And
Burnt Corn." That was a nearby community, tiny but still something
listed on maps. We laughed together about some of the colorful place
names in Alabama. She lamented that local flavor was being lost. Later,
she noted how developers often named new subdivisions for what they
had destroyed to create them. As Lee put it, many paved Oak Groves
stood where oak trees had fallen.

Mayor Daley wasn't the only prominent Chicagoan to have pro-
claimed his love of *To Kill a Mockingbird*. Oprah Winfrey spoke of the
influence the novel, one of her favorites, had on her. I'd heard she'd
wanted to pick the novel for her immensely popular televised book
club but that the novelist declined.

Lee confirmed this. "I met her. We had lunch together." The two
discussed Winfrey's request over lunch in New York at the Waldorf
Astoria, she said. Lee declined her request but was impressed by Winfrey's knowledge of her characters, and her passion for the book.

"What did you think of her?" I asked.

"Well, for a girl, a black girl, growing up in poverty in Mississippi
when she did to accomplish what she has . . ." Her voice trailed off. "It
is remarkable."

Winfrey had been a cultural force as long as I could remember. It
was easy to forget—unless you remembered the place and era in which

Winfrey grew up—how unlikely it was at the time that she would become a cultural figure of influence and wealth beyond all imagining.

Lee mused aloud as to why Alice and I developed a quick rapport. With her index finger stabbing the air as if she were pressing an invisible doorbell—a gesture, I'd come to learn, that was as automatic to her as breathing—she delivered a true compliment, given the character of the woman to whom she compared me.

"I know what it was," Harper Lee said. "Quality met quality."

I had never heard that formulation before. It might have been particular to her.

I was surprised, once again, that she seemed in no hurry to leave. When she did stand to say good-bye, I thanked her and she wished me safe travels.

But she had one last surprise.

She hugged me. I hoped I didn't look startled. And then she was gone.

Chapter Four

Already I found myself fascinated by Harper Lee and Alice Lee as sisters. Even at their ages, it was clear Alice was the steady, responsible older sister, and Nelle Harper the spirited, spontaneous younger one. Born fifteen years earlier, Alice was as much mother as sister to Nelle. Alice had lived most of her life in Monroeville, and she and Nelle shared her home several months of the year. The rest of the year Nelle lived in her New York City apartment. Alice handled, in large part, Harper Lee's financial affairs. Her sister had no interest in that, Alice said.

They were utterly different in temperament and the paths they chose. Nelle left Monroeville in 1944 to attend Huntingdon College, as Alice had done, in Montgomery. After a year, Nelle went on to the University of Alabama in Tuscaloosa and studied law. The summer of 1948, she studied at Oxford and fell in love with England.

Both she and Alice were fascinated with English history and English literature. Their own English roots went deep, back to the barons of Runnymede, the feudal landowners who made history by forcing King John to accept the Magna Carta, limiting his powers, in 1215. The more Nelle and Alice learned about British history, the more they wanted to know. It was true when they studied it in high school and college, and it was true in the decades of personal reading that followed. Alice's research into the family's origins led her to believe they also had an ancestor who, four hundred years later, was one of the scholars to help translate the King James Version of the Christian Bible for the Church of England. Nelle believed this translation to be simply the best, hands down, no argument.

After Oxford, Nelle returned to her legal studies in Tuscaloosa but left a semester before she would have gotten her degree. The philosophy and human drama of law interested her. The dry technicalities did not. Alice recalled, "She got an itch to write."

Or, rather, to devote herself to writing. She had dabbled in it before, starting with the stories she and Truman made up as children. At the University of Alabama, she wrote for and edited the *Rammer Jammer,* a student humor magazine. Like Alice, she was also a lifelong correspondent. "Her letters," her friend Tom later told me, "are like short stories. Her powers of description are extraordinary."

And so the dark-haired young woman was off to New York, at age twenty-three, to a walk-up, cold-water flat and a job as an airline reservations clerk. It was several years before she was able to quit that job and start writing full time, in a turn of events worthy of an O. Henry short story. On Christmas Day in 1956, Harper Lee was spending the holiday at the home of her friends Joy and Michael Brown. She found an envelope addressed to her on the tree in their living room. Inside was a simple message: "You have one year off from your job to write whatever you please. Merry Christmas."

Lee wrote about that turning point, calling it "a full, fair chance for a new life," in the December 1961 edition of *McCall's* magazine. "I went to the window, stunned by the day's miracle," she wrote. "Our faith in you was really all I had heard them say. I would do my best not to fail them." They meant it to be a gift, but she insisted on repaying them. The Browns remained lifelong friends and a surrogate family in New York. When Nelle went to the White House in 2007 to receive the Presidential Medal of Freedom, the Browns were in attendance.

Nelle extended the same kind of gift to many others. Alice told me her sister gave very generous sums to charities, behind the scenes, and I came to learn she had educated many people who never knew she was their benefactor. She preferred to do her charitable giving quietly. Some of it was distributed through the Methodist Church. Other regular contributions went, quietly, to local charities and other organizations. But that came later. When she moved to New York, she had little money and lived frugally. Even after the unexpected success of her book, she still lived frugally when it came to spending on herself. In Monroeville, she bought clothing at the local Walmart and the Vanity Fair outlet. In Manhattan, she took taxis on occasion but mostly rode the bus.

Lee's initial efforts, living in New York in the 1950s, were short stories. Then, at the suggestion of her literary agent, Maurice Crain, she expanded one of them into what would become *To Kill a Mockingbird*. For a time, the title was simply *Atticus*. She wrote the novel in Manhattan and Monroeville, where she spent time helping out after her father fell ill. When she had first submitted the novel to J. B. Lippincott Company, she was asked to rewrite it. It was finally published in June 1960. She expected the work to be met with "a quick and merciful death at the hands of the critics."

It was not. Nelle Harper Lee, the onetime tomboy roaming Monroeville by foot and the world at large by vivid imagination, was now Harper Lee, literary celebrity. The *New York Times* review praised her "level-headed plea for interracial understanding" and her "gentle affection, rich humor and deep understanding of small-town family life in

Alabama." The reviewer, Frank H. Lyell, also wrote, "The dialogue of Miss Lee's refreshingly varied characters is a constant delight in its authenticity and swift revelation of personality." Lyell did judge, however, that "the praise Miss Lee deserves must be qualified somewhat by noting that oftentimes Scout's expository style has a processed, homogenized, impersonal flatness quite out of keeping with the narrator's gay, impulsive approach to life in youth. Also, some of the scenes suggest that Miss Lee is cocking at least one eye toward Hollywood."

I'd sent along a photocopy of the *Chicago Tribune* review, an unqualified rave of an "engrossing first novel of rare excellence," with the materials I mailed to Alice Lee before my trip south.

Whatever her discomfort with public speaking, the Harper Lee of those early years after the book's publication granted interviews and even, in 1965, gave a speech to several hundred West Point cadets.

"This is very exciting," she began that day, "because I do not speak at colleges. The prospect of it is too intimidating. Surely, it's obvious— rows of bright, intense, focused students, some even of the sciences, all of them analyzing my every word and staring fixedly at me—this would terrify a person such as myself. So I wisely agreed to come here, where the atmosphere would be far more relaxing and welcoming than on a rigid, strict, rule-bound, and severely disciplined college campus."*

The cadets roared.

She came across as quick-witted and passionate. In more than one interview, she admitted to being fearful of how a second novel would fare. But she gave little indication of the toll that, privately, was being exerted by the publicity and demands of her success.

Lee dutifully made the rounds promoting the book. She sat for

* Gus Lee, *Honor and Duty* (reprint, New York: Ivy Books, 1994), pp. 149–50.

radio and print interviews and showed a writer and photographer for *Life* magazine around her hometown. She appeared at press conferences and book signings. Several years after the book was published, she still was fielding questions and replying with a characteristic mix of low-key erudition and self-deprecating wit.

People wanted to know more about the dark-haired woman from Alabama whose first book was becoming a phenomenon. What were her plans? Did she date? Did the characters' relationships in the book reflect those in her own life? What would she write next?

She was also spending long hours responding to fan mail and requests for additional interviews and appearances. Capote wrote a friend that he wished she could enjoy the fruits of her success. Instead, she seemed hassled. He reveled in his literary fame. She endured hers.

For someone who disliked dressing up and fussing over her appearance, that aspect of life in the spotlight was one more reason to dislike public appearances.

One reporter at a Chicago press conference to promote the film took note of her weight and the fact that she didn't curl her hair. "Chicago Press Call" included this description by a reporter for *Rogue*, a Chicago-based men's magazine, in its December 1963 issue: "Harper Lee arrived. She is 36-years-old, tall, and a few pounds on the wrong side of Metrecal." Metrecal was the Slim-Fast diet shake of its day. "She has dark, short-cut, uncurled hair; bright, twinkling eyes; a gracious manner; and Mint Julep diction."

Asked if she found writing her next book slow going, Lee answered, "Well, I hope to live to see it published."

Questions about her second book began to rankle. She wasn't making the progress she hoped, and preferred not to disclose the specifics of the novel she had been working on for more than a year at that point. The expectations of a second novel were overwhelming.

When you start at the top, she told those close to her, there is nowhere to go but down.

Her decision never to publish another book took on the aura of a dramatic decision she had made early on after the overwhelming success of *To Kill a Mockingbird*. Her choice to live out of the public spotlight and begin a half century of silence seemed equally stark.

But the decision not to publish again was far more gradual than that. As I got to know Nelle and her friends, I learned that, rather than a grand decision, the shape of her life was dictated by a series of small choices made at different points along the way. For many years, she thought there might be a second book.

At age thirty-four, Harper Lee had a stunning achievement behind her, and a world of promise before her. Naturally, she planned to write more. She would turn her keen eye once more to the complexities of character and community. In *To Kill a Mockingbird* and in future work she envisioned, the rich particulars of her corner of the Deep South could illuminate something universal.

"I hope to goodness every book I write improves," she told an interviewer, only half in jest, in 1964. "All I want is to be the Jane Austen of south Alabama."

Then: silence.

"There were so many demands made on her," Alice recalled. "People wanted her to speak to groups. She would be terrified to speak."

Lee withdrew from public view and never published another book.

And so for a half century now, readers and reporters alike have asked the question that drives any good mystery: Then what happened? She wasn't telling, at least not publicly.

Chapter Five

The Lees' onetime pastor and longtime friend Thomas Lane Butts called. He was back from preaching out of town, and he would come by the motel and drive me to dinner. Alice hadn't wanted me to leave town without talking to him, as he was a close friend to both of the sisters. What was it he would have to say? And why were they asking a good friend to sit for an interview about Harper Lee, on the record, the very thing they usually discouraged?

As a Methodist minister assigned to different congregations in south Alabama and Florida over the years, Tom came to know Alice well back in the 1970s. Like the Lees' father, she was deeply involved in the affairs of the Methodist Church in Alabama and northern Florida. Tom had been the pastor of the Lees' church, First Methodist, for several years. Technically, he was then the pastor emeritus, although Alice chided him about his "alleged" retirement.

Tom and his wife, Hilda, became friends with Nelle Harper in the 1980s, when Alice fell into a coma, apparently from a virus that was not responding to antibiotics. Finally, after a few weeks, she regained consciousness. By then, her sister and the Butts had spent long hours together at the hospital, getting to know one another over stale dough-nuts and endless cups of coffee, worried sick about Alice.

There weren't many people in Monroeville with whom Nelle could enjoy long conversations about her favorite writers and historians, people like Macaulay and British cleric Sydney Smith, his nineteenth-century contemporary. She found a kindred spirit in Tom, someone whose wit, intellect, and lack of pretense were a good match for her own. He and Nelle were just as happy fishing together and trading stories of their Alabama youth as they were discussing the King James translation of the Bible or Macaulay's voluminous history of England.

Tom and Nelle grew up just one year and fifteen miles apart. But it was far from assured that their paths as adults would intersect the way they did. He was a country boy growing up in a sharecropper's home in which the only book for many years was the Bible. She lived in town, the daughter of a lawyer in a family that loved to read. "In one way," Tom said, "we grew up the same. But in another way, we didn't."

Tom's family, in *To Kill a Mockingbird* terms, was closer to the fic-tional Cunninghams, poor folks who eked an existence out of the land, than the Finches, who derived a modest income from the law and so-cially were a notch or two above.

Among white families in Maycomb, the violent, foul-mouthed wid-ower Bob Ewell and his passel of unkempt children are at the bottom of the heap. They even live next to—and off of—the town dump. At age nineteen, his oldest, Mayella, is trapped. Trapped by poverty, by circumstances, by her abusive father. She grows red geraniums in a chipped chamber pot, cultivating what little beauty she can in a bleak existence.

As a pastor, Tom had known versions of all three families. "I've been knowing Mayellas all my life," as he put it.

Earlier that day, though I didn't know it then, he had spoken with Lee about what to say, and what not to say, when I interviewed him. I later learned what the list included. He could talk about the book and their friendship, but she didn't want him to give specifics for the newspaper story on where she spent time around Monroeville. Otherwise, those restaurants and even the homes of her friends might be subject to visits by reporters or tourists in search of a Lee sighting. Already reporters had been known to visit David's Catfish House and Radley's in hopes of encountering her. In her absence, they asked waitresses and other customers about the town's most famous resident.

He was surprised that both Lees encouraged him to speak with me and, more so, to talk freely about most topics pertaining to them. It turns out he was as curious about me as I was about him.

I waited for him at the front entrance of the motel. He pulled up in a roomy gray Buick and stepped out to greet me. He was short, only five feet four inches, not much taller than I am. He was what used to be called a natty dresser. Italian leather loafers, a crisp shirt and designer tie, navy blazer pressed just so.

"Miss Mills," he said, and extended his hand. He was more formal than I expected there in the parking lot under the Best Western sign. Every now and then I felt I was glimpsing the Monroeville of another era.

"Have you been to the South Forty?" he asked me. I hadn't. The restaurant was a fifteen-minute drive from Monroeville, near the tiny town of Repton.

The South Forty was a down-home place, with a rough-hewn front porch, light oak tables and chairs in a bright room, and the day's specials listed on a whiteboard. We took a table against the wall in the back.

"I don't know why Alice and Nelle have opened up to you the way they have," Tom told me. "They are two of the most interesting, intelligent women you will ever meet and they have remained so private all these years. I get after Nelle Harper about it. I say, 'You need to be out there, teaching or talking to people.' She says, 'I value my privacy too much.'"

So why help out on a newspaper story now, and why me? The reverend speculated that the sisters were pleased by the One Book, One Chicago program and figured if there was going to be a story, it might as well provide some insight. The letter I sent to Alice's post office box, letting her and her sister know I would be in town and why, might have helped pave the way, he said, since it struck the right tone: polite and not wheedling or demanding. They got a lot of the latter. Once Alice and I developed that quick rapport, other doors opened.

"I think after that first day or two you were here, word also got back that you were an intelligent, charming young lady who seemed like a thoughtful person as well." They were kind words, though I suspect "right place at the right time" was a factor.

Whatever the reasons, the reverend said he was thrilled that Alice was willing to speak on the record at some length, that Nelle Harper had been willing to get together, and that both sisters had given him their blessing to speak to me.

Butts told me Nelle Harper liked to tease him if he missed a literary reference, such as the time he came up short on his knowledge of the writing of Sydney Smith.

"She'll say, 'Dr. Butts!'" He mimicked her mock outrage. "'I thought you were an educated man.'" Once, on the way back from fishing at the home of a mutual friend, he was pulled over for a rolling stop at a stop sign. His passenger turned to him as the officer approached their car.

"Quick," she said, according to his recollection. "Don't you have a clerical collar in the glove compartment or something you could put on?" She was kidding. Maybe.

Butts said he helped administer charitable donations, through the Methodist Church, that Lee didn't want to carry her name. Neither sister talks much about their faith, he said, but their ties to the Methodist Church are strong. That is how they were raised.

"They are very traditional in some ways," Butts said of Alice and Nelle Harper. "They tithe. They like good, old-fashioned preaching. They don't believe in spending a lot on themselves, although they could."

"And then, in other ways, they seem so different," I said.

"Miss Alice is very calm and deliberate, and yet powerful in the statements she makes," Butts said. "Whereas Nelle Harper has more hell and pepper in her. . . . She has that public reserve but her feelings get expressed rather graphically sometimes. An injustice stings her to the bone.

"And, of course, Alice is a very systematic person," Butts added, "whereas Nelle goes at [a task] like she's fighting a fire and then won't do anything more about it for a month or two. When she's going somewhere it's always a last-minute struggle to get ready."

If Alice had an event to attend or a trip to make, she was ready a week ahead of time. When Nelle Harper prepared to return to New York each year, she spent the last few days in Monroeville rushing around and muttering about all the boxes she had to ship, the bags she needed to pack, the loose ends she needed to tie up.

Like all of Nelle's friends, I would come to know this quirk of hers. "Can't talk. Fifty-eleven things to do before I leave," was her flustered greeting when she was preparing to return to New York.

I asked Tom about Nelle's life in New York, where she had a small one-bedroom apartment on the Upper East Side. For many years,

Nelle had divided her year between her home in New York and Monroeville. She would say she was going south to look after Alice. Once Alice no longer drove, Nelle would take her to and from the office, "Driving Miss Alice," as she said. Among her friends, the feeling was that Nelle needed Alice as much as, if not more than, Alice needed her.

Once home, they would get to clucking over each other, Alice telling Nelle to drive carefully and Nelle telling Alice not to work herself to death. The two women had this much in common: Sisterly admonitions aside, they did as they saw fit. As Nelle prepared to go back to New York, Julia teased her about that. "You know she's going to be back to it," Julia said, "as soon as your feet hit the street."

Tom had spent time with her in New York the previous month. He served as guest preacher for a few Sundays at Christ United Methodist on Park Avenue, as he had done every summer for more than fifteen years. He stayed in the apartment of the regular minister, who was away on vacation with his family. Tom's grandson, fifteen-year-old T. L. Butts, visited from Mobile.

Nelle, whom he described as a "rabid Mets fan," nonetheless took the reverend and his grandson to the place the young man wanted to visit: Yankee Stadium. The three took the subway there and back and sat in the bleachers, apparently drawing not a single second look. "We go all around," Butts said, "and no one even knows they are seeing one of the great literary figures of the twentieth century."

Nelle Harper, he said, dressed in jeans and a T-shirt much of the time. She liked to go to the Metropolitan Museum of Art, and took the bus there. Tom and Nelle would take a bus to the casinos of Atlantic City as well. They both loved a gambling trip, and they'd indulge on the Mississippi River, too. In Atlantic City, they played the machines, met up for lunch, went back to their favorite machines, and hoped they could find each other before it was time to go home.

Once, they located each other right before the bus would have left without them.

"Thank God," Nelle told him. "I thought I was going to have to call Alice and tell her I'd lost you."

"That's exactly what I was thinking," Tom told her. "I didn't want to have to make that call to Alice."

Tom and I looked up from our conversation and saw that we were the last ones in the restaurant. They needed to close.

"I hope we can talk some more, by phone and when I come back," I told him.

"Definitely," he said. "See that you hurry back."

By the time he dropped me off at the motel, went home, answered e-mails, and wrote in his journal, it was past midnight.

After I began work on this book, he gave me permission to read and quote from his journals. That night, he sat at his kitchen table and wrote the day's entry in his slim, hardcover journal. Two rows of the journals, with "Record" embossed in red on the covers, resided in one of his many bookcases.

"Took a package to Harper Lee that had been delivered to me," he wrote of that day. "We talked for a while about the Chicago Tribune reporter and what she would like me to say and not say. To my astonishment, NHL spent two hours with the lady—not in an interview but in a visit. I've never known her to give a reporter the time of day."

Of that evening he wrote, "I hope she does a good job with this series of articles, because NHL has put lots of trust in her integrity. I would hate to see NHL wounded by any of this."

Nelle asked that Tom not reveal when she was in New York versus Monroeville and that he not disclose the restaurants and other spots where journalists or tourists might find her.

This was becoming a different story than my editors and I first envisioned. It was unprecedented for Alice and Tom to say this much on the record about Harper Lee. With the author's trusted circle usually unwilling to talk, Tom pointed out, "Those who know don't speak and those who speak don't know."

As far as I could tell, two better sources of insight into the author's life didn't exist. Alice was as much mother as sister. She had vivid memories of Nelle Harper when she was the age of Scout in *To Kill a Mockingbird*, about six. The attorney knew their father, the model for Atticus, better than anyone and shared her home with Nelle Harper part of each year. For forty years, she had been deeply involved in handling her affairs.

Tom Butts, meanwhile, knew Nelle Harper in the way almost no one else did: He spent time with her in both Monroeville and Manhattan. Few, if any, of Nelle's Manhattan friends spent time with her Monroeville circle and vice versa. Tom knew her in both contexts.

My editors agreed it was worth delaying the story to take up the Lees on their invitation to return. I could fly South again in a week or so, and research a longer profile of Harper Lee. One Book, One Chicago would continue into October. We had a little time.

I told the Lees and Reverend Butts I would be in touch about a possible date to return, and Terrence and I made our way back to Chicago.

Chapter Six

B ack in Chicago, Terrence and I were surprised when photos of Nelle being inducted into the Alabama Academy of Honor went out on the wire. He had suggested staying on to photograph her at that Montgomery ceremony, since she did not want him to photograph her in Monroeville, as he had done with Alice and the other interviewees. It was no surprise she would not want to be photographed for my story; our meeting was off the record for newspaper purposes, after all. But now Terrence had missed his chance.

I mustered what gumption I could and faxed the author. The letter, addressed "Dear Ms. Lee," said,

> *I'm writing with a request: Would you consider letting Terrence pay you a very brief visit in the next few days? He stayed away from Monday's Montgomery ceremony at your request, but then was chagrined to see the Montgomery newspaper publish that photo of you that went out on the news wires. That happens; and we, of course, are most grateful for the help you and the others have been in our research . . .*

I went on to tell her about the next steps in the One Book, One Chicago program, including a story I was writing about the staff of a children's hospital reading the novel to their patients.

Lee's sense of fairness, and her distinctive style, were abundantly clear in her reply. It arrived the same day. The one-page, handwritten letter began with high praise for Terence, whom she called "a latter-day Alfred Stieglitz" and whose portraits she and Alice thought were "unfailingly wonderful." She was certain that they were taken through cheesecloth.

She consented to be photographed and noted that she and Alice didn't wish to be photographed together. I learned later that they didn't want their ailing other sister, Louise, to feel excluded.

She signed the letter with her full name and in parentheses added, "And call me Nelle—for goodness' sake."

Terrence flew down soon after, and spent a day with her. "She was actually a lot of fun," Terrence said. "She knew I had a job to do and we drove a number of places." She teasingly gave him the nickname "Terrible T."

For my part, it looked like the second week in September might work out for a return trip. Before then, Alice and Nelle Harper would be with their sister Louise. She lived in Eufaula, two hundred miles away. We agreed that a return flight on September 12 would work.

But on Tuesday, September 11, as the horrifying footage of the World Trade Center played nonstop on television, I faxed the Lees. It would be all hands on deck at the paper for a while. With planes grounded I wasn't sure when I'd be able to reschedule the visit.

Nelle called Tom the following day, September 12, when she and Alice returned from Eufaula. Nelle wanted to seek her solace at the catfish ponds on the rural property of their mutual friends Ernie and Angie Hanks. The following day, the preacher and the writer cast their lines in those tranquil waters. Their bobbers left only small ripples in the surface. Neither could think about much except the horror in New York, but they did not discuss it at any length.

"She didn't really want to talk about it," Tom said. "She just wanted some peace. That's how she deals with those things."

The first week of October, I made the return trip to Alabama. I would interview Alice again and do more reporting in Monroeville. Tom suggested another form of research: fishing with Nelle. If she was up for it.

As research goes, I decided that fishing with Harper Lee would beat an afternoon in the library.

Tom invited me to join him at their usual spot. If Nelle wanted to join Tom and me, the three of us would go. If she preferred to do her fishing without the likes of me, understandably enough, I'd still see their favorite spot and she and Tom would go another time.

"Nelle is in her element there," Tom had told me. "I'd like you to see that if it works out. And if not, you'll still have a good afternoon."

I waited in the glass-front entryway to the Best Western. A gray Buick made a left turn off Alabama Avenue, or Highway 21, as it was considered here on the outskirts of town. The Buick crossed the large parking lot and pulled under the portico. Nelle was in the passenger seat. She had on faded blue jeans and a T-shirt. Behind the wheel, Tom was in overalls and a white T-shirt.

I raised my hand in greeting and slid into the backseat. "Hey, girl," Tom said. From Nelle: "Hello, child." I was excited she was joining us but wanted to be low-key. She might be skittish, liable to dart away if she felt crowded. "Hi, there," I said.

"You ready to catch some fish?" Tom asked.

He turned and looked at me over his shoulder for a moment. I could see he was pleased, proud he had been able to make this happen.

"You bet," I said, as casually as I could, but with a look that telegraphed "Thank you, thank you, thank you."

Nelle asked what I had been up to the last couple of days.

I began to tell her about my interviews, leaning forward in my seat a bit and raising my voice to be heard.

She was chatting, in good humor, but she also was gathering intelligence. What had I heard lately from the people at the Old Courthouse?

She also didn't want our fishing trip to be in the story in a way that revealed I was there with her. We worked it out later that I could describe the outing by attributing the description to the friends and not spelling out that I was there, too. She also asked me not to identify the friends hosting us that day. "I don't want people showing up there, looking for me or bothering Ernie and Angie." Long after the newspaper story ran, she gave me permission to include outings such as this one in the book.

Not that many out-of-towners would be able to find Nelle's fishing hole anyway. It was well off the main road to the nearby town of Lenox. A wooden sign nailed between two trees formed a rustic entrance to the property. Emblazed on the wood was SWAMPY ACRES. It wasn't swampy, though. A couple of large ponds were surrounded by large oak trees. Beyond were Ernie and Angie's carefully tended rows of corn, watermelon, and tomatoes.

Before we arrived, Tom told me that Ernie's left leg had been amputated below the knee, a complication of his diabetes. With the help of his prosthesis, and a beat-up golf cart, he still spent long hours puttering around the gentle slopes of the property. He grew up near here, played in these woods as a boy, searching out enemy soldiers lurking behind the tree trunks. He met Angie, the woman who would be his Yankee bride, when he was in the service. She was a fun-loving, petite, dark-haired girl from a big Italian family. They both liked to laugh.

"Do they still have figs?" Nelle wondered aloud as we drove the final stretch of dirt road to the Hanks' home. They did, Tom said, and some days they could be eaten warm off the tree.

Tom pulled up to the gravel area by the house, a one-story ranch with brown and beige bricks. Ernie was waiting for us, ready to fish. He was tall and wearing denim overalls like Tom's. A large straw hat shielded his reddened face from the sun. We made our way down a small slope to one of the two large catfish ponds. The oak trees around the ponds were reflected in their placid, dark surfaces. "Do you know what we use for bait?" Tom asked me. Nelle waited for my answer, looking mischievous. Tom pulled out several small plastic Baggies.

"Hot dogs!" he said. He doled out the small chunks of wieners from the Baggies and we slipped them on the fishing hooks.

I stated the obvious. "It's beautiful here."

"I never get tired of this," Nelle murmured.

They both caught a few fish. My casts were falling short. I tried again, casting more energetically, and caught my line in the branches of an oak.

As dusk fell, we trudged back up the gentle slope for dinner around the kitchen table. Ernie took the fish we'd placed in a white bucket and put some on ice. The rest he gave to Angie. She coated the fish in bread crumbs and lightly fried it, along with a pile of sweet potato rounds. We feasted that night.

"Delicious," Nelle pronounced.

Tom took his glass to the sink and dumped out the ice cubes. He hesitated, then retrieved them and rinsed them off.

"Angie, do you want me to . . . ?"

Angie laughed. "Sure."

Tom put the cubes back in the freezer. "Old habits die hard." He looked sheepish, then amused.

Ernie was chuckling. "I catch myself doing the same thing."

Nelle tipped her head back and laughed. "Oh, Tom."

He explained. When they were children in the 1930s, getting ice, and keeping it, was a lot of work. And it cost money. The rolling store came through town twice a week, selling its wares, and so did the ice truck. It was out of Evergreen, the Conecuh County seat and home to the railroad station from which Nelle later set out for New York. The iceman hauled big blocks of ice in the back of the truck. He stretched a canvas tarp over the top to keep them cool, or as cool as they could stay under the Alabama sun. Air-conditioning didn't come in until the 1960s, and even then it was enough of a novelty that businesses that had it advertised the fact.

So used ice was something to rinse off and keep, not toss in a sink to melt. Tom's mother washed off any ice that remained in a glass and put it in a sawdust-lined hole in the ground. Then she covered it with cloth. She would no more let ice melt down a drain than she would throw away the scraps of cloth she stitched into quilts.

On hot days, which were most days, nothing was as refreshing as a chip of ice dissolving on your tongue and running cool down your throat. Just the sound of it clinking in a glass of sweet tea made you feel cooler. It was civilized.

This was the first of many times I would find myself around a kitchen table with Nelle, enjoying the sound of laughter and old friends trading stories of the way things used to be.

It was pitch-black outside now, and time to go home.

"Angie, you are a marvel," Nelle said, pushing back from the table. "I don't know when I've enjoyed a meal more."

"You come back quick, Nelle," Angie said.

Ernie walked us to the car and opened the passenger door for Nelle. "Don't be getting into any trouble now," he said.

"Heavens, no," she said, laughing.

"I can't make any promises," Tom said.

It was their usual give-and-take. Nelle fumbled to fasten her seat belt by the car's interior light. She feigned indignation. "Tom, what in the world?"

He reached over and guided the seat belt into the buckle.

Nelle rolled her window the rest of the way down and reached over to put her hand on Ernie's sleeve. "You take care of yourself, Ernie. Thank you for a wonderful time."

Ernie nodded and glanced at the backseat. "You find your way back here now, you hear?"

Nelle and Tom chatted the whole way home about people they had in common with Ernie: who had been feuding with a neighbor, who had remarried, who had come into a small inheritance, and whatever happened to his cousin?

The names didn't mean anything to me. But I listened to the easy banter between the two, even as I got sleepy in the backseat. Tom was right. Nelle was in her element here.

We followed our headlights through the dark back to Monroeville.

On that trip, I was able to spend more time with Alice and Nelle. Once they passed, Tom pointed out, the tangle of myths and half-truths that have flourished amid Nelle's decades-long silence would only grow. He worried about that.

"When she and Alice go, people are going to start 'remembering' things as they didn't happen, or outright making things up, and they won't be here to set the record straight. So keep taking notes, girl."

One afternoon, I had a message from Nelle. Since I would be in town awhile longer, would I like to go for breakfast? If so, she would swing by the motel the next morning and get me. Once again, I found myself waiting in the glass vestibule of the Best Western, not sure what to expect.

She was right on time. She pulled up in a dark blue Buick sedan and motioned for me to get in.

"Good morning."

"Morning," she said. "Have you been to Wanda's?"

I hadn't. We made a left onto Highway 21 and, a short distance later, just past the intersection with 84, turned into a large gas station parking lot. Behind it was Wanda's Kountry Kitchen, a low-slung diner painted yellow. Nelle glided into a parking spot and glanced over at me.

"It's not fancy. But it's good food. More or less." She gave a wry smile. "You've discovered Monroeville's dining options are limited?" This was a statement more than a question.

A sign posted near the front door had the silhouette of a video camera and a warning: THESE PREMISES PROTECTED AGAINST BURGLARY, HOLDUP AND VANDALISM.

Nelle opened the door for me. "Proceed."

I proceeded. Cigarette smoke greeted us, and the din of regular customers at their usual tables. A gentleman with an enormously round belly and scraggly beard was holding court, loudly, at a table of several men. In one corner, a group of older women was deep in conversation, flicking cigarettes in a couple of ashtrays in the middle of the table. Half of the other tables were occupied. To our left, the woman behind the counter looked up.

"Anywhere," she told us.

Nelle and I slid into two empty places along the far wall. Our waitress was a slim woman in her fifties or sixties with a tanned, lined face. She set two large plastic menus in the middle of the table.

"Hi, hon," Nelle said.

"How y'all doing this morning?"

"Tolerable."

"Coffee?"

"Please," Nelle said.

I studied the menu. It was standard fare: eggs and hash browns and hotcakes, along with that Southern staple, grits. Nelle barely glanced at the menu and set it aside. The waitress returned with the coffee carafe and filled our cups, the thick white mugs of diners everywhere. Small curls of steam rose from the mugs.

"Bless you, hon," Nelle said. She wrapped her hands around the mug.

Now Nelle was spooning a couple of ice cubes from her water glass into her coffee. She looked over at me. "Do you need a minute?"

"No. That's all right. You go ahead and I'll be ready."

The waitress pulled out her pad.

"I'll have two eggs, over easy," Nelle said. "And a side of sausage. And a biscuit."

"Gravy?"

"Yes, ma'am!"

I was pretty sure ordering my trying-to-be-healthy usual— scrambled egg whites, a piece of wheat toast, and a side of fruit— violated the spirit of this place. It could mark me as a city girl or a granola head, neither a popular demographic around here. I set down my menu.

"I'll have the same, please. But with bacon instead of sausage, please."

I wondered if Nelle had invited me to breakfast to ask me something specific or just to continue our conversation. Those eyes of hers, brown and penetrating, could be unnerving but at the moment they were sparkling. She smiled broadly.

"Have you had sawmill gravy?"

"No, I haven't." Sawmill gravy . . . sawmill gravy. I should know what this was. Was it mentioned in *To Kill a Mockingbird*? This was lumber country, after all, sawmill country.

"You're in for a treat."

Nelle was draining her cup as we spoke. When the waitress stopped by, Nelle tapped lightly on the side of her mug. "Keep it coming, would you, hon?"

I'd studied Nelle, subtly, I hoped, at the Best Western, at the catfish pond, and now here at Wanda's. Each time her humor and her down-to-earth demeanor struck me.

There was an edge there, too, though, of suspicion or impatience, and I didn't want to set it off. Tom had warned me she had a temper. When something set her off she could get creative with her cursing, her salty "Conecuh County English," in Tom's words.

"Have you been back to the courthouse?"

"Yes, I was there and I stopped in the history room in the library. I spent some time with Dale Welch."

Nelle's expression softened.

"Dale's a good egg. She was a librarian, you know. And she taught. She's a reader, unlike most of the people around here."

As I was recounting my conversation with Dale, our food arrived, and I had my first look at sawmill gravy, poured over my biscuit. It was thick and white with bits of sausage. I had never learned to like gravy of any kind. At holiday time, my family knew not to pass the gravy boat my way. But if this was part of local culture, and possibly a test of my willingness to partake, I was going to eat it all and look like I was enjoying it, no matter what.

It was viscous stuff. I swallowed hard.

Nelle dug into her own biscuit and eggs with gusto. That surprised me a bit, because I'd read so much about her reserve. But that was at public events, I suppose. In person, her heartiness was appealing: her relish of the food and coffee; that big laugh; her obvious affection for Alice and Julia and Dale and Tom. I had assumed I would have to keep my distance from the famously private Harper Lee but I couldn't help but enjoy her company. She might have been prickly but she was a delightful companion.

I did some more reporting around town for a couple of days. As I was walking from the car to my motel room one afternoon, I felt a lupus flare taking hold, worse than usual. I didn't know if I'd be able to make the long drive to the airport the next day. It meant a trip to the local emergency room.

I knew this sensation. It was mounting. I'd been pushing through the fatigue. I recognized the characteristic shooting pains in my fingers and toes

I'd been more tired the last few days but now it was what the doctors call wipe-out fatigue. Walking to and from the rental car felt like trudging through molasses. Even lying in bed I felt slammed.

I faxed the Lees that I would have to cut my stay short and thanked them for the time they'd spent with me. Because of their failing hearing, faxing was our most reliable mode of communication. I apologized for rushing off—this was a standard-issue lupus flare, for me, and once I got treatment at the ER I'd be fine and on my way. I'd fax them once I was in Chicago, and keep them posted as I put together the stories.

I drove the short distance to the hospital and filled out the paperwork to be evaluated in the emergency room. A nurse took me to one of the private areas and drew blood. I conferred with the white-smocked doctor making his way from one curtained area to the next. We agreed this was probably a flare that could be treated. I'd get home and then deal with my doctors there if needed.

The nurse started an IV and I started figuring whether it would be realistic to try to drive to the airport later that day. I was resting on a gurney when I heard a voice.

"Child, what have you done to yourself? Heavens."

I knew that husky voice. Nelle had materialized by the gurney.

I was stunned, and embarrassed. I didn't want her to go to this trouble or to see me like this. I stood up to greet her and blushed on the spot.

She gave me a quick hug and then stood back, taking the measure of how I looked.

I was hoping the hospital's tile floor would open up and swallow me. Knowing how the Lees felt about journalists, I had taken extra care not to impose on their time and goodwill. For their sake, and mine, it was best I be professional, together, and outa here. This had no place in that picture.

Instead, here I was, a pale-faced girl in a hospital gown, shaky and embarrassed that Nelle had gone to the time and trouble of driving to the emergency room.

"You're so kind to come out here. But really, this is just standard stuff. I've dealt with it before."

She looked at me skeptically.

"They'll do some labs, see where things are. They'll probably give me a little bit of IV steroids and I'll be fine."

She glanced over at the nurses. She lowered her voice and leaned in closer. "If anyone asks, I'm your mother-in-law. Otherwise they won't let me stay back here with you. Only relatives. Rules." She spit out the last word. I smiled.

Before long, Nelle was on her way, and I was on the mend.

In Chicago, I faxed the Lees on my first day back at work to let them know I was feeling better. As it turned out, ongoing health problems and other assignments conspired to delay the publication of the stories even longer. Finally, in September 2002, I began final fact-checking on the articles we were preparing to publish.

I wanted to spell out in the story that Nelle consented to be photographed. Otherwise, I thought, readers would wonder why a story in which she had no comment, as usual, was accompanied by *Tribune* photos clearly taken with her permission. Not at all usual.

Nelle questioned if that explanation was necessary but gave her consent in a one-page, typewritten letter spit out of a *Tribune* fax machine.

In the letter, she did two seemingly contradictory things. She made clear her low regard for newspaper reporters. She also indicated she might be open to talking with me some more.

I sat at my desk and read the fax. As would happen many times in the years to come, I was unsure, and anxious, about what Nelle would have to say this time around. I needed to honor my agreement with her and Alice. At the same time, I had to write a journalistically sound article, not a puff piece.

She began with kind words. I had returned to work after a short stay in the hospital. She and Alice were endlessly patient as my health problems slowed the process of getting the story ready to be published.

She wrote that she was "appalled by the viciousness of lupus" and was encouraging about the way I'd dealt with setbacks. "You are a most remarkable young lady. Bless you" I was to make it "Quaker plain" that she declined to comment for the story.

For my edification, she outlined the decline, as she saw it, of journalistic standards. "The files on one Harper Lee," in fact, were a useful case study of the fall. She had no patience for New Journalism. She lamented the passing of an era she said I was too young to remember, one in which a reporter's first and only job was to get the facts right, not to inject personal opinion. After reflecting on her treatment in the press, she began the next paragraph, "Therein you should see the possibilities of another story."

I remembered the case in general in which the U.S. Supreme Court widened freedom of the press, making it more difficult for public officials to win libel or defamation cases against news organizations. I looked up the specifics. The *Sullivan* case focused on civil rights coverage in the segregated South, but its ruling applied more broadly to what some perceived as a lowering of standards regarding both accuracy and malicious reporting. Plaintiffs had to prove "actual malice" by reporters and editors, the hard-to-prove action of setting out, deliberately and knowingly, to publish inaccurate reports in an effort to defame public officials.

I didn't agree entirely with her view of my "once reputable profession" but I knew what she meant. And as a practical matter, I was hugely encouraged that she was bothering to teach me what she saw as the relevant history of my career. I read the letter a second time. I appreciated the comments about dealing with lupus. More important, in the story soon to go to press, I could state that she had consented to be photographed and thereby resolve that issue.

And those magic words, unlikely as they were coming from Harper Lee: "You should see the possibilities of another story."

———————

The main article, with a few sidebars, was to run Friday, September 13, 2002. I flew to Montgomery Thursday afternoon, as planned, with the preprinted feature section in hand. After so much time, theirs and mine, spent reporting the story, I wanted to face them after they read it, whatever their reaction. And I didn't need to be asked twice when they encouraged me to come back when I could.

Friday, at Barnett, Bugg & Lee, I found Nelle slouched in a chair in Alice's office after a morning running errands. Alice sat, as always, facing the doorway, her deeply veined hands folded on her desk's little return table. We exchanged greetings and the usual catch-up on weather, travels, health. Nelle nodded at the copies of the *Tribune* I held in my hands.

"You are a brave woman," Nelle said. "You have come to face your accusers."

The way she phrased that, I thought, sounded like something out of the British histories they read. I pictured the two sisters in the white wigs worn by British jurists.

I wasn't feeling all that brave. Would they think the story was fair? I thought so, but I couldn't be sure. Accurate? Better be. But so much conflicting information had been published about Nelle Harper over the years. I was wary that an incorrect date or a long-exaggerated anecdote could survive the fact-checking I had done, somewhat awkwardly, by fax.

I figured a few things in the story might bother Nelle. But they came from Alice and their preacher friend, Tom Butts, speaking on the record. Already, I was feeling the uneasy tug between inquisitive journalist and protective friend.

The story, "A Life Apart: Harper Lee, the Complex Woman Behind 'a Delicious Mystery,'" took up the front page of the section and another two full pages inside. The section front included a large, close-up photo of Nelle, gazing with those penetrating eyes, arthritic hands folded in front of her on an unseen restaurant table at Radley's.

The story traced Harper Lee's path to being such a famously private author and gave details of her day-to-day life in Monroeville with Alice, from feeding the ducks to collecting mail at the post office. It described the toll the press of attention had taken on both sisters. One sidebar story described the fishing outing, another Nelle's long friendship with Gregory Peck. Per our agreement, I did not include my meeting with Nelle.

While they read it, I left to photocopy an essay about local history that Alice wanted me to read. Not everything in the story was flattering, though much of it was. I didn't know how Nelle would feel about all Alice had said on the record. I dallied by the photocopier so they could read the piece without my standing there.

When I returned to Alice's office, Nelle looked up from the newspaper. She read quietly for a few more minutes. "B plus," she said when she finished. From Alice, "Good job." They seemed generally pleased, perhaps relieved.

Nelle did have one complaint, about the way I described Alice's accent in this sentence: "'Nelle Harper is very independent. She always was,' says Alice Lee, who, with her Alabama inflections, pronounces the name 'Nail Hah-puh.'"

Wrong. "Nail Hah-puh" was closer to the way some people I interviewed pronounced her name, but not Alice. There was something soft, something Southern, in her pronunciation, but it was more subtle than I had been able to capture phonetically. I'd seen her name spelled phonetically like this in other stories and remembered the moment I sat at my desk quietly repeating aloud the name as I remembered Alice saying it. Not quite it, I thought to myself at the time. But as close as I'm going to get. Now I regretted it.

"You dropped her two social classes with one syllable," Nelle said.

I was chagrined. Even so, I had to admire her admonishment. It was succinct and delivered its sting with a dash of wit. Classic Nelle.

I tried to imagine the correction the *Tribune* could run. "An article in the September 13 *Chicago Tribune* mischaracterized the way Alice Lee pronounces the name of her sister Nelle Harper Lee. Alice Lee says 'Nelle Harper,' not 'Nail Hah-puh.' The *Tribune* regrets the error."

Absurd? Maybe I could come up with a better way to word it. Maybe not.

Don't bother, Nelle said. She'd rather leave it be. I let it go. But I made note, ever after, of the myriad accents freighted with meaning within the 1,035 square miles of Monroe County, Alabama.

Chapter Seven

The Lees invited me on a drive the following day to see one of their favorite historical spots: the grave of Creek Indian Chief William "Red Eagle" Weatherford. Dale and Tom would join us as well. Nelle drove Alice, Dale, and me. Tom trailed us in his Buick. About an hour out of Monroeville, we came across the small town of Stockton and the Stagecoach Cafe.

The decor of the Stagecoach Cafe was pegged to its history as a stopping place for the covered wagons making their way across this part of the state. Even the salad bar was shaped to resemble a giant (and very long) covered wagon. The five of us sat at a long pine table with a red-and-white-checked cloth. We ordered sweet tea and baskets of fried oysters.

Nelle ate the last of her oysters with relish. She pushed her chair back with a small groan. They were good, and they were filling. Alice took small bites from her plate. It took her longer to eat less. Before we left, Alice rose to use the ladies' room. I went with her.

It isn't easy navigating a restroom with a walker. By the time Alice made her way to one of the sinks, I had washed and dried my hands. The surface around the sinks had the usual splashes of water, and stray strands of hair. You wouldn't want to set down a pocketbook there. The paper towel dispenser was on the wall, several steps from where Alice stood. To reach it, she would have had to grip her walker with wet hands. I handed her a paper towel.

Alice dried her hands and then matter-of-factly wiped clean the area around the sink. This hadn't occurred to me to do. I was in a hurry or someone else left the mess or I was paying no attention. Pick your reason. But this was routine for Alice, an extension of being a good citizen, really. It was a small thing. And yet it wasn't.

She ruined me for leaving public sinks the way I find them. Years later, I'll be in the ladies' room at a restaurant or the movies and notice the counter around the sink is wet. "Oh, forget it this once," I'll think and begin to walk away. Then, ashamed, I'll turn around and dry the sink.

Fortified by our big lunch, we climbed back into the two vehicles and pointed toward the main destination that day: the grave of Creek Indian Chief Red Eagle. A green Baldwin County park sign pointed the way to the grave.

We had talked, on country drives, of the heritage of the area, of Creek Indians and white settlers, many of them Scottish, Irish, and English. Of the people who arrived not by choice but by slave ship and melded African traditions with those forged in the hardships of their new existence.

"There's a reason for the Southern tradition of storytelling," Nelle explained. "We are Celtic," she said, "and African."

And contrary, she added, especially when it comes to edicts from above. "When Southerners know they have to obey the law, they do it, without much enthusiasm. Though segregation has ended, that doesn't mean there isn't a terrific social stratum still in place."

Nelle idled the car by the grave sites. A simple gray slab was engraved with "Red Eagle" in large letters. "William Weatherford" was carved above it, and his birth and death, "1765–1824," were below. The slab was embedded in a thick pillar of stones. Next to Red Eagle's grave was that of his mother, Sehoy Weatherford, with no dates given. A small distance away, a large green plaque contained several paragraphs about Red Eagle's colorful life. It also gave a short history of the chief's mother.

I walked the short distance from the car to the plaque and began reading.

"The son of a Scotch trader, Charles Weatherford, and a Creek Indian Princess, Sehoy Tate Weatherford, William was destined to become one of the most powerful leaders of the Wind Clan of the Creek's Indian Nation."

I glanced back at the car. Nelle made a motion that indicated "Keep reading. We're fine." So I did, trying to concentrate on the words and not the sledgehammer heat or the surprise of being invited on this outing.

"During the early 1800's conflicts, usually over land, between the Creek Indians and the white settlers erupted into open warfare. After having led his warriors in the attack on Fort Mims, in August of 1813, he was known to have grieved at the viciousness of the attack. Over 500 white settlers, men, women and children, and several hundred Creek Indian Warriors were killed in this historic battle."

Nelle was captivated by local history. She admitted to feeling the hair on the back of her neck raise sometimes when she drove past the site of the Fort Mims massacre. Her reading of Albert J. Pickett's two-volume *History of Alabama* brought to life the horrors of the bloodshed between the white settlers and the Creek Indians.

"I feel presences there," Nelle said.

I was still concentrating on Red Eagle's story and withering in the

September afternoon sun when Nelle yelled from the car window. "Child, come here immediately," she commanded. Something in the way she said it made me dash to the car without saying a word.

Another order: "Get in the car."

Only then did she point out the four-foot rattlesnake that had been curled at my feet.

Smart move, I realized from the safety of the Buick's backseat. If she had called out, "Rattlesnake—watch out," I would have been looking around, alarmed, instead of simply darting to safety.

"You scared me to death," Nelle said. I couldn't tell if she was angry or relieved. Some of both, I decided.

With me safely in the backseat, Nelle began scolding Tom. The preacher had gotten out of his car. Armed with rocks, the seventy-two-year-old Tom inched a little closer to the snake.

A rattlesnake nearly killed his sharecropper father years ago when he reached his hand into a woodpile and was bitten by the snake. Tom still remembered his father's arm swelling grotesquely as his sons rushed him to the home of Dr. Carter, the only physician for miles.

This day, the good reverend had a plan. He wanted to stone the snake to death. He gathered rocks, then aimed and missed a couple of times.

"Tom, stop that right now." This was foolishness.

He complied.

It was frightening for a moment but, more so, it was encouraging as Nelle and Alice both seemed enthusiastic about showing me around the area.

Back in the car, Nelle issued an invitation.

"Do you have plans? Would you like to go to dinner with Tom and me?"

"Well, yes, I'd love to, thank you."

"Does the South Forty sound all right?"

"That sounds great."

Alice would stay home since it was after dark, Nelle said, but her sister wanted us to go. Alice liked at least a window of solitude in her day, time to settle into her recliner with no distractions as she tended to her correspondence and read. Tom would go home to change clothing and then drive the three of us to the South Forty.

Nelle did have a request. Would I mind terribly if we bypassed the Best Western until after dinner? It would simplify things if I waited with them at their house while Tom went home to freshen up. That way he'd have to make only one stop.

I sat with the Lees in their living room before going to dinner; they both wanted to get back to the books they were reading. Alice offered me that day's *Mobile Register,* and motioned to the plaid sofa next to her chair. "Please make yourself comfortable."

She took her usual spot in the recliner and pulled the lever to raise the leg support. She resumed where she had left off in one of the four books she had going. As usual, Alice's focus was on nonfiction. "Real life is so interesting." She appreciated good fiction, of course, as did Nelle, whose reading tastes were more varied.

Alice was the picture of relaxation, somehow, despite the skirt and jacket and pantyhose, her everyday uniform. Her outstretched legs were crossed at her slender ankles. As always, white Reeboks completed the ensemble.

Nelle had gone down the hallway to freshen up. She returned and sank into her reading chair across from Alice with a loud "Oomph. I'm bushed." We'd had quite a day. Nelle made a face, then brightened and chuckled. She shot a look of—what?—merriment, perhaps, at Alice and then me. Perhaps because their hearing made small talk a hassle, especially across even a small room, they managed to convey a lot with just a look or a gesture. I was learning to be more comfortable with silence around them, to resist the impulse to begin chatting out of politeness or habit.

Nelle, too, had a side table with a smaller stack of books and some papers. She opened a small hardcover. The only sound in the room was me turning the page of the *Register* as quietly as I could. They were reading peacefully, companionably, as they did so many evenings. Routine for them. Magical for me.

The Lees encouraged me to pay another visit to Monroeville, a social call this time, now that the newspaper story had run. This was new territory for all of us. The work, as such, was completed but a friendship had begun, one that, against the odds, felt natural, unforced. They urged me not to "disappear back to Chicago."

I was touched by their sincerity. I had loved hearing their stories and, of course, wanted to get to know both of them better. I wasn't thinking or talking in terms of a book at this juncture, but as a journalist I wanted to continue our conversation. With Alice being ninety-one years old, there was always an urgency to these conversations. In retrospect, I think the Lees and their friends chose to open up to me in part because they knew Alice might not be long for this world.

By that point, the Lees had already begun assigning me Alabama history books to make up for my woeful ignorance of their local heritage. I noted in a fax to them that my copy of Pickett's history was on the way. This was the book Nelle wrote about in an essay presented in Eufaula, Alabama, in 1983, and later published. "In what would occupy a few paragraphs of an American history survey," she wrote, "Pickett took 669 pages to unfold a story that is more hair-raising than anything yet seen on television. Indeed, in today's terms, it is almost as though Pickett trained a camera in relentless, unblinking close-up on a period of Alabama history that we seldom think about anymore, a period that sometimes seems to live only in our place-names and on roadside markers."

Throughout our friendship, the Lees assigned me history books to read that they deemed essential, including Carl Carmer's *Stars Fell on Alabama,* W. J. Cash's *The Mind of the South,* James Agee and Walker Evans's *Let Us Now Praise Famous Men,* Harvey Jackson's *Inside Alabama,* and Wayne Flynt's *Alabama in the Twentieth Century.*

Nelle recommended fiction as well, including Alabamian Mary Ward Brown's *Tongues of Flame,* a collection of short stories. I lingered over the one about a Yankee reporter who makes a fool of himself by making assumptions about the small Southern town he is visiting. She'd blurbed Roy Hoffman's *Chicken Dreaming Corn,* about an Eastern European Jewish family in the Mobile of the early 1900s.

Their reading tastes were varied and fascinating. It's a safe bet that the Lee home was the only one in Monroeville getting a steady stream of British periodicals. They subscribed to several. Among them: the *Spectator,* the *Weekly Telegraph,* and the *TLS,* or the *Times Literary Supplement.*

Magazines would pile up on the floor by the reading chairs, on kitchen counters, on the bookshelves. American periodicals arrived in abundance, too. They got the *New York Times Book Review, New York,* and *Newsweek,* as well as *Vanity Fair.* And then there were the newspapers that Julia fetched from the front porch early each morning: the *Mobile Register,* often left hanging over the arm of the plaid sofa, and the *Montgomery Advertiser.*

A treat I always brought them from Chicago's Midway or O'Hare airport was that day's *New York Times*—handed to a grateful Alice or Nelle, or left in a plastic bag on their doorknob.

At times, when I'd see Alice or Nelle reading one of the papers, I was reminded of the scene in *To Kill a Mockingbird* after Sheriff Tate comes to tell Atticus that Tom Robinson is being moved to the local jail that night. A crowd of local men stand in the yard, trouble brewing. Atticus thanks the sheriff and goes back inside.

"Jem watched him go to his chair and pick up the evening paper. I sometimes think Atticus subjected every crisis of his life to tranquil evaluation behind *The Mobile Register, The Birmingham News* and *The Montgomery Advertiser.*"

Nelle wanted to make sure I had read William Faulkner and Eudora Welty, to better understand the South. She liked Flannery O'Connor less, particularly the Catholic element in her books. Plus, O'Connor had once said that *To Kill a Mockingbird* was a good book— for children.

Alice was fascinated by crime stories. As a young woman she closely followed, along with most of the country, the trial of Nathan Leopold and Richard Loeb, charged with murdering a fourteen-year-old Chicago boy in 1924. Clarence Darrow defended the two young men who spent seven months planning the perfect crime. Alice recalled her anticipation each day, coming home from school as a thirteen-year-old, to read that day's coverage of the trial.

But she loved English history most of all. In an early visit, Alice told me she was reading *The Asquiths* by Colin Clifford. It's exactly the kind of book that intrigued her—a sweeping saga about the remarkable British family in the early 1900s, headed by Margot and Herbert Henry Asquith, who became prime minister. A fax she sent to me in Chicago ended with this:

"I almost feel that I am a member of that family! No fiction can match the story of their lives. That is why I love history and biography."

Alice and Nelle's shared interest in the Asquiths goes back a long way. In an essay Nelle described spending Christmas with her good friends Joy and Michael Brown and their young children in New York, noting that "we limited our gifts to pennies and wits and all-out competition. Who would come up with the most outrageous for the least. . . . Bedlam prevailed until they discovered there was more. As their father began distributing gifts, I grinned to myself, wondering how my exceptionally wily unearthments this year would be received. His was a print of a portrait of Sydney Smith I'd found for thirty-five cents; hers was the complete works of Margot Asquith, the result of a year's patient search."

The books that Nelle read in childhood had a recurring theme— one of adventure and getting out of predicaments, without the moral tone of some earlier children's books.

She later described her early reading life in a July 2006 letter that ran in *O, The Oprah Magazine,* that began, "Dear Oprah, Do you remember when you learned to read, or like me, can you not even remember a time when you didn't know how?"

Her family read aloud to her, she said, and her childhood friends circulated their scarce books among themselves. As time went on, they swapped books in order to acquire a full set of a series.

"Now, 75 years later in an abundant society where people have laptops, cell phones, iPods, and minds like empty rooms, I still plod along with books. Instant information is not for me. I prefer to search library stacks because when I work to learn something, I remember it."

Alice had me read *The Ballad of Little River* by Paul Hemphill, about a south Alabama black church burning in the 1990s. Nelle later took me to the area where the church was located. Friends Ila and Judy joined us, too. When we went to the Dixie Landing rural café, Nelle had me stuff my copy of the book in my purse. It was not a popular book around there. Only the top peeked out of my small purse. I rested my hand on it.

Chapter Eight

When I was in Chicago, we kept in touch by fax. I told Alice and Nelle, for example, about additional newspapers that had run my story. Alice was a regular correspondent, keeping me up to date on how she and Nelle were doing and what was happening in Monroeville. I began to get a deeper appreciation for the way in which meaningful friendships once blossomed via letters. It allows time to reflect, and to reveal oneself gradually.

In July 2003, I made it back to Monroeville. I saw Dale Welch and drove with Tom to see Alice honored in Mobile with the Alabama Bar Association's second annual Maud McLure Kelly Award. The honor was named for the first female lawyer in the state.

This was the first and only time I saw Alice wear footwear other than her trademark white Reeboks. She had on white flats for the occasion. They complemented her lavender suit. She stepped more gingerly without the traction of the Reeboks.

I glanced around the room and saw lawyers and judges, and Lee friends and family. This was, everyone understood, a day to honor Alice while she was still alive to enjoy the tributes.

"I don't see Nelle," I told Tom.

"I noticed that. It's a long trip by train, though. And I'm guessing she wanted the focus to stay on Alice today. Anytime she's in a room, she is going to be the star attraction."

Nelle's best tribute to Alice was in the pages of *To Kill a Mockingbird*. All those years ago, she dedicated the novel to her and their father. The simple dedication was "for Mr. Lee and Alice in consideration of Love & Affection." A. C. Lee, Nelle made it clear from the start, was the inspiration for Atticus Finch. And Alice, in Nelle's words, was "Atticus in a Skirt."

Tom took to the podium to introduce Alice, and to recount the legal career being celebrated that day. When it was time to deliver a sermon or give public remarks such as these, he lowered his voice an octave or two and put a little more English on the ball, linguistically speaking. He called this his "stained-glass voice."

"Let me tell you something about the journey of this unusual woman, who is the uncontested, quiet queen of the courthouse, the Methodist Church, and the community where she lives."

Both Alice and her father started their law careers later in life, after working in other capacities. A.C. was a bookkeeper for a lumber company before studying law. Alice graduated from high school in 1928 at the age of sixteen and went on to Huntingdon College in Montgomery. When the Depression hit, she returned to Monroeville before graduating. A.C. had purchased the *Monroe Journal*. She worked there seven years, doing whatever needed to be done, as she put it. She spent the following seven years in Birmingham. She went to work for the Internal Revenue Service in the newly created Social Security administration. From 1939 to 1943 she attended night school at the Birmingham School of Law. The bar exam, in 1943, was an ordeal. She told the audience assembled at this Mobile hotel for the Maud McLure Kelly event of the four anxious souls taking the exam. Three young men, all 4-Fs, disqualified from service in World War II due to physical problems, and one Alice Finch Lee.

"I don't recall a single one of us completing a single exam, a factor that caused considerable anxiety as we had no clue as to how it would affect the examination. Four examiners, sixteen exams, and at five P.M. on the afternoon of day four we were finished. It is my private opinion that Lance Armstrong, who is currently looked upon as the epitome of stamina and endurance, is no more fatigued at the conclusion of one of his races than we were at the end of day four."

She passed.

"Something called the Victory Tax had just become law," Tom told the crowd. "All income over six hundred dollars became taxable, and people who had never filed a federal tax return had to file. There was no CPA in Monroeville, but it was commonly known that Miss Alice had worked for seven years for the IRS, so people assumed she was well versed in income tax law. They didn't know that her work for the IRS had been in the Social Security division and that she had never filled out an income tax return other than her own. Tax clients poured in. Miss Alice studied the tax code by night and did tax returns by day. She became the tax lady."

As much as she was known for her legal work, Alice's role in the Methodist Church was probably the defining work of her life. When Tom asked Alice for a list of offices she'd held in the Methodist Church, she said simply, "Well, I've never been the pastor." She served on every committee they could come up with, much as her father had.

Tom took special pride in recounting her actions at a regional Methodist conference. "It was in the midsixties when the rhetoric of racism was loud and vitriolic. A committee report concerning the problems about our racially divided church and society had come to the floor. Amendments had been made and debate had started. And the advocates of continued racism were poised and ready to try to drag the church deeper into institutional racism. But before their leader could get to the floor, a wee woman from Monroeville, Alabama, got the attention of the presiding officer of the conference. Miss Alice Finch Lee went to the microphone to make her maiden speech to the Alabama–West Florida conference of the Methodist Church. Her speech electrified the seven or eight hundred delegates there—I was there. It consisted of five words. She said: 'I move the previous question' and sat down. The conference applauded enthusiastically and voted overwhelmingly to support her motion and then adopted the committee report without further debate. The advocates of racism were left on the sidelines holding their long-prepared speeches. Miss Alice became the hero of the conference and from that day on the enemy of the racists. She's always been a person of few words but important words said at the right time and the right place."

It wasn't an impassioned speech, but the Southern Methodist Church was deeply divided on the question of race in the 1960s. Alice's stand carried quite a lot of weight with the congregation. It's an example of the quiet work for equality that has been a hallmark of the Lee family. The sweeping change that came to the South in the 1960s was largely the work of the civil rights movement and its brave leaders. But people like the Lees played an important role behind the scenes. Of course, Nelle's novel itself was influential for generations of Americans in how they understood the questions of civil rights.

One of the more common criticisms of the character of Atticus Finch is that he did not do enough to fight the racism of Maycomb. His way was to do so rather quietly, and behind the scenes. A.C. and

Alice were cut from that Atticus cloth. Or, rather, Atticus was cut from the A.C. and Alice Lee cloth.

A year after the Lee profile ran, I was on to other topics and continuing to struggle with my health. I was in the hospital and at home more and at work less. Periodic inflammation in the lining of my lungs wasn't serious, but it was painful and tiring. Nausea was a problem. I'd had a few surgeries in recent years and now underwent a few more, one to repair a femoral artery damaged during a diagnostic procedure and a couple of others to repair stress fractures in my left foot that were slow to heal. I spent a fair amount of time on crutches or in a walking cast.

My editors were mostly understanding, but in 2003 they told me I needed to go on the *Tribune*'s medical disability plan. It was a blow. I didn't want to leave a job I liked, even though it had become a test of will to work through the periods of wipe-out fatigue. I was hopeful I could return in a couple of months or a half year, tops. My list of story ideas, things I wanted to write about for the feature section, grew longer, but after a year of rest and additional treatments, I was no closer to being able to return. I still had good days but they were unpredictable.

But what if I was in Alabama for those good days? Alice's willingness to share her stories with me in her nineties was a gift. It was also an unexpected opportunity to research and write at a slower pace on a project that felt tailor-made for someone like me. Nelle had already told me several things she thought I could write about and correct regarding "the forty-year file on Harper Lee."

Just as Nelle's retreat from fame was a series of small decisions, as opposed to one sweeping pronouncement, their decision to let me into their lives as fully as they did had not stemmed from one grand declaration but, rather, was a gradual process. They kept encouraging me to come back south, and on each trip they would share more of their lives and their history with me. Slowly but surely, the idea of a longer sojourn in Alabama took hold.

Chapter Nine

E ven before my move, I was becoming part of the Lees' social circle and, as such, was included in their regular get-togethers. In
early 2004, I was staying with Haniel and Judy Croft. Haniel was the
retired president of what was then the Monroe County Bank. They
invited Nelle and Alice and me to watch the Super Bowl on the big-
screen television in their living room. We'd settle in to see the New
England Patriots play the Carolina Panthers in Houston and then have
dinner. "Marvelous," Nelle said of that invitation.

I looked forward to it as much as they did that week, even though
the only Super Bowl games I remotely enjoyed watching over the years
were in Black River Falls. Those I enjoyed not for the football but for
the sound of my grandfather's deep voice mixing easily with my
father's and brother's above the television commentary and the din of
the crowd.

For years, Nelle and Alice had their own tradition for watching
football games. They loved watching the Crimson Tide in particular.
They had no television in the house, Alice told me, until Julia was
hired in 1997 and insisted. Nelle had suggested the same more than
once, but it took Julia to get a small set across the threshold. She was

not about to miss her game shows. After that, during football season, Alice would join Nelle in the back bedroom to watch the games. Before the dawn of the television age in the Lee home, the two sisters would make the seven-block drive to the Monroe County Bank building, below Alice's law office, and watch the weekend's best games in a conference room.

Sometimes Nelle watched University of Alabama games at the home of her high school English teacher, Gladys Burkett. This was in an old house on North Mount Pleasant Avenue, a few blocks off the town square. It was there that Nelle got to know Dale Welch. They met over football but bonded over books. "I think she appreciated that I was a teacher and a librarian. We had a lot to talk about," Dale told me. A friendship quickly blossomed and soon they were meeting for coffee or lunch at Radley's.

Like many in their circle of friends, the Lees were a mixed family when it came to football in Alabama. Their brother had attended Auburn. That gave it special status. But Nelle had attended the University of Alabama, and she and Alice gravitated to the Crimson Tide. If you ever want to drive down an empty thoroughfare in Monroeville, do so when Alabama is playing Auburn.

Their other great sports passion was golf. In fact, both Alice and Nelle had once played the game regularly at the Vanity Fair golf course. Nelle told a journalist in the early 1960s that the course provided her a quiet place to think. They particularly looked forward to the Masters every April. As Alice told me, "We usually root for the underdog." Later that same spring, the Lees got a thrill cheering for Phil Mickelson at Augusta, where he won his first major at long last.

As was often the case in Monroeville, I was reminded on that Super Bowl Sunday that I was a foreigner. The temperature in snowy Black River Falls, my father's hometown, barely reached into the twenties.

On Alabama Avenue in Monroeville, the Monroe County Bank time and temperature sign showed it was fifty degrees. We settled into the Crofts' comfortable living room to watch the game. Haniel Croft took a wing-backed chair. His wife, Judy, and I were on a coral-colored sofa, Nelle across from me. Alice preferred a chair to sinking into a sofa. As soothing as the sounds of the three generations of menfolk in my family had been to me, my own voice sounded distinctly midwestern, almost clunky, in a room of softer Southern accents.

In lighter moments, my otherness—my Yankeeness—was a subject for good-natured joshing. Didn't I know what butter beans were? Or that "mashing a button," an expression I first heard from Judy, simply meant pressing a button? Not pushing it hard, again and again, as I had guessed. Or that the Civil War, as Alice never called it, might better be referred to as the War Between the States? We had a running debate. Which was more extreme: the oppressive heat of Monroeville in August or the bitter chill of Chicago in January? I thought Monroeville took the title in that one. The others were skeptical.

As I spent time with this circle of friends in Monroeville, I was aware of a mutual wariness of the sensibilities on the other side of the Mason-Dixon Line, at least as we had experienced them. I was a blue state woman in a red state town and reminded almost daily of the cultural differences. In my piece for the *Tribune*, Tom had called Nelle socially liberal but politically conservative. She later chided him for the comment. Her politics were not that black and white.

It still surprised me how many public events here began with a Christian prayer. I was accustomed to prayers being private or an ecumenical blessing at most. My father's family is Methodist and my mother's is Catholic but I was raised in a Unitarian Universalist congregation. I was pretty sure my Methodist credentials, from the church my extended family belonged to in Black River Falls, were held in higher esteem than my upbringing in a Unitarian Universalist congregation in Madison.

This was a day just to kick back and enjoy the warmth and ease of that group. Lamps cast a glow on the wood paneling in the room. The large oak bookcase and cabinetry that housed the big-screen television was the painstaking work of Nelle and Judy's friend Ila Jeter's husband, James. On one side, he used tiny screws to affix a small metal plate engraved with the date, his name, and the names of the friends for whom he spent long hours making it. He did the same for the Lees with the wide, chest-high bookcase that dominated their entryway. In a place of honor, on a corner display shelf of the Crofts' cabinetry, was their copy of *To Kill a Mockingbird* with Nelle's inscription.

For many years after the publication of *To Kill a Mockingbird,* Nelle willingly signed thousands of copies of the book. Alice once told me she had even given herself tendonitis in her wrist from the long hours she spent fulfilling autograph requests. It was one of the many ways she tried to be a good steward of the tremendous affection her novel had engendered. The book exerted an unusually strong personal pull on readers and Nelle didn't want to disappoint her public. The volume of requests, letters, and books sent to the Lees' small post office box in Monroeville was overwhelming and showed no sign of stopping even four decades after the book's initial publication. Alice toted them all home in plastic grocery bags.

"Did you ever think about hiring an assistant to help with all this?" I asked Alice.

"No," she said. "It wouldn't work too well, because there is no uniform way of handling it. Each thing, almost, is different."

Their generosity was not always met in kind. In the 1990s, a local shop owner took advantage of Nelle's efforts to help out Monroeville brick-and-mortar establishments by signing books to be sold there.

The shop owner sold some of them, marked up, on eBay, Nelle discovered. She was outraged. Some book buyers did the same. After that, she mostly stopped signing books. Behind the scenes, she still autographed books in special cases, but she had a public policy of no longer signing books.

Before the game got under way, I grabbed another Diet Coke from the kitchen and took my place near the Crofts' son Kenny. He loved to be a part of any gathering and he loved football. So today, as his father said, he was in high cotton. Kenny, with the unusually flexible joints characteristic of Down syndrome, sat cross-legged with his knees all the way to the Oriental rug on the floor. He was a yogi in Auburn's orange and blue.

Kenny looked up at Nelle as she began to read aloud from Doris Jay's "Rocky Hill News" column in that week's *Monroe Journal*. This was, hands down, Nelle's favorite part of the paper. The column detailed the comings and goings of an extended family who lived in the area known as Rocky Hill, southwest of Monroeville.

"'Jan. 1: Dale and Brenda Jay had dinner with his parents Thursday.'" Nelle read this first sentence matter-of-factly. "'Jan. 5: Calvin and Doris Jay made a trip Monday to Atmore on business.'" Here she began to falter. "'Jan. 7: Philip Jay had dinner Wednesday with his parents.'" The chuckle was building. Nelle took off her glasses, leaned her head back, and let loose with a deep laugh. She had the rest of us laughing, too. This wasn't mocking laughter. It was the kind of affectionate amusement I'd come to recognize, an appreciation of what was both absurd and deeply human about this kind of thing.

Nelle collected herself and continued. "'Dale and Brenda Jay visited Wednesday afternoon. Doris, Lisa, M. C. Cauly, and children visited with their grandmother, Effie Lee Dunn, recently.'" Nelle was gone again. When her laughter subsided into controllable chuckles, she de-

livered the news of January 10. "'Dale and Brenda Jay attended a singing in Mobile Saturday night. Joe Shiver has an appointment with his
doctor in Mobile. He accompanied Slick Linam to the doctor earlier in
the week in Pensacola.'"

One more visit to parents plus three more medical appointments
and Nelle had taken us through the rest of the "Rocky Hill News." Her
laughter was contagious. Kenny joined in. I did. And Haniel, with his
low chuckle.

"Oh, bless their hearts," Nelle said. She was still chuckling when
she set down the *Journal* and rose to duck into the other room for a
minute. She gave Kenny's crew cut a playful rub on the way out.

Then the ads for erectile dysfunction began. This was the first
Super Bowl in which Viagra and its like were staples of the commercial breaks. The ads are so common now that the surprise and unspoken embarrassment we shared at the time seem almost quaint. I gave
silent thanks that Alice's poor hearing meant she wasn't much interested in straining to catch the commercials. It was jarring when pre-
scription drugs were first advertised heavily on television. But now
this? Nelle walked back into the living room a couple of minutes into
the commercials. She stopped and peered at the screen. "Is that an ad
for . . . ," Nelle began to ask, puzzled. She paused. Got it. Judy glanced
down at Kenny and then at me. I shrugged my shoulders.

It was a relief when the television screen flashed back to the football field. We stopped talking, mostly, to listen. The crowd was loud.
Commentators pressed one hand to their earpieces as they speculated
the game could turn on the Panthers' running game.

At halftime, the Panthers were leading, 14–10. Janet Jackson took
center stage with Justin Timberlake. They rocked out to her "All for
You" and the infectious "Rhythm Nation." Singing the final line of his

own hit, "Rock Your Body," Timberlake yanked at Jackson's bustier. What happened next apparently was not planned. "I'm going to have you naked by the end of this song," he sang, and, rip, there was Jackson's right breast. The television cameras quickly cut away.

I didn't see this. I had been in the kitchen helping Judy and returned to the living room, which was suddenly abuzz. "Was that?" someone asked. "I think so," came the answer.

If Alice was taking it all in, she gave no indication. Nelle appeared to experience these Super Bowl developments with a mixture of surprise, consternation, and barely suppressed amusement, in that order. Not that we spoke of it again. She told an off-color joke in private now and then but also lamented the erosion of a particular kind of public propriety. "She grows frustrated," Tom told me in one of our first interviews, "with a country and a culture grown coarse and obscene."

Alice spent the commercial breaks and halftime show in conversation or absorbed in the coffee table book I had given her as a belated Christmas gift. She ran her arthritic fingers across the photos in Thomas Pakenham's *Remarkable Trees of the World,* and studied the text. On the cover, an older man in hiking boots, gazing upward, stood dwarfed at the foot of an enormous redwood. I bent over Alice a bit and raised my voice so she could hear better. "In honor of your most remarkable tree," I told her.

"Alice's tree" is what her friends called a giant, sheltering live oak people guessed might be a couple of hundred years old. The tree didn't belong to anyone she knew. It wasn't even on a main road. It shaded a good portion of a large yard in the town of Uriah, a forty-five-minute drive southeast of Monroeville. It was just something striking she had come across years ago and liked to check on, to appreciate out on drives. The oak prompted Nelle, on an earlier Sunday drive, to observe about the two sisters, "One thing about us, we can appreciate beauty without needing to possess it." The moment she said it, I knew that comment would stay with me.

The game turned out to be memorable for more than the brief nudity and the novelty of the men's pharmaceutical ads. The score was close. The Patriots narrowly beat the Panthers, 32–29. Soon it would be time to take our places at the more informal of the Crofts' two dining tables, this one on a large rug between the kitchen and the living room.

Following some postgame analysis, Alice again was absorbed by her new book of photographs. Nelle leaned over Alice's chair and put her left arm on the backrest to brace herself. This way her face was closer to Alice's.

"Alice," Nelle asked her tenderly, amused, "are you ready to surrender your trees?" Alice smiled. She was not. Not just yet. It was almost time to eat, though, and Nelle was getting hungry. A few minutes later, her voice tinged with exasperation, she tried again.

"Alice, will you surrender your trees?"

She did.

As we lingered at the table after dessert, Nelle warmly thanked Haniel and Judy. "I suppose we should be on our way," she said. She pushed back a bit from the rectangular table. I could see the mirth in her eyes when she explained.

"One of us at this table has to be at work in the morning."

There was silence at the table for a moment and then a ripple of appreciative laughter. All eyes had come to rest on Alice. The ninety-two-year-old was the one who had to be at work in the morning.

That night, with the three Crofts sound asleep, I lay awake in the guest room. It was close to midnight, dark and silent. The best days always lingered in my memory as sounds, even a day like this that just ended.

The sounds were still in my ears. Before the game, Nelle's slightly husky voice reading aloud the "Rocky Hills News," unable to finish before that infectious laugh took over, with Judy joining in. "Oh, Nelle."

During a commercial, Haniel leaning over Alice to comment on a play, his deep voice mixing with her soft rasp, for the time not banker and attorney who had worked together but old friends talking football on a relaxed Sunday afternoon. Kenny's muted *rat-tat-tat* of his drumsticks against the living room rug.

Nelle's circle of close friends was a down-to-earth group, eclectic in that it included a retired hairdresser, a pharmacy clerk, a one-time librarian, and a former bookkeeper who also was the wife of a retired bank president. None cared too much about status. Nelle got a kick out of it when one of the town's socially prominent women referred, a bit dismissively, to Nelle's unpretentious running buddies as "that crowd."

Nothing about the day spent with that crowd—not the ease of it, not the familiarity of it, certainly—would have been imaginable two and a half years earlier when Terrence and I rented a car in Atlanta and bent over a map to find Monroeville. I had been surprised—pleased, sometimes thrilled, but always surprised—as strangers I didn't expect to meet opened the doors to their homes, and as people I spent time with, to discuss the Lees and the area, became new friends. In several cases, those new friends, with time and talk and shared experiences, began to be good friends.

Chapter Ten

I was back in Chicago to build stamina to return to my newspaper job. But my friendship with Alice and Nelle offered a glimpse at life before the onslaught of modern communications. Not until a year later, in 2005, at the urging of Gregory Peck's wife, Veronique, would Nelle finally give in and get a cell phone for the long Amtrak journey she was undertaking from New York to Los Angeles. She was going there for Peck's library fund-raiser. Otherwise, at home in Monroeville, the Lees stuck with the telephone in their hallway nook.

But we shared a favorite mode of transportation: trains. Railroad tracks connected the places that mattered in their world in the South. They connected Evergreen, thirty miles from Monroeville, to Selma, and Selma to Birmingham, Birmingham to Atlanta. The rails also connected one generation to the next in their family as well as mine.

Before passing the bar in 1915, A.C. kept books for Barnett & Bugg and did work for the Manistee & Repton Railroad, a client. A train gave the young Alice and her friend Evelyn Barnett the thrill of their lives when A.C. took them along on a trip to St. Louis. Years later, when Nelle set her sights on being a writer in New York, like her friend Truman, A.C. dropped her off at the Evergreen train station for the long journey east. Alice made it through the twentieth century without boarding an airplane. Her doctor told her flying would be a bad idea due to an ear condition. Nelle did fly, for a time. She worked as a reservations clerk for the British Overseas Airways Corporation for several years, after all, to pay her rent in New York. That's the problem, however, with working for an airline. She learned too much about what could go wrong and cause an airplane to crash. After BOAC, she abandoned the skies. Amtrak took her back and forth between New York and Alabama, between one way of life and the other. She made that overnight train trip through her thirties, her forties, her fifties, her sixties, and her seventies, when I met her.

I was looking to return to my job, to keep up with the rigors of newspaper reporting. Well into a period of convalescence, though I was still in bed a lot and no closer to that goal. As my rheumatologist predicted, I'd have to stay on disability leave for the foreseeable future. I decided to explore with the Lees the idea of spending more time in Monroeville, and perhaps renting a place there.

If nothing else, I thought I could begin gathering information for a book about *Mockingbird* country, captured as the fictional Maycomb County in the novel. I didn't know at that point if Nelle would want to be much involved, but Alice was a remarkable story in her own right. As she entered her tenth decade and our rapport grew, she was ready to talk candidly. Friends of the Lees predicted that Alice would be steadfast in her view of my undertaking and Nelle would run hot and cool on her enthusiasm for it.

I was stunned Alice hadn't committed their family stories to paper. She knew the family background she shared with Nelle was of lasting interest. *Mockingbird*'s importance in American culture ensured that.

She wrote exceptionally well. Nelle, in fact, once said to me, "Alice is the real writer in the family." Alice cherished history. She knew history. She could recount these stories as no one else. She had an eye for details and the memory to do them justice.

"It just wasn't for me," she told me when I asked her about that. She didn't explain why. For years, friends and family had been gently suggesting she put the recollections on paper. She was the authority on Lee family stories and most of the community's history as well. Precision mattered to her, and accuracy. When she wasn't sure of something, there was no fudging of facts or embellishing of tales. She found the answer or made it clear she didn't know.

On days when I was up to it, I pulled out my tape recorder and began the slow, deliberate, and often enthralling project of recording oral histories of Alice Lee and her friends and neighbors in Monroeville. As I did, I could almost feel an invisible hand pushing me. I knew I had to hurry. Alice would one day be gone, and her stories would go with her.

"You know that African proverb 'When an old man dies, a library burns to the ground'? When Alice dies," Tom said, "it will be like a library burning."

A motel wouldn't suffice for a long-term stay. Yet my search for short-term rentals led to a series of sketchy apartments and depressing dead ends. I hoped to find a mother-in-law-type apartment above someone's garage or a tiny guesthouse behind a family home. Those existed here and there. Friends asked around for me and I followed a couple of leads, but the places either were occupied or not something available to be rented. If nothing else, I was learning my way around Monroeville's residential streets and getting a sense of what were considered desirable neighborhoods and not, and why.

I talked to Tom about any older people around town who might be willing to rent a room and grant kitchen privileges to me. It wouldn't be ideal but it could be workable. The problem was the couple of people who might consider that also were looking for some live-in assistance from such a person and I didn't want to commit to any particular schedule.

One lucky day, Dale Welch told me about a house that might be available two doors down from the sisters. She knew the owners. They were fixing it up to sell but might consider renting it to me.

Naturally, my first thought was, No way. The Lees, I assumed, would be less than thrilled at the prospect of having a Chicago journalist as a neighbor, even one with whom they'd formed a friendship.

I was wrong. Nelle and Alice were pleased with the idea.

They weren't so pleased, however, with the $650 a month rent the owners proposed. "Highway robbery," Nelle said, indignant. Dale wondered aloud what I already was thinking: What about the other house, next to the Lees, that also was for sale? I didn't want to even ask the owner unless the Lees approved. They encouraged me to check it out and offered themselves as references to their former neighbor, a young man named Wes Abrams. Would he consider renting it? Turns out he would, and for $450 a month.

The day I met him, Wes wore a camouflage shirt and jeans. His big dog, Buck, happily followed him from room to room in their old house. A year earlier, Wes was transferred to Jackson, Alabama, an hour's drive from Monroeville. After finding a place there, he put his house up for sale. In a sluggish market, the one-story, three-bedroom home in one of Monroeville's less glamorous neighborhoods was a tough sale. Priced at eighty thousand dollars, the house sat across the street from the junior high school and featured a screened breezeway off the eat-in kitchen and built-in bookshelves next to a fireplace. In the high-rise where I live in Chicago, not a fancy one by downtown standards, eighty thousand dollars will get you two parking spaces in the underground garage.

Wes and I agreed I would rent month to month while the house remained up for sale.

The house had been empty for several months before I moved in. Well, empty of human occupants, anyway. But I was not alone. I came to realize that my residency was preceded by that of scuttling spiders, alarmingly big cockroaches, and aggressive mildew brought on by storm damage. The formerly living things were no better company. Wes loved to hunt, and these were his trophies. A large deer head sporting an impressive set of antlers was mounted high on the wall of the small room where I put the folding table that served as my desk. What looked to be a stuffed bobcat watched me from a shelf in another room; another crouching creature via taxidermist—I had no idea what—perched nearby. In the kitchen, even the green and white dishes had a duck theme.

I didn't have much to unpack. I stacked my books, including my paperback copy of *To Kill a Mockingbird,* its margins now filled with my scribbled annotations, on the shelves, hung up my clothes, and made up the bed with the butter-yellow sheets that Dale Welch had lent me. The bed was rather high off the ground, with a white metal frame. When I sat on the edge of the bed, my feet didn't quite reach the floor. As I settled in, it seemed to me that the unblinking eyes of the animals, as cold as marbles, followed me ominously around the house.

I briefly considered draping towels over their heads, the better to escape those eyes. That would be even creepier, I decided. So I just tried to ignore them.

That first night, sleep felt like a long way off. Perversely, I found I missed the familiar cacophony of Chicago's streets.

So there I lay, in the white-frame bed in the house next door to Nelle and Alice Lee. I snuck glimpses at Nelle's window, a tidy square hung with blinds that didn't quite manage to keep the light from escaping. We were close enough to rig ourselves a child's primitive telephone. Who needs a cell phone when you've got two tin cans and a hunk of string? It was just the kind of thing Scout and Jem would have done.

I was having an awful time trying to fall asleep. The silence intensified all around me. Occasionally it stopped, replaced by the compact chaos of a cricket's lament, but then the silence returned, wider and deeper and more enveloping than ever.

And then it hit me: I was journey proud.

Nelle taught me that phrase early on in our friendship. Part of my role at the *Tribune* had been to write a column I initiated on language. Both Lees enjoyed teaching me new phrases, like "pounding the preacher," an old Southern expression for paying the preacher with a pound of chicken or vegetables or the like when money was in short supply.

For them, language was play. A person who tosses and turns on the night before a trip, she explained to me, is journey proud. And I was on a journey. A journey that was entertaining, but that also made me bristle with anxiety. What if Nelle suddenly decided, as she had been known to do, that I was no longer trustworthy, that I was not someone she wanted to spend time with after all? What if Wes sold the house, forcing me to move elsewhere?

What if my own health declined while I was down there, many hundreds of miles from my doctors at Northwestern Memorial Hospital? Well, then I'd move back to Chicago and that would be that.

I love the phrase *journey proud*. I love it for its simple colloquial beauty. I love it the way I loved so much of what I was learning here, day by day, taught by a couple of Southern women who opened up their lives—and now their neighborhood—to this Yankee newcomer.

The first day waking in the new house, November 22, I found a yellow Post-it note from Nelle on my kitchen table. I didn't hear her knock or slip in to leave the note. Her message instructed me to meet her next door at six that evening for a dinner she'd host at the country club. I faxed back my thanks and walked over at the appointed time.

I raised my hand to knock and stopped. It occurred to me my cardigan might smell like the mildew that was my unwelcome roommate for the time being. The baskets of scented Walmart pine cones I placed strategically around the house only meant that the place now smelled of mildew with an odd note of cinnamon. Me, too? I lifted my forearm to my face and sniffed. Not great but passable. I knocked.

No answer. I hesitated to press the doorbell. That would make the floor lamp next to Alice's recliner blink on and off. She would have to do that small rocking motion to get to her feet and make her way with her walker or cane to the door. I knocked again, loudly, so there would be a better chance that Nelle would hear me. She did. "Hoo-hoo-hoo," Nelle said by way of greeting, much as she did with the ducks at the lake. She told me to say hello to Alice and she'd be back in a minute. Alice was staying home this evening after a long day of work.

"How is it coming?" Alice said. Her voice was especially raspy this evening, almost a croak. "There is so much to do in your position."

I pulled up the rocker, close enough that my knees brushed against the footrest of her recliner. "I'm getting there," I said. The water, electricity, and gas were in my name now. A woman from an industrial cleaning service had sprayed disinfectant on the walls and ceiling, a formula that was supposed to kill the mildew and keep it from coming back. "Oh, heavens," Alice said.

"It was fun to unpack my books and get settled in. Wes has those built-in shelves in the living room." Alice knew the house. She knew the family who lived there before Wes, and the family who lived there before that. People still called it the Snowden house, after the original owners. The Snowdens moved to the neighborhood, then on the woodsy outskirts of town, about the same time Alice and her father did.

That was fifty-two years ago, when Alice was forty-one and A. C. Lee was seventy-two and newly widowed. I realized then that I was the same age Alice had been upon moving to West Avenue. I tried to picture Alice back then. Her hair was still dark, her hands not yet lined with age. She had cat's-eye glasses, I had seen a photo. Ed's death, at age thirty, was still a fresh grief, alongside the loss of Frances. Louise was thirty-six, living in Eufaula with her husband and two children. Nelle, at twenty-six, had been living in New York for three years at that point.

When I thought about them as young women, I wondered about their romantic lives. Dating, either as young women or in later years, never came up in conversation with either sister. It didn't seem to be a topic up for discussion. Finally, I asked Nelle if Alice had dated at some point. I asked Alice the same of Nelle. A little, was the answer both gave. And that was that.

The specter of A. C. Lee loomed large for both Nelle and Alice. Both sisters often mentioned him in conversation and absolutely lit up whenever an acquaintance or friend shared a memory of their father. Their mother's legacy was more complicated and both sisters curated it carefully. Neither of them mentioned her often, and when they did, both were careful to refer to her as a gentle soul.

In part, the sisters were wary of doing anything to sully the image of their mother, which had taken a beating at the hands of biographers and Truman Capote himself. Capote told his biographer Gerald Clarke that Frances twice tried to drown a young Nelle, a story the sisters vehemently denied.

In her recollections of her mother, Alice focused on her musician-ship and her love of reading. She also spoke of how A.C. cared for and protected his wife. Frances's delicate nature was not always a good fit for the role that was available to a Southern woman at the time. In many ways, her youngest child shared her sensitivity. But because of the extraordinary success of Nelle's novel, she was allowed a latitude that was never afforded to her mother. Nelle, of course, had a fierce-ness and an independence that her mother seemed to lack, too. Alice, like her father before her, did not share her sister's need to roam outside their hometown. From an early age, she followed in A.C.'s footsteps.

Alice adjusted the precarious pile on the side table next to her. Through some feat of creative engineering, she was able to pile her books and papers into haphazard stacks that threatened to topple over but didn't. On top of a couple of hardcover British histories she had piled yellow legal pads, manila file folders, handwritten correspon-dence, a Smithsonian catalog, a sheaf of papers, and another couple of books. She didn't seem to lose track of those things, though. She sim-ply remembered where she put them.

Alice nudged back into place a book that threatened to slip off the pile. I took the opportunity to wipe away the sweat already forming on my upper lip and then swipe my hand on my pants, my usual furtive gesture so that Alice wouldn't see how warm I was.

"Problem is," I told Alice, "I'm already accumulating more and more books." Alice's eyes crinkled at the corners. "At this rate, I'll have to check out the space in the oven soon." She chuckled. "As long as you don't cook any more than we do," she said.

Nelle reappeared from the hallway in the back. I stood up and dragged the rocking chair back to its spot by the piano. "All righty, you have a good time at the club and you call us if you need anything," Alice said.

Nelle leaned over Alice and spoke loudly. "Don't get into any trouble now while we're away, Bear," she said. The name seemed incongruous for someone so petite. I asked Nelle early on where the nickname came from. "That's for me to know and you to find out," she said. I didn't press it. It wasn't until the two of us made a day trip to Montgomery that Nelle gave me a clue to the origin of her name for her big sister.

The family had rented a home in Montgomery one summer when A. C. Lee was serving in the legislature. Nelle was just a little girl, but an early memory was going to the zoo with Alice and seeing the bears.

Our ride was here, idling in the driveway. Jack and Julie—if I have their names right—greeted us. Jack was a lumber or paper company executive originally from Detroit, and his wife, Julie, a secretary, was from the area.

"I have another Yankee for you," Nelle told Jack.

He dropped the three of us off in front of the white brick country club and went to park. Dale was already seated at a round table in the back room. A dinner buffet was set up there. Sunday brunch buffets were in the front room.

As we settled into our chairs, Nelle said firmly, "You are my guests." She wanted no fighting about who would pay for the meal. Jack joined us at the table. We stopped talking long enough to survey the menu. Dale, Julie, and I made our way to the salad bar. "That's what I should be eating," Nelle said, but she stuck to the fried catfish that soon arrived.

Nelle told Julie and Jack about the newspaper story I had written. "She's a contradiction," Nelle said. "She's a class-act journalist."

"Thank you for the compliment," I said. "To me if not my profession." She laughed and the others joined in.

"Miss Nelle," Jack said, mock scolding. The "Miss Nelle" or "Miss Alice" that sounded natural coming from local people seemed stilted somehow the few times I heard it used by a northerner. Which was worse, I wondered, to risk sounding contrived or to bypass a local courtesy? Nelle and Alice had told me to call them just that, and so I stuck to it. I had to hope that if this ever sounded impolite to other ears, I'd be given a Yankee special dispensation.

Jack had wondered the same about all the "yes, ma'am's" and "no, sir's" that laced conversation around Monroe County. It is a different culture in some ways, he said. Those "yes, sir's" and "no, ma'am's" that sounded respectful here could sound almost mocking where we were from.

The dining room wasn't full this evening. Another group of four took a table near ours. Nelle protectively scooted her black handbag closer to the leg of her chair, then laughed at herself.

"I think I'm in New York," she said.

I glanced down at her handbag, pleasantly worn with long, sturdy straps. She wore it diagonally across her chest sometimes. I thought of the purse story someone had told my mother. "My mother heard about a woman in Black River Falls . . ." I faced Nelle when speaking so she could hear better. I glanced at Jack and Julie and added, "That's the little Wisconsin town where I have family.

"The woman—this was an older woman—was terribly afraid that someone would break into her house to steal her purse. She couldn't sleep out of fear that an intruder could break in and hurt her in the process of trying to steal the purse. He could have it; what she feared was violence. Finally, she came up with a solution. Every evening, she would walk out on her front porch and deposit her purse outside the front door. If a thief wanted her pocketbook, he could get it without breaking in. She slept better after that."

"Oh, that's marvelous," Nelle said. "I love that." She let loose with that slightly husky, contagious laugh of hers.

Later, as we stood to leave, I glanced around at the other tables. My impression was that those who recognized Nelle were paying her the courtesy of pretending not to. Others simply didn't know who she was.

I appreciated Nelle introducing me to Jack, someone closer to my age, and a midwesterner. "I fear you don't have young people here to be with," she told me. I never did get together again with Jack and Julie, as it happened.

Beyond a shared passion for stories, for learning, it turned out that I had an awful lot in common with this gray-haired crew, with Alice and Nelle, Dale and Julia, Tom and Hilda, and others. Their joints hurt, too. They didn't have the energy they once had, either. We all were more familiar with doctors' waiting rooms than we wanted to be. These were my people.

And they had time for me, time for someone who, like them, was not raising a family or, with the exception of Alice, going into an office every day. They were in a different stage of life from my peers in Chicago.

I was researching a project about aging once at the *Tribune* and interviewed Mary Pipher, the psychologist who wrote the bestselling *Reviving Ophelia* about pressures on teenage girls. Pipher had just written a book about aging and the generation gap that often divides baby boomers and their parents, many of them in their eighties and nineties, who grew up in another time with another sensibility. It is as if the older people, often isolated by age and challenged by health problems, inhabited some other territory in their day-to-day life. She called the book *Another Country.*

Short of moving into an assisted living center, I was learning about that world, too. Not just about what it means to live in the Lees' small hometown in Alabama but what it means to be among the old in a nation geared to the young.

Chapter Eleven

B y this point, the Lees were excited for me to discover their Monroeville. True to their personalities, Alice was more steadfast and
constant in her enthusiasm, while Nelle was often inspiring and helpful but could also be distant about it. Sometimes I sensed that her old
trepidation about the press got the better of her. But the many days
she was keen about the project were magical. As she came to know me
better, we had more of those days.

Even in her later years, Nelle retained a childlike enthusiasm for
things: for exploring, for good meals, and, as time went along, for my
book. In my early days in Monroeville, she began to want in on the fun
that Alice and Tom and I were having on Sunday drives.

"Do you mind if I join you?" she'd ask. I didn't mind.

She was an enthusiastic guide, on drives and when she was giving
me assignments of where to go and whom to see if I had any hope of
really understanding this area, her family, and her own experience.

One afternoon, Nelle arranged for us to meet with Margaret Garrett, an old friend who lived in Stockton and was related to Chief Red
Eagle Weatherford. In her nineties now, Garrett was a good storyteller
and she remembered what it was like here when she was young.

We spent a few hours with her, the stories flowing back and forth between Margaret and Nelle, and Nelle was elated on the drive back to Monroeville.

I took my eyes off the road to glance over at her. "I think we got great stuff, don't you?" she said, tapping her index finger on the dashboard for emphasis.

"The part about the hair?" she said. "Oh, that was great."

Margaret's parents brought her home from a Montgomery boarding school when, feeling modern and bold, she had cut her hair into a bob. In that era, they figured it was the first scandalous step on a young woman's road to ruin. She continued her schooling back home, where her parents could keep an eye on her. The story said a lot about the social mores of the time for a young woman growing up in Alabama.

I glanced over at Nelle when Margaret was telling us about that. Nelle shot me a "good stuff" look and made a quick scribbling motion, meaning "Make sure that's in your notes."

She loved that part of the reporting process, it was clear. It gave me just a glimpse, in my own humble circumstance, of what it must have been like to work with her in Kansas all those years ago when she and Capote spent long hours around the kitchen tables of the people they were interviewing.

In later years, Nelle made no bones about all the aspects of publishing a book that she was glad to leave behind: the spotlight on her personal life, the demands on her time, the way people just showed up at her door, wanting something.

But on that day, I saw the downside of her decision—her series of decisions over the years—not to publish again, or to collaborate the way she did with Capote for *In Cold Blood*. Anxieties and frustrations aside, she loved the work.

I was accustomed by now to Nelle's wry way of introducing me to people as "a contradiction in terms: a class-act journalist." I remembered her letter to me, back in 2002, when she wrote about "the decline of a once honorable profession."

She'd observed that decline, as she believed it to be, from a unique perch. For forty-two years at that point—more than half of her life—she had avoided interactions with the press and yet been written about regularly. Being written about and, in the absence of firsthand information, speculated about, bothered her deeply.

"Some of that is our generation," Tom told me one day over burgers and onion rings at the South Forty. "The idea that some stranger would speculate in print about whether she is gay just appalled her, embarrassed her." He paused.

"Not that younger people want their sexuality speculated about, either, but for someone who grew up in the time and the place that we did, it was really jarring to her. She didn't grow up with things like they are now, where people discuss the most personal stuff on TV and all that."

People sometimes asked Tom whether Nelle had dated and, if so, what her orientation was. "I tell people I don't know."

It's the kind of question, he said, that would bother someone of Nelle's sensibilities regardless of orientation.

Only a couple of other tables at the restaurant were occupied, but there at our back table, we lowered our voices. It was a sensitive topic, but this was part of Nelle's difficult experience with fame.

I took a sip of my Diet Coke.

"Why all the speculation, do you think?"

"Well, she never married and no one seemed to know about her dating life, if she had one. Scout was a tomboy, and so was she, and she kind of kept that almost masculine way about her as an adult. She's not a dainty person. Especially back when she first got famous, she didn't fit the stereotype of a ladylike Southern woman. Remember, that was 1960. I don't think I've seen her wear a piece of jewelry as long as I've known her except something simple for an appearance. She doesn't wear makeup, hardly. You know how she dresses. Always pants and kind of baggy clothes sometimes. Even the way she moves, you know, there's just something almost masculine about it. And that stood out more back then than it does now. People forget how times change."

Nelle endured other speculation in the press, of course. Whether Capote had a hand in writing *To Kill a Mockingbird*—though everyone in the know agreed he did not—and whether she simply gave fictional names in her novel to people taken directly off the streets of Monroeville.

Even in those articles that didn't indulge in speculation, Nelle found she was misquoted at times, or that incorrect names and dates and other inaccuracies appeared in print. The Internet only made the problem worse, as a mistake or rumor in one article would then be picked up and copied in a dozen others, and personal blogs meant unedited copy circulating without any form of fact-checking or editorial control.

Nor did Nelle think much of the way a narrative approach to nonfiction had become popular both in newspapers and in journalism as practiced in magazines and books.

"Having been around for 30-odd years, the New Journalism is your heritage," Nelle had written in that 2002 letter.

One thing that intrigued me about this was that the New Journalism, as it often is called, had its origins not only with journalists such as Tom Wolfe but with Truman Capote and, specifically, the book Nelle helped research and report, *In Cold Blood*.

She and Capote delved into the kind of reporting that allowed his narrative approach to the book. With a level of detail and effort to understand people's motives and mentalities, Capote was able to write the story as what he famously called a "nonfiction novel."

And this was reporting about a husband and wife, and two of their four children, who were murdered in their home. Even more than a private author such as Nelle, these were people who had no chance to protect their private lives from what others might write. I saw the irony there, or at least a contradiction. Didn't Nelle?

I approached the subject gingerly in one of our long, later conversations.

"You were practicing journalism doing that research, wouldn't you say?"

Nelle looked at me evenly. "There was a difference."

"A difference?"

"I knew when to stop."

I wasn't sure Herb and Bonnie Clutter would agree with that assessment but I wasn't going to press the point. Nelle did say she felt Truman exaggerated the emotional instability he described plaguing Bonnie Clutter in the years before she was killed.

Nelle believed, she said, that Bonnie Clutter had endured the hormonal changes that come with menopause, and perhaps some moodiness, but that her emotional health was not as fragile as Truman depicted it.

She might have questioned his work on that point, but on the whole, she was proud of their work together in Kansas.

Chapter Twelve

Those first several weeks of settling in were full of errands, chores, and possibility. One afternoon, Judy stopped by with small Tupperware containers of homemade vegetable soup. "You take care of yourself, girl," she said. "What do you need? What can I get you?" Kenny accompanied her. He was anxious to secure my promise that I would leave Wes's Auburn sun catcher in the kitchen window. The sun catcher was a large, decorative rectangle of stained glass, with "AU" in Auburn orange and blue. The first time Kenny walked into the house, he spotted it right away. It was the only thing he needed to see to know this was the right place for me.

I knew the Auburn decoration would get me grief, though, from the University of Alabama fans in my slowly widening circle of friends. Football was second only to God in inspiring devotion around here, and even He had to be relieved the annual showdown between Alabama and Auburn didn't conflict with Sunday services. People wouldn't dream of dropping by during those games, any more than they would bother the sisters once the Masters was under way. Later that year, Alice got a huge kick out of Alabama native Warren St. John's *Rammer*

Jammer Yellow Hammer, about the subculture of die-hard 'Bama fans that follow the team in RVs.

Methodist or Baptist, Alabama fan or Auburn. These things mattered. They determined who your people were. In a way, I had a clean slate.

"I haven't decided about that," I told Kenny. "What about the Alabama fans?"

I was teasing but he looked genuinely alarmed.

"I give you my word, Kenny."

He brightened. "You my sister."

He gave me a hug good-bye. Kenny's hugs weren't perfunctory. He wrapped his arms around me and gave me what my three-year-old nephew Andrew would call a squeeze hug.

When Kenny and Judy headed home, I was alone again in this unfamiliar house. I wanted voices in the room with me. Storms had claimed the antenna. I could get one channel, CBS. It was full of static. I decided not to bother with television. I'd already watched enough *Law & Order* episodes for one lifetime. I asked around: How might I get my transistor radio to tune in to NPR? No one knew. This was puzzling; Hilda Butts had her kitchen radio permanently tuned to NPR, so there must be a way. I asked Tom the next time I was at his house. Turns out they had a special rooftop antennae that allowed them to tune in the NPR affiliate in Tuscaloosa, 150 miles away. Hilda made it the one condition of their transfer to Monroeville.

"There is one trick you can try, though," Tom said. "Hold it against your body like this." He held an imaginary radio against his rib cage. "And point the antenna toward your backyard."

That evening, alone at home with my thoughts and the whooshes and clanks of the furnace, I gave it a try. I climbed onto my bed and stretched out, looking up at the ceiling. There was a cobweb there I hadn't noticed. I pushed myself back so that only my lower legs dangled off the end. My clog slipped off my right foot and dropped to the wooden floor with a thunk. I kicked off the left shoe and scooched back more so I could try this with my knees bent and my feet flat on the mattress. I tuned in the radio, rested it on my ribs with my left hand, and, with my other hand, pointed the long silver antenna over my right shoulder toward where my backyard met the Lees'.

It worked. Victory! I listened to the smooth, low-key voice of a news commentator out of Tuscaloosa. Hardly any static, and a familiar lilt to the radio host's voice. Did NPR send people away to boot camp somewhere to acquire that public-radio way of speaking? The accent was different here but the slightly professorial, low-key intonation, the NPR-ness, was familiar. The tone of it was ripe for parody, especially around here, and I didn't broadcast my preference for it any more than I did my Unitarian Universalist upbringing. I lay on the bed, luxuriating in the static-free reception as the radio rose and fell softly on my ribs. I'd be able to get *Fresh Air* this way at last. Problem was, I had to stay like that or I lost the reception. The position got old in a hurry. I stood back up. Defeat.

I mentioned this to Nelle one day. A couple of days later, she called. We had tentatively planned on coffee that morning at my place. I knew when I lifted the receiver who it was and what she'd say.

"Hey. You pourin'?"

"You bet. The coffee's brewing."

I put out the duck teacups and saucers and fished a couple of teaspoons out of the top drawer to the left of the sink. I left the kitchen door ajar so Nelle could walk right in. She poked her head across the threshold, keeping her white sneakers planted on the little screened porch. I was in the dining room for a minute, hunting for a place mat for the middle of the table.

"Woo-hoo," I heard.

"Come on in," I said, and closed the door to the large, dark buffet where I'd found the place mat. Nelle closed the door behind her. "Here," she said, handing me two cassette tapes in plastic cases. "These are for you."

Nelle had come bearing the remedy for my NPR withdrawal, for the desire to have voices in the room other than those to be found on the evangelical and country music radio stations. Even with the white hair and aging hands, when she was up to mischief, or giving a gift, you could see the girl in her.

I turned over one of the cassettes to read the cover.

"Kathryn Tucker Windham," Nelle said. She beamed. "She's wonderful."

"Wow. Thank you." I read aloud from the cassette covers. *"At Home with My Daddy's Stories."* And the other: *"Women to Remember."* I knew of Windham, just in passing, the Alabama newspaperwoman and storyteller, now in her eighties. I'd hear snatches of her on NPR now and then. Her voice was as comforting as an embrace, and the stories of small-town shenanigans and growing up near Selma poured out of her. The tales were popular with NPR listeners and had become a staple of national storytelling festivals. She was nostalgic without being sentimental. Human nature amused her.

She had that in common with Nelle, who had taken her usual seat at the table. She pushed her teacup toward me, a supplicant for coffee. Once she smelled it brewing, she didn't like to wait.

I set down the cassettes and picked up the glass carafe.

"Strong coffee, coming up."

"Please."

Nelle didn't stay. She was there just long enough to gulp one cup and go over the logistics of our upcoming movie night with Judy and Ila. We'd watch Christopher Guest's satirical *Best in Show*. I ordered it from Netflix and a few days later the rectangular red envelope showed up in my box at the post office. Nelle thought this was a more involved process than it was. She always gave me props for procuring her movie requests, as if it required more than hitting "rent" on the Netflix site. I started to explain how easy it was but she waved that away. It was the Lees' need-to-know approach to technology. If they didn't need to know the specifics, all the better. As long as the movies showed up, the *how* didn't matter. I was curious to see what else she would request. The next ones she suggested were *A Mighty Wind* and installments of the British television comedy *Yes, Prime Minister.*

Her appreciation of satire was reflected in her choices of British and American films. During my time in Monroeville, those included *Wallace & Gromit, Kind Hearts and Coronets* (an Ealing British black comedy with Alec Guinness playing eight different members of the same family), *Fargo, Heavens Above!* (a British film in which a minister is accidentally appointed to a snobbish parish, starring Peter Sellers), *Heaven Help Us,* and Guest's *Waiting for Guffman.*

I stood at the sun catcher window and watched Nelle start back across my front yard. I picked up the cassettes and carried them down the wide, wood-floored hallway to my bedroom. I kicked off my clogs and climbed onto the bed. It was still morning but I was feeling the short night of sleep. I slipped *At Home with My Daddy's Stories* out of the case and into the tape player and pushed it to the other side of the bed. Windham's voice, warm, almost golden, was in the room.

I reached over for the green fleece throw and curled up on my side, gently hugging a pillow. I closed my eyes and listened.

"I'm Kathryn Windham in my home in Selma, Alabama [long pause], remembering tales about my father, other members of my family [pause], sitting in his rocking chair, talking about stories he told me and stories I heard about him and learned from him [pause] a long time ago in Thomasville, Alabama."

The stories poured like honey: smooth, then faster, then slower.

"Every now and then somebody will say to me, 'I notice when you tell stories you always pause and there are periods when you don't say anything.' And it occurs to me that may be because my father would pause in his storytelling while he lighted his pipe to get it going again. And though I don't smoke a pipe"—Windham laughed—"that may have influenced my storytelling."

Nelle later requested Windham be inducted into the Alabama Academy of Honor, and attended the event.

Chapter Thirteen

Nelle told me to come by at three that afternoon. We'd stop off at McDonald's for a cup of coffee and then collect Alice at the office and head over to the lake to feed the ducks and geese.

Nelle came to the door practically clucking. I don't know if it struck me that way because we were off to feed the ducks later but it was as if her feathers were ruffled and she was deciding whether to talk about it or not.

She apologized for the delay in answering my knock. She had been on the phone. Then, with no other preamble, she paused and said, "Do you know the dirtiest word in the English language?" She stood just inside the house.

I thought quickly. I wanted to see if I had the knowledge, by this point, to guess correctly what she would say.

Bigotry, I thought. No, maybe *poverty*. But there was a moral indignation to the way she posed the question, so maybe . . .

She answered before I did. This was rhetorical, anyway.

"Entitlement." She spit the word out.

Instead of asking, especially when she was irritated or angry, I'd learned to wait for her to volunteer details if she wanted to do so. She didn't, at least not on that day, but it was a topic she would refer to again and again.

One afternoon, Nelle glanced at the *Mobile Register* on my coffee table. The paper had another story about the trials of Richard Scrushy, former CEO of HealthSouth, the large health-care company, and a co-defendant with former Alabama governor Don Siegelman. Known for extravagant personal spending, Scrushy and the governor were eventually convicted in 2006 of federal funds bribery, conspiracy, and fraud.

"Greed is the coldest of the deadly sins, don't you think? At least lust, gluttony are . . ." She paused. "Human."

I had to think what the other cardinal sins were. Unitarians aren't big on those. Our Sunday school classes never touched on them.

I knew, at least, that there were seven deadly sins. So what were the four others besides greed, lust, and gluttony? Sloth was one. Envy another.

I had to Google the other two later. Pride and wrath.

Greed, especially, did gall Nelle. In part, that was because on occasion people took advantage of her goodwill to make money.

"She'll give you the shirt off her back," Hilda Butts told me for the newspaper story, "but don't try to take it without her permission."

Love of money and the things it can buy didn't motivate Nelle. She just wasn't interested in luxury, though she did value the opportunity to give bountiful sums to charity and to educate people behind the scenes.

The fortune she earned from the book did afford her the opportunity to live her life, from her midthirties on, without having to worry about money, or holding down a traditional job. And that was something she cared about, deeply: the ability to live her life on her own terms. She answered to nobody. She had no husband or children. No boss. With her withdrawal from public life, she rarely committed to public appearances or other obligations of that sort. She did look to Alice for guidance and support, and was keenly aware of Alice's high standards of personal conduct. But Nelle's life, and her choices, were her own.

Chapter Fourteen

Those first weeks I got by with a rental car and then one borrowed from the Crofts. But I needed my own wheels. I never cared about cars. I was nearly thirty when I got my first one, and only got it then because there was no public transportation to my job. Living in downtown Chicago, as I did when I decided to spend more time in Monroeville, I could again get by without one.

But there was no getting around the need for a car in Monroeville. I wanted a car that Alice and Nelle, Dale and Tom, and the rest of my gray-haired posse could get in and out of without need of a crane or orthopedic surgeon. That narrowed the field. Nothing that rode too low or too high.

I test-drove a few cars at the dealership while Tom rode shotgun. I tried a bigger car with a bench seat. I was used to smaller Japanese cars. This felt like driving a parade float down the street. I glanced over at Tom.

"I feel like I don't know where my sides are."

"You'd get used to it."

I made an awkward, wide turn at the intersection and he qualified his prediction.

"Or maybe not."

We tried a 2001 Dodge Stratus with sixty thousand miles on it. It was smaller, more familiar. It was in my price range.

"Okay, Tom. What do you think? How is it for getting in and out?"

"It ain't a Cadillac. But it ain't bad, either. I think this'd do fine."

I paid seven thousand dollars for it. Tom and I puzzled over what color it was. Silver is what the title said. And it did look silver, sort of, from some angles. In other light it was closer to metallic blue. After a few months, when the car had more miles and some Monroe County red clay dust on it and the air conditioner would blow only full blast or not at all, Tom started calling it "Old Blue."

I faxed the Lees about my progress. "Dear Alice and Nelle, Hallelujah! I now have a car and fridge, phone and fax. Feels luxurious . . ."

With Christmas getting closer, we were exchanging more faxes about logistics. By that Wednesday, December 22, the rain was cold and steady. It wasn't good weather for travel but Nelle and Alice were headed out with a nephew to Jacksonville, Florida, where Louise was now. I read the latest from Nelle. It referred to the little wooden Christmas ornament, a violin, I had found for them at the gift shop of the Chicago Symphony Orchestra.

"Thanks for the info and the Strad—it's lovely." She outlined their plans and ended with a cheery "Merry C. & love, Nelle."

The three Lee sisters remained close throughout their lives, but Louise, in marrying and having a family, had chosen a more traditional path for a woman of her era. Alice and Nelle, in choosing to pursue male-dominated professions, made their own way. Their mother did not want them to have the same limitations she had. It galled both Lees that Frances did not get the credit she deserved in that respect.

Growing up, Frances had wanted to be a nurse. It didn't happen. Her parents agreed with the prevailing wisdom that this was not a job for young ladies. It wasn't proper, not with bed pans to empty and patients to bathe, and all the rest.

"She felt that disappointment throughout her life," Alice told me. "And she made sure all four of us felt free to do whatever we wanted."

Frances Lee wasn't the only one thwarted in her career ambitions. Just as nursing wasn't considered ladylike, being a secretary was off-limits for Ida Gaillard, a Lee family friend who had taught at the local high school. Both Alice and Nelle remained close with her.

"You should talk to Ida, no question," Nelle had told me. "Don't wait too long on that one. She's ninetysomething, you know."

Nelle and Alice were both matter-of-fact about the issue of age, Alice advising me to interview one retired doctor "while he still has his marbles," and Nelle, a Pentecostal preacher "while she's still above-ground." The same words accompanied the stories Alice told me about people she grew up with. "He's dead now." Or, "She's gone now."

Ida Gaillard not only was aboveground and in possession of her marbles, she was enthusiastic about an afternoon of storytelling. Nelle called ahead to tell her about me, and to let her know it was all right to share memories of Nelle and the Lee family.

At ninety-eight, Ida still lived, with help, in the home in which she was raised. The white house with a large front porch was near Perdue Hill, twenty minutes outside Monroeville.

"I always wanted to do secretarial work. But my father said no. I finished high school when I was sixteen and he didn't want me to go into an office so young. In those days they didn't think young girls ought to do things like that."

Maybe after she got her degree, he said, she could consider it. But it wasn't to be. She went a more traditional route, earning a college degree and then teaching from 1928 until she retired. The closest she got to working in a business office was teaching typing to her students.

She remembered the four Lee children as students, especially the three girls. Ida first met Alice when Ida was teaching and Alice was in senior high. "She was one of these quiet studious people."

Louise was more outgoing. "I'll never forget Louise. Louise was a pretty child, and we'd have football games and they'd have Coca-Cola— it came in bottles then. She was serving the Cokes at a football game and reached down to get a Coke out of the tub of ice water and the thing blew up and cut her face on her cheek. She always had a scar from it. It was the first that I'd ever seen Coke blow up."

"Ed Lee was all about football," she recalled.

And Nelle, well, Nelle stood out in her own way. "Nelle was always the tomboy. She was always—getting into something. If somebody picked on her she'd jump on 'em and fight 'em. So a bunch of the boys decided one day they were going to get the best of Nelle. So one was going to start it, and then the others were going to jump in and help him. But she jumped on that first one, and then the others came in and she jumped on them." Ida laughed. "And they didn't jump on her anymore! She was quite different from Alice. Growin' up, she was a tomboy."

As she spoke, all I could think of was Scout. Scout, who got into school yard dustups with boys from her class. Scout, who wanted to do what her brother did and not be confined by dresses and ladylike manners.

Chapter Fifteen

A s I began to spend more time with the Lee sisters, I was mesmerized by the stories they told and by the way they told them, in beautiful, fluid language rich with the flavors of the South. They spoke with a playfulness, too, a sprightly humor that turned even mundane events into wry tales. Our days fell into a rhythm, punctuated by the daily drive to Whitey Lee Lake to feed the ducks and geese.

I often found myself standing at the edge of the small lake, just a few minutes from Alice's law office, watching Nelle summon ducks with her distinctive call:

"Woo-hoo-HOO! Woo-hoo-HOO!"

While calling the ducks, Nelle shook a Cool Whip Free container filled with seed corn. The ducks responded to the rattle. Alice stayed in the car, peering out her open window. The small, grassy slope down to the water's edge couldn't be navigated with her walker. Nelle stood on the small bank. She would focus on one duck, then another. She was studying, as she always did, how they interacted.

Nelle was counting the ducks, too. The difference in her approach to life as compared with her sister's was in evidence even here, counting ducks. Alice did so silently and methodically, and then repeated the process. Nelle, standing a few feet from me and a tad closer to the lake, counted rapid-fire. I could hear, without a breath between the numbers, "Eleven, twelve, thirteen, fourteen." It was tricky counting moving ducks. She started again, and then once more.

She turned to me, exasperated. "You have young eyes. How many do you get? I only count sixteen."

"Let me see." I performed my own count at a pace between the two sisters'. A couple of the smaller ducks strayed closer to the water's edge after I counted them, and then hustled back to the larger group.

"I counted seventeen but I think I counted one twice."

"What?" she said, straining to hear. It was irritating not catching things the first time.

She moved closer and I raised my voice to repeat what I had said.

She nodded. I began the count again.

"You're right. I only get sixteen."

"Eaten by a fox, maybe."

I wasn't sure if Nelle was kidding. Were there foxes around here? These residential areas were wooded. Maybe so. I didn't ask. I'd revised my usual thinking about posing such questions on the spot. Better to find out another way. I had the feeling one or two ignorant questions would get me a demotion.

Something startled the geese into a cacophony of honking. Whatever prompted the ruckus, it was quickly dismissed as neither threat nor possible source of food. They returned to pecking at the ground.

Nelle gave an audible sigh and walked over to Alice. "Well, are you about ready to go, Bear?"

"Yes, I believe so." She said "I b'lieve so," minus one syllable in *believe,* like my grandfather. "How many did you count?"

"Only sixteen. Marja the same."

"I fear one has gone missing."

I slid into the backseat as Nelle walked around to the back of the car and put the Cool Whip container in the trunk. She got behind the wheel with a loud "oomph."

"Home," she said, and we were off. I looked back at the ducks. From a distance, they all looked alike.

No detail in these interactions was too small to escape their attention or pique their interest. Once, when one of the ducks had an injured wing, Nelle watched to see how "the little fella would get his food." She noticed him the first time because he was trailing behind the feathered flock in the rush for the corn kernels.

The next time we spotted him, he brought up the rear but hung with the other ducks and geese closely enough to stake out his share of corn and peck away. The others didn't give him leeway, nor did they take advantage. It was simply competition as usual.

Another day, Alice gazed out the open window from her usual vantage point, the passenger seat. She chuckled softly. "Look at them follow momma duck."

After the rush for corn, the mother duck made her way back down to the lake, ducklings waddling after her in ragtag fashion. The little ones knew to keep up with her. She didn't look back. In the water, they fell effortlessly into orderly formation behind their mother. To human eyes, anyway, they were the picture of a contented family, a page out of *Make Way for Ducklings*, Robert McCloskey's 1941 classic set in Boston.

The sisters noticed the aggressive ducks and the more passive ones. Nelle commented on the way one new goose briskly circled the lake, small head held high above a slim, regal neck. He was showing who was top goose, she speculated, and Alice agreed. Or maybe he was just checking out the new territory. The interpretations were the Lees'.

They did the same around town, keenly observing the

interactions—in government, at church, and in personal circles—among the leaders and the followers, the newcomers and the established, the injured parties, socially speaking, and the top dogs. That eye for the way hierarchies and influence form and slowly shift in a community infuses *To Kill a Mockingbird*.

In the community of Monroeville, information about Nelle was currency. It could be spent, traded, or saved for the right moment. Demand exceeded supply, especially because her good friends kept their interactions with her largely private. People were curious about where she went, whom she saw, what she said.

"I've just learned not to even mention it to anyone, usually, if I have coffee with Nelle," Dale Welch told me. "People talk if you do that, and she doesn't want that."

Perhaps that's why her friends were interested in long conversations about Nelle and Alice. Early on, Nelle and Alice told them it was okay to speak freely with me, and so it was a chance for them to compare impressions with someone else, to share favorite stories that they didn't with others.

"I'd like you to meet some people," Nelle had told me on that visit when I delivered the published story.

I didn't know where she was taking me, or exactly why, but I didn't ask. I just followed her to her Buick. She drove me to three homes and introduced me to close friends Judy Croft and Ila Jeter, and took me to Dale Welch's house to get to know her better.

It was lost on none of us that this was an unusual decision on her part. That day marked the beginning of a new phase in my getting to know the Lees' world in Monroeville. These were good friends she was introducing, telling them I was looking to do more research in Monroeville. Alice had begun sharing more stories of her life, of Nelle's, of their family, and of the area. Nelle, too. They both encouraged me to talk to their friends there, especially the older folks who remembered Monroe County in the 1930s. These weren't stories that could be told quickly. Our conversations usually were two or three hours long. Now in their seventies, eighties, and nineties, those friends might otherwise take some of their firsthand knowledge of the Lees and old Monroeville to the grave.

Chapter Sixteen

Julia Munnerlyn, the mystery woman in the kitchen making fried green tomatoes that first day I met Alice, welcomed me into her life. She would take me to her church and her home. She proudly showed me the flowers she tended at both places, as well as at the Lees'.

Julia grew up in the area, the youngest daughter of six Stallworth children. "Four boys, two girls," she told me. "I'm the baby girl and I had a brother under me."

Their father farmed and logged at a sawmill camp. "But our livelihood was farming. Oh, we made everything. We grew everything. We didn't have to go to the store to buy too much, just sugar or something like that. We'd raise hogs and butcher the hogs and make up our own cracklins'"—she chuckled at the memory—"and make our own lard."

"It sounds like a lot of work," I told her over coffee at my kitchen table one August afternoon when Julia walked across my parched yard from the Lees' house and rapped on the kitchen door. I had asked her over, and we settled in at the kitchen table, tape recorder rolling.

"No, it was fun. Because, you know, it was your main source [of fun] that you invented. Today's children, they don't do anything but put their hands on things they're not supposed to. We didn't have a problem back then. Everybody worked together and everybody—well, if this family over there sees these other children doing something wrong, you got a whipping from them. . . . The children obeyed. I don't know how the news got home so fast—we didn't have no telephone—but when you got home it would go like this:

"'Uh-huh. What'd you do at Sadie's house?' 'Oh, we didn't do noth . . .'

"'Uh-huh. Come on, young lady or man, you're gonna get it.' And you would [get it] again."

Julia met her husband when she was on a Greyhound bus bound for a town near Memphis. He asked for her address. She figured she wouldn't hear from him, but he surprised her with a letter three or four months later. "He was more serious than I was," she said. "I wasn't thinking about settling down." She was twenty-two when they married.

They had eight children. One of their children, a daughter, was killed by a school bus on the road near their house. Julia has lived with that memory, that loss, ever since. It isn't one she discusses much. Now her husband was gone as well.

Julia had been taking care of people one way or another all her life. Before doing the kind of work she did for the Lees, she worked twenty years as a licensed practical nurse at the local hospital. Before that, she was a midwife, delivering babies at home when that was common practice. People still walked up to her, introduced themselves, and said, "Remember me? You delivered me. My momma's name is . . ." She'd delivered a whole lot of babies. Sometimes the name brought it all back to her, though, a delivery forty years earlier, a moaning young mother in a bedroom, pushing and perspiring and worrying, and then the tiny human being Julia would wash and weigh and speak to softly. Softly but not so softly the mother couldn't hear. "You're a healthy little one, aren't you? Yes, a fine baby boy. Mm-hmm. A strong little guy."

"Just makes you feel good," she said, "bringing someone into this world safely. No telling what happens to them after that, though. Lord have mercy."

Julia's work life would always include caretaking. When she started working for Alice, she was still taking care of her grandchildren during the day. These were the children of her son, Rudolph, the police chief. "I had to get up early," she recalled. She'd get ready, drive into town to take Alice to work, and then pick up the children and take them to her house. "Later, I'd go back to pick up Miss Alice at work, drive her home, and then get the children home. It worked out fine."

Eventually, when she wasn't needed for child care, she stayed with Alice at night while Nelle was in New York, taking over Nelle's bedroom.

She was definitely not one to dwell too much on Nelle's celebrity. When Julia mentioned that day that she hadn't yet seen the *Mockingbird* play, I asked if she had read the novel. "No," she said. "But I mean to."

After she had been working for Alice for a few years, Rudolph asked her if she didn't want to retire. She was in her seventies, after all. Julia said she preferred to stay on with Alice.

"I think she needs Miss Alice," Rudolph told me, "as much as Miss Alice needs her."

Julia had also worked for the hospital as a nurse's aide. She remembered one man as the cruelest of the cruel to blacks in her area. Decades later, he showed up, old and sick, at the Monroe County Hospital. She recognized him, recalled his name. She remembered the brutality he inflicted.

"He had been so bad," Julia said. "He had lived a raggedy life. . . . He would beat people up," people he called "those niggers." As the man's body and mind failed, his victims turned the tables on him and set chase. The only way Julia could pacify him was to pretend to kill them. So there in his hospital room, she would reassure him his pursuers were gone and he was safe.

"I just had to beat so many up and kill them because it worried him when he got really bad. He would holler, 'Whoa, whoa, whoa! Don't let that nigger get me.'"

Julia looked pained, and then amused, at the irony. "It was unfortunate," she said, a wry smile breaking into a laugh, "I had to be the one to take care of him." Her job was her job. She did it. Bathed the man, fed him, chased away his imagined enemies. "They ran him to death day and night," she said.

Like Julia, her supervisor, a white woman, usually knew instinctively when a patient was near death. "One night, when I was taking care of him, the head nurse come in there and [said], 'Julia? He is going to die.'

"I said, 'Yes, ma'am, I know that.'

"She said, 'Okay. You need me, you call me.'

"I guess she was gone out of his room about an hour. He got straight out of that bed.

"'Oh, those niggers are gonna get me.' He was staggering around, then back in bed, then up again. I'd just grab him and he'd put his head on my shoulder. That's the last thing he did," she said. "He died on my shoulder."

Julia called for the head nurse. "She said, 'Told you he was going to die.'

"And I said, 'Yes, ma'am. I knew he was going to. But I didn't think he'd die on my shoulder.'"

Vicious as he had been in life, Julia felt sorry for him in death. "I wouldn't want to leave this world in that kind of shape," she said. Julia shook her head at the memory. "Oh, my, I tell you," she said, and paused.

She looked as if she were resurfacing at the kitchen table from that long-ago hospital room with the tortured end of a raggedy life. And the violent racist seeking his final comfort on the shoulder of a black woman who knew his history.

Julia grew pensive about death as she told me that story. "It's terrible to die remembering bad things you've done to people," she said. "So when I get angry"—she laughed—"I ain't gonna kill nothing but the snakes. And I've killed a lot of them. I'm still killing them."

I asked her how she kills a snake. "A stick, or a hoe," she said. "Or I shoot 'em." She paused. "Now, you certainly have to approach a rattlesnake. You don't ever go up behind him. You have to face him direct." Julia said this emphatically, "DIE-rect."

She told me about her history, how her mother was born in 1889, so her mother's mother had to have been in "the last tickin' of the slavery time." Slaves often took the last name of their owners, so the area has both black and white Stallworths, her maiden name.

It was remarkable how different her life had been from that of the Lees, with whom she spent her days. Yet at the same time, there was a tremendous amount of shared experience between them.

"I hope she knows how much we love her," Nelle said over coffee one day.

Chapter Seventeen

Nelle pulled into the driveway next door and, with a wave, she and Alice disappeared inside.

Alice explored the world from that modest house. She did it year after year, her appetite undiminished, from her perch in the living room, in those classic suits and panty hose, one slim ankle crossed over the other.

If the gray recliner was command central, as I came to think of it, it also was a nest, the reading chair with the floor lamp on one side and the mounting stacks of books, always threatening to topple over, on the other.

Nelle's life in a wider world, her singular experience being Harper Lee, with all that meant, expanded Alice's world, too. So many of her stories unfolded as Alice sat in that same living room chair, Nelle in her own reading chair across from her, telling her about the famous people she met, the trips she took to England, the things she did in New York, and, yes, the books she was reading.

It wasn't the same, of course, as if she had poked around those English villages in person, or walked the streets of all the other places she visited by books and imagination. But I was struck by how fully she seemed to have experienced the world.

"This is how I've traveled," Alice told me that first evening I met her, running her hand across a row of books.

"You know," Tom said one day, "here Nelle Harper is this famous author who has traveled all over and met so many famous people. And I used to wonder if that wasn't a little hard for Alice, who knows more about English history than most British people and never has gone there. But I've never seen any envy there. She gets such a kick out of Nelle's stories but I don't think there's ever been resentment about that."

On one Saturday afternoon I was recording Alice's stories about the Lee family when she told me about the letter Nelle sent home the summer she was studying at Oxford.

"The American students that were over there that summer—see, it was still close enough after the war that everyone was still rationed and gas was still—you went everywhere on bicycle, nearly. Occasionally, Nelle Harper would see one of those big hogs on wheels—one of the Rolls-Royces."

It turned out, Alice told me, that one of the Oxford boys was going to London because he had a letter of introduction to a member of Parliament. "Something had happened that his girl couldn't go," Alice said, "and he asked Nelle Harper if she'd like to go. And she went. I think maybe they bicycled all the way in but, you know, it's not far. And they were having tea on the terrace and this man who was hosting them excused himself from the table for a short time and returned with somebody."

Alice paused and looked at me with the relish of a cook about to serve something special. "And that somebody was Winston Churchill."

She continued, "Nelle Harper was so shocked and so overcome she couldn't remember what she said because it was just a brief thing: somebody doing it to give college kids a thrill. . . . Nelle Harper's letter back home said, 'Today I met history. I met history itself.' "

Alice flat out knew more about the Lee family, past and present, than anyone else. No one else even came close, Nelle included, as Nelle herself acknowledged. More than once, Nelle laughed about that. She was telling me about their aunt Kitty over a hamburger at Radley's. "I'll ask Alice," she said. She laughed. "That's always the answer, isn't it? We'll ask Alice."

And she did. So did their nephew, dentist Ed Lee, when he wanted to know about his great-grandparents. So did Tom Butts when someone needed to know about the last-minute rescue of the stained-glass windows at the turn of the century as the Methodist church burned.

Alice knew a lot more about her mother's parents than her father's. Nelle and Alice's maternal grandparents were younger and lived closer. A.C.'s family was hundreds of miles away in Florida.

On one of our Sunday drives, Alice pointed out where a cotton gin used to be, the one that her grandfather Finch operated. He was targeted, Alice told me, by a man named Sam Henderson, who delivered the mail to the Finches and other families in the area. It was a sociable job, and the Finches considered him a friend. It made no sense that he would try to harm them.

"It was ginnin' season. My grandfather was in the gin with two black men who were working that day. They said, 'Mr. Finch, Mr. Sam Henderson is out there, looking for you to kill you.' And my grandfather said, 'No way, he's my friend. He wouldn't kill me.' They said, 'Mr. Finch, he's got a gun and something is wrong. He's going to kill you.' Well, Mr. Henderson was at the only exit, the entrance to the gin.

"And the men finally convinced my grandfather that his life was in danger. And they worked away and loosened some of the side and got him out. And they stayed in the front and kept Mr. Henderson involved. My grandfather slipped out and went up to the house and got my grandmother and they went down through the pasture behind the house for a couple of miles.

"When the men got ahold of somebody who went to the phone and called the sheriff, and when it was safe for my grandparents to go back to the house, the glass in the front door had been shot out. A bullet—the house had a room that extended out, you know, in a porch on this side"—Alice gestured—"and he had shot through that room right where the head of my grandparents' bed was. The man spent the rest of his life in Bryce Hospital, insane."

The incident was horrifying for those involved but a captivating story to hear growing up, as Alice, Louise, Ed, and Nelle Harper all did.

"Nobody ever knew what his grievance was. My grandfather never knew. He was so shocked. Something gave way and the man went stark raving mad. And as long as my grandmother lived, every Christmas she sent a check to Bryce Hospital that Mr. Sam Henderson might be supplied with some candies and Christmas presents. That's the way my grandmother was."

Alice said this—"That's the way my grandmother was"—with such affection in her eyes, it gave me a pang.

"He had been their friend and what he did was something that was beyond his right mind. No grudges. I was very conscious every Christmas of what my grandmother Finch was doing. But I never asked anything beyond what I've told you."

In that, the grandparents, like Alice and Nelle's own parents, took a progressive view of mental illness for the times. They saw not a character defect but a condition the man suffered.

Those grandparents had two daughters: Frances, born in 1888, and, two years later, Alice. Aunt Alice was the young Alice and Nelle's only aunt on their mother's side. No matter. She was enough fun for five aunts.

Frances and Alice were close, but not alike. Alice was the more outgoing of the two. The two Finch sisters went off by riverboat to a private boarding school in Mobile, much as the ultraproper Aunt Alexandra had done in *To Kill a Mockingbird*.

There was no driving to Mobile because there was no bridge over the river and delta along the way. And there was no public school for them to attend. The high school in Monroeville wasn't established until 1911, the year Frances and A. C. Lee had their first child. They named her Alice, after Frances's sister.

"I'm the first person in my family to have been educated in public school." Alice noted this with pride. Her feelings for public education never wavered. Nor did her disappointment in seeing a private school spring up the year desegregation came to Monroeville.

Before their mother and Aunt Alice went to study in Mobile, schooling took place at home with a few other white children. There was no thought then of white and black children going to school together. That wouldn't happen for fifty years.

"There were just a few white young people their age over there, and they'd get together and employ a teacher. When it came time for high school, Mother and Auntie went to Mobile and boarded with friends who had at one time lived in Finchburg."

The Finch sisters went on to study at a women's college, what eventually became the coed University of Montevallo, and marry before graduating. In 1910, Frances wed A. C. Lee at the family home in Finchburg. Alice married Dr. Charles McKinley and they made their home in Atmore. As women, just as when they were girls, the Finch sisters were close to each other yet had distinct personalities. Alice remained the more gregarious of the two.

"Auntie had a marvelous sense of humor. Well, Mother had it, too, but she did not create as much as Auntie did."

"Create as much mischief, you mean?"

"Did not create as much humor as Auntie did. Auntie would make up these funny words and things like that. Mother was more proper." Alice laughed.

Nelle and Alice, even in their eighties and nineties, reached into their aunt's improvised vocabulary. They knew what the other one meant, even if no one else did. Their favorite word of hers was *cyphaloon,* which referred to weather so bad it might as well be a cyclone crossed with a typhoon.

One afternoon, Nelle, Alice, and I were making the short trek from their front door to the driveway. We stepped outside and saw dark clouds hanging low. A faint breeze carried that feeling of a storm brewing. Nelle looked skyward but said nothing. The Lees had installed a few wide, unvarnished wooden steps up to the front door. They took the place of the original cement ones. When Alice was concentrating on taking those steps carefully, anyone with her waited until she was in the car to address her.

Nelle walked with her to the passenger seat and handed me the walker. I folded it and placed it in the trunk. Once we were in the car, Nelle turned to Alice and said in a raised voice, "Cyphaloon coming." From the backseat, I heard Alice's low chuckle.

"I b'lieve so," she said.

Frances Lee had four children. Alice McKinley had five, all of them boys. Hers was a rambunctious household.

Until the last four years of her life, Frances took every chance she got to spend time at the Gulf shore. Sometimes the whole family went. Other times, A.C. or a friend would accompany her so she would not be alone. It was the only place she got relief from terrible allergies.

Where rows of condos now stand near Destin, Florida, seaside cottages back then offered a peaceful retreat.

"Life was one big sneeze for her and when she would get within ten miles of salt water, she'd be free. So she would spend not only the summers but some of the cooler weather down there across from Pensacola. That was the only time she had any pleasure, when she would not sneeze. She was allergic to everything. Everything they could test for she was allergic to. Salt water stopped it."

Aunt Alice survived Frances by thirty years, decades in which she shared any number of misadventures with her adoring nieces. Alice McKinley was older and arthritic when she and Nelle would set out on one of their country drives to ride past places like an old Scottish church they both liked.

The bonds of the family were strong, in part because of the terrible events of the summer of 1951. Every family has its defining events, and for the Lees, that summer held two of them. Frances Lee's death in June was an unexpected blow. Her youngest, Nelle, was only twenty-five; her oldest, Alice, almost forty; Louise was thirty-five, and married with two young sons. Ed, thirty, the only son, also was married, and had a young daughter and baby son. Six weeks after Frances's death, the still grieving family got that shocking news from Montgomery. Just the evening before, all had been fine when Ed chatted by phone with his wife in Monroeville.

That summer had begun as usual, with A. C. Lee a delegate to the Methodists' regional annual conference, this time in southwestern Alabama. It was business as usual for Nelle, too, in New York, where she'd moved in 1949 to pursue her writing while working as an airline reservations clerk. She lived in a small apartment on the Upper East Side and had resumed her friendship with her old neighbor and now rising literary star, Truman Capote.

The Lees' doctor in Monroeville, Rayford Smith, advised that Frances Lee go to Selma for tests. These days, people in Monroeville travel to Mobile or Pensacola for specialists they can't find in town. But in Frances's day, Selma was the place. A.C. dropped off his wife at what was then Vaughan Memorial Hospital in Selma on that Wednesday and then continued along to the conference. A few days of tests would, they hoped, explain why Frances was feeling ill.

On Friday, conference business concluded, A.C. drove to Selma to pick up Frances. He was not prepared for the grim news that greeted him.

"He was told she was in the last stages of malignancy in the lungs and the liver," Alice said. "She probably had three months to live."

A.C. drove back to the house on Alabama Avenue and broke the news to Alice. They made the difficult calls to Louise in Eufaula, Ed in Montgomery, and Nelle Harper in New York.

"We called Nelle just to alert her, and said, Don't come yet."

They'd know more in a day or two, when she could plan accordingly. Alice and A.C. spent a restless night at home. They drove to Selma the next morning. Louise and Ed met them there.

Alice fell silent for a few moments as she recalled the scene. Nearly fifty years removed from the event, her sadness was still palpable. "Sometime in the afternoon we went out to get some food, and when we got back to the hospital, Mother had gone," Alice said. Frances had suffered a heart attack and did not regain consciousness. "She was unconscious when we returned to the hospital," Alice said, "and died that evening.

"Then we called Nelle Harper so she'd have time to get money out to come home," Alice continued. "Fortunately, she was working at BOAC at that time and they made arrangements for her. And we had to make arrangements for [the funeral]." Perhaps the only thing worse than being with their mother in Selma that day was, in Nelle's case, not being there.

Nelle never spoke of that time; only Alice did.

Still reeling, Alice and A.C. found some comfort in returning to the routines of their law office. Nelle stayed on a while with the family before going back to Manhattan, to her typewriter, to her friends, to her airline job.

Six weeks after Frances's death, Nelle's day began like any other. Her life as an aspiring writer in New York City was not as predictable as her father's and Alice's. But weekdays were routine as Nelle rose and dressed for her job at the airline. She could look at her watch at any given hour on any given workday and know what the two of them were doing back home.

A blink ago there'd been three in Monroeville, with Frances at home while A.C. and Alice practiced law in their office two blocks away. Now father and daughter found solace in the familiar. At Barnett, Bugg & Lee, there were, as usual, clients to see, documents to draft, cases to research. Both A.C. and Alice were creatures of habit. Now their routines were something more: a relief, something useful to do as they adjusted to the loss.

That July morning father and daughter were at their desks in adjacent offices when the call came from Montgomery. It was 8:30 A.M. "We were both there, but for some reason I answered the phone," Alice told me, "and this voice identified himself as the commandant at Maxwell Air Force Base. Could he speak to Mr. Lee? I called Daddy and said, It's for you."

Something told Alice to stay on the line. "I don't know why," she says. "I never did that. I heard the commandant say, 'I'm sorry to tell you, but your son did not wake up this morning. He was found dead in his bunk.' So there we were."

An autopsy revealed that Ed had died of a brain aneurysm, probably several hours before his body was discovered on the morning of July 12.

If Alice and A.C. took comfort in the routines of the law office, Nelle found solace with artistic expression. For a time, she wrote less and instead painted. The sea scene she painted as she coped with the losses hangs above the living room piano in the sisters' home. I'd seen it a hundred times before I thought to ask Alice its provenance. I could hear the pride of an older sister in her reply.

Nelle's creativity always had extended beyond writing and her foray into painting. She was musical. On our drives, she sometimes sang random lines of the hymns of her childhood. Or show tunes from the Broadway shows she saw as an adult. One day, under her breath, she began singing "Love Lifted Me." She picked up the lyrics partway through the hymn. "Dah dum, sinking to rise no more." Another time, more playfully, it was a jaunty line from *The Pirates of Penzance*. "I am the very model of a modern Major-General." I couldn't get that tune out of my head for the rest of the day. Despite her vocal ability, Nelle's early efforts to learn the violin did nothing to further their mother's desire to have another musician in the family. Nelle sawed away at it as a girl, and then gave it up. Nobody tried to talk her out of it.

As a family, they loved the literary arts, of course. A. C. and Frances Lee devoted lots of time to reading to their children. When Louise and, later, Ed both married and had children, A.C. read to his grandchildren. He was a somewhat formal man, even at home, but his lap was a welcoming place to enjoy a book.

The sorrow over Ed's sudden death, with his children so young, was something to be borne, not gotten over. Ed's widow, Sara Anne, went on to marry again, a man who also had lost his spouse and was raising a young child, Stella. John and Sara Anne went on to have a fourth child, Martha. A.C.'s oldest grandchild called him "Opp," a mispronunciation of "Pop" or "Poppa." He became Opp to the other grandchildren when they came along.

A.C. wrote a letter to her in her new life that Sara Anne shared with me all those years later. It is on Barnett, Bugg & Lee letterhead. His distinctive blend of formality and affection is evident.

The stationery notes in smaller letters on the upper left the names of four lawyers, two of them living: J. B. Barnett (1874–1952); L. J. Bugg (1870–1938); A. C. Lee; Alice F. Lee. (Two minor spelling errors are corrected below.)

LAW OFFICES OF BARNETT, BUGG & LEE

October 25, 1955

Addressed to Mr. and Mrs. John A. Curry Jr.,
310 Woodfield Drive, Auburn, Alabama

Dear John and Sara Anne:

As I grow older, I become more thoroughly convinced that the policy of passing out flowers during life time is wise and proper.

I am not given to lavish flattery where not deserved, yet I feel that we should recognize well earned meritorious accomplishments as we see them. With this idea in mind I take this method of conveying to you two my earnest congratulations and high appreciation for the outstanding job you have done and are still doing in the matter of welding two families into one.

And in this connection I would not overlook the part Stella has played in this accomplishment. You can easily understand my keen interest in observing the situation from its inception; and I have always recognized in her a most commendable attitude, and a desire to promote the development of the new family relationship.

I now say again, I want the whole family to feel that our home is your home too; and particularly, I want always to be "Opp" to all the children.

With love for the entire family,

Very sincerely yours,

A C Lee

"I can't tell you what that meant to me," Sara Anne said. "What it meant to us. It was typical of him, even when he had lost Ed."

I first interviewed Sara Anne in the Monroeville dental office of her son, Ed, just a baby when his father died. Sara Anne and her husband, John, had driven from Auburn for the day for dental work and a visit with the family.

She and Nelle had been classmates when she was Sara Anne Mc-Call. She married Ed Lee in the summer of 1947. The Methodist church grew so hot that June day she told me, that the candles melted and fell over to one side.

The personalities of the four Lee children, as Sara Anne observed them, were in full force by the time they reached young adulthood. Alice, from an early age, was responsible, steady, one to look after the others in the family. Louise was the prettiest of the girls, lively and social. Ed was the all-American who loved football, studied engineering, and went off to serve in Europe in World War II. Nelle, even as a girl, was the nonconformist, feisty and independent.

When she was ten, Nelle was feeling put out as Christmas approached. Usually this was a festive time of year for the Lees, even during the Depression, and a season rich in anticipation for the youngest among them. That year, however, 1936, all the family's energies were devoted to the upcoming wedding of twenty-year-old Louise. Or at least that is how it felt. Nelle groused that this wasn't going to be much of a Christmas.

On Christmas Day, out of nowhere, a red bicycle appeared. It was a gift from her parents. Nelle was thrilled. They had kept their secret well, and in an instant her dejection turned to elation.

"She rode off," Alice said with a chuckle, "and we didn't see much of her for a while after that."

Later, Nelle recalled her childhood Christmases in an essay for *McCall's* magazine. "Christmas to Me" appeared in December 1961, amid perhaps the most eventful period of her life.

What I really missed was a memory, an old memory of people long since gone, of my grandparents' house bursting with cousins, smilax, and holly. I missed the sound of hunting boots, the sudden open-door gusts of chilly air that cut through the aroma of pine needles and oyster dressing. I missed my brother's night-before-Christmas mask of rectitude and my father's bumblebee bass humming "Joy to the World."

That Christmas of 1961, *To Kill a Mockingbird* was still on the bestseller list seventeen months after it was published. The book was proving to be a genuine phenomenon, with all the attendant adulation and money, demands, and hassles.

Perhaps the harshest critics were in her hometown. Some resented the focus on racial injustice in their part of the world. Others thought the to-do over the book by Mr. Lee's little girl was plain silly.

That year, *Writer's Digest* asked several authors, "What advice would you offer a person who aspires to a writing career?"

Lee's response was telling. "I would advise anyone who aspires to a writing career that before developing his talent he would be wise to develop a thick hide."

In small type below her signature, the magazine identifies her as the "author of *To Kill a Hummingbird*."

(In 2012, the magazine's editors, recalling that 1961 survey, wrote about her long public silence. "Here's to hoping it wasn't because we cited Lee as the author of 'To Kill a Hummingbird.' Oy. Some 50 years later, WD still regrets [and heavily cringes at] the error. Sorry, Harper!")

In Hollywood, meanwhile, the filming of *To Kill a Mockingbird* was under way, as was a close friendship between Nelle and its star, Gregory Peck, and his wife, Veronique. Nelle told interviewers of her struggle, and determination, to produce a second novel.

The following year, 1962, she lost the father on whom she had based her beloved character Atticus. A.C. had been ailing and died on April 15. Eight months later, in December, the film was released.

That year also marked the beginning of a tradition, one that yielded an abundance of adventures, misadventures, and, always, stories. For the decade after their father died, the three Lee sisters took annual trips, seeing much of the country by car, train, and even riverboat.

At this time in their lives, the difference in their ages mattered less. And Nelle's celebrity status not at all. In this group, she was the baby sister, plain and simple.

So Alice, Louise, and Nelle would plan and correspond, talk and anticipate, and then meet up in the designated city. They would look around if any museums or restaurants drew their interest. But then they would take to the open road or board a train. One vacation would

The Lee sisters took me on extraordinary guided tours of a rapidly disappearing South. Alice often led the way as we explored the red dirt roads of the Lee sisters' youth.

In a departure from her usual policy, Nelle Harper allowed the *Chicago Tribune*'s Terrence James to photograph her for my 2002 newspaper story. *From The Chicago Tribune, September 13, 2002 © 2002 Chicago Tribune*

Photographs of Alice and Nelle's parents, A. C. and Frances Lee,
hang in the entryway of their home; Methodist minister Tom Butts
(right) has been a close friend of both Lee sisters for decades.

From The Chicago Tribune, September 13, 2002 © 2002 Chicago Tribun

Nelle enjoyed a good laugh at dinner with her sister, Alice, at Radley's
Deli (named for the reclusive Boo Radley of *To Kill a Mockingbird*).

From The Chicago Tribune, September 13, 2002 © 2002 Chicago Tribun

Nelle found another home when she moved to New York City
in 1949, and she split time between the city and Monroeville for
many years.

When Nelle was in New York, Julia Munnerlyn took her
place driving Alice to the office and staying overnight in
Nelle's back bedroom.

The Lees' dining room also served as storage for their many, many books.

The Lee house is several blocks from the town square and on a quiet street across from Nelle's former high school.

Nelle told me that this home, on Claiborne Street,
was the inspiration for Boo Radley's house.

Tom and Nelle loved going fishing; reading widely and
discussing history and religion; exploring the area; and
swapping stories of colorful characters from 1930s Monroe
and Conecuh counties. They also enjoyed exploring New
York together on Tom's regular visits there.

In May 1961, Nelle posed for *Life* magazine in the balcony of Monreville's old courthouse. *Donald Uhrbrock/Time Life Pictures/Getty Images*

As a young couple, Frances and A. C. Lee shared this house with the Barnett family, lifelong friends.

In this photo from 1961, the year she won the Pulitzer Prize,
Nelle relaxed on the side porch of the Lee home on West Avenue.

Donald Uhrbrock/Time Life Pictures/Getty Images

Gregory Peck would win an Oscar for his iconic role as Atticus Finch; Nelle joined him on set of the film. © *Bettman/Corbis*

A letter from "the real Atticus Finch," A. C. Lee, father of Nelle and Alice. The letter is addressed to his daughter-in-law, Sara Anne.

end and they'd begin thinking about where to go next. By this time the oldest, Alice, was settled in Monroeville. Middle sister, Louise, lived in Eufaula, Alabama, two hundred miles away. Nelle, the youngest, was in New York. The trips stopped when the uncertain health of Louise's husband meant she no longer felt comfortable being away for long.

As different as the three sisters were, they all had their Aunt Alice's sense of adventure. They could squabble with the best of them, but their pleasure in one another's company, the way they made their own fun, was obvious. On one such trip, in 1965, the observation came from a fellow steamboat passenger they hadn't even met. For a change of pace that year, they boarded a Mississippi riverboat, the *Delta Queen*.

"I never shall forget the morning we were to get off the *Delta Queen*."

"I never shall forget." I didn't know anyone besides Alice who used that phrase. A story followed, always.

Five years after *To Kill a Mockingbird* was published, the three sisters met up in Ohio to take a riverboat down the Mississippi to New Orleans. From Alabama, Louise and Alice took the train north to Cincinnati. Nelle arrived by rail from New York and met them there. They boarded the *Delta Queen* on a Saturday for the eight-day trip to New Orleans.

That last day, as they waited for their luggage before getting off, the three women did what they had been doing all along. They reclined in chairs on the deck, soaking in some sun, laughing, talking, finishing one another's stories.

A passenger they had not met approached the sisters.

"She said, 'Do you mind if I speak to you?' And we said, 'Certainly not.'

"She said, 'I've been watching you all week. You have never [mixed] with anybody. You haven't participated in any of the entertainment, as most of the passengers have done. And yet you seem like you've had the best time of anybody.'

"And we just said, 'We're three sisters and we live in different parts of the country and when we get together this is what happens.'"

Another time, Louise and Alice met Nelle in New York. The three rented a car for a drive through the autumn blaze of color in New England. In Connecticut, they saw a farmer in a field with his horse, not an uncommon sight. As they got closer, the horse suddenly bolted for the road and ran smack into their rental car. The ladies were unhurt; the horse seemed okay, too. Alice wondered aloud if the clerk would believe them when they returned the car and had to explain the dents. Nelle was persuasive.

"You're not going to believe this, but a horse ran into us. We didn't run into the horse. It ran into us."

Another year, the three took Amtrak's Empire Builder from Chicago up through Minnesota, west through North Dakota and Montana, all the way to Seattle.

On one of their last trips together, Nelle's agent, Maurice Crain, joined the sisters for a swing through the South. Word got back to the sisters that upon his return, Crain had this to say about the three of them: "They laugh all the time. They don't agree on anything, not even the temperature. But they have the best time of anybody you ever saw."

Even so, this trip was bittersweet. Maurice already was in failing health and didn't have his usual stamina. He died a couple of years later, in 1970. He was sixty-eight. Nelle would grieve his loss for a long time.

Perhaps the most animated I ever saw Nelle was in, of all places, the darkened, charmless parking lot at the Walmart strip mall off Alabama Avenue. Tom and Hilda Butts and Nelle and I had lingered over dinner at China Star, the storefront Chinese restaurant a couple of doors down from Walmart. Only a few other tables were occupied that night, and it afforded privacy.

Nelle had been telling us about Crain's experiences in World War II and continued the conversation as we walked to our cars. A native of Texas, he spent time in a German prisoner-of-war camp.

"Can you imagine being a young man from Texas," Nelle said, "in those conditions, not knowing if you will survive, and if you do, what will happen?" She could listen to him talk about it for hours, she said, but he didn't speak about it all that much. "That was true of a lot of the men when they returned, you know."

I nodded.

"And then to think Jewish men returning home from the war were still treated like second-class citizens when they wanted to move into a certain building or join a country club. Just nonsense."

Nelle cut herself off.

"Listen to me going on and on," she said. "We should be going. I don't mean to keep you."

With a hint of a warm breeze, and Nelle in high spirits and a talkative mood, there was no place I'd rather have been than standing in that strip mall parking lot under a blanket of stars.

Chapter Eighteen

Predicaments make for the best stories. One wrong turn was all it took for Nelle to drive into trouble years ago near the tiny town of Tunnel Springs. The misstep left Nelle and their Aunt Alice alone in a quandary on a cold night.

"It had rained heavily," Alice said, "and as they started down a hill, they realized how deep the stream was at the foot of it.

"Nelle Harper was afraid to go down for fear the car would drown out. Well, she had started down the hill. It was slick. And she couldn't back up. There was nowhere to turn. She either had to go through the water or back to the top. Well, she said something told her not to get in the water. She had no idea how deep it was."

They waited for another car to come along, but it turned out they were on a little-used logging road and no one came.

"Nelle Harper was afraid," Alice said. "It was spring so they had only lightweight garments on when they set out, but it was going to get cool at night. And Auntie was very crippled from rheumatism and could not walk—her knees—she could not walk distances. Nelle Harper was afraid to leave her there by herself while she tried to walk out. They had no idea how far they'd gone in. So they just had to spend the night in the car.

"The timber was high on each side of the road and the only thing they could see was the sky above them. Occasionally they'd see lights from an airplane, and they heard all the sounds of the night."

They got cold, afraid of carbon monoxide if they kept the heater on too long.

"Now, this was in the spring of the year, during turkey hunting season," Alice explained. "And if you know anything about turkey hunting, people go into the woods before daylight and sit and wait for the turkeys to come off the roost.

"At first light, Nelle Harper started out walking and ran into a turkey hunter. She told him her predicament. He went on down there and was able to back up the car and get it out, because the road had dried some during the night. Nelle Harper measured on the car odometer how far they were from the highway. They'd gone six miles.

"The turkey hunter and his young son had gotten everything fine for 'em. Back in those days, we had evening services at our church. We don't have 'em anymore in the evening, not a church service. But when I came back to Monroeville that Sunday afternoon, Nelle Harper was sitting on the front steps. She said to me, 'I'm going to church tonight. I want to tell Fletcher—the minister—not to fuss at his congregation—this man and his little boy were Methodists—not to fuss at his Methodist members who turkey-hunted on Sunday morning. They might be friends indeed.'"

All these years later, Alice had a big laugh about it again.

Predicaments also inspire the best humor.

Late one morning, Nelle and I were taking the long way back from McDonald's to West Avenue. Instead of making the usual right onto

Alabama, Nelle took the back way out of the McDonald's lot. She made a left onto the Highway 21 Bypass. We sped along past the Subway sandwich shop and the Ace Hardware store, both to our left, and up the incline to the intersection with Pineville Road. The Bypass ended here. Turn right and you were on the rural stretch of highway to Julia Munnerlyn's house in the country and, just beyond, to the tiny town of Peterman.

Turn left on Pineville, as we did, and you were headed toward the Methodist church. Immediately to our right, we drove past a couple of abandoned structures, a weathered house and a dilapidated gas station, neither of which looked to have been occupied since the Depression, give or take. We passed Dale's large redbrick Baptist church on our right. Nelle slowed and glanced over at me. We were coming up on First Methodist, its white steeple stately against a blue sky.

"Do you mind if we stop off in the cemetery?"

I did not mind.

She knew her way around the cemetery and idled the car in front of a few headstones. They weren't names I recognized. She didn't volunteer information about the interred and I didn't ask. Something reminded her of a story and a smile spread.

"Has Alice told you about our Aunt Alice and Cousin Louie encountering a problem at the cemetery?" Nelle laughed.

I'd heard about other Aunt Alice capers, to be sure, but none in a cemetery.

"You see, Cousin Louie took Aunt Alice and a couple of other old ladies to pay a visit to the cemetery." This was not in Monroeville but, she thought, Atmore. They paid their respects at a number of graves, and were having a perfectly pleasant outing, as cemetery visits go. Then Louie, who was driving, got the underside of the car caught on a mound of grass—more of a small, steep hill—she tried to drive over. The car was stuck there, like a turtle on a short pole.

Louie tried to go forward. Nothing. She tried to put the sedan in reverse. Nothing. They were stuck. The ladies peered out the car windows. They would have to half-step, half-drop out of the car to get out. And then there still would be the problem of what to do next.

Louie clambered down onto the grass from the driver's seat. She took several steps back and surveyed the situation. She walked around the car, perched firmly atop the grass mound, and issued her report to the others, who remained in the vehicle.

"What confronts us," Louie declared, "is a problem of physics."

Nelle dissolved into laughter as she said this, so much so that I never did hear the solution.

Years later, Alice found herself in a predicament of her own, one that involved Nelle only after the fact.

Alice was about seventy years old then. She was heading back to Monroeville from yet another Methodist conference, this one in Dallas. She was getting ready to board a Greyhound bus when she realized her pocketbook was open and her wallet was missing. Someone had slipped in a hand and snatched it.

"I'd already given the bus man my ticket, but there I was with no ID." And not a penny for the journey home. She took a seat.

A hand appeared over her seat back. A sympathetic stranger had realized Alice's situation and offered a twenty-dollar bill. Alice was relieved and grateful. She tucked her benefactor's address in her purse to reimburse her later. Meantime, she'd have food money along the way.

Once she was home, Alice set about replacing her driver's license and the other contents of the stolen wallet. She wasted no time sending the woman a check to reimburse her, as well as a gift to say thanks.

It was a nightgown and robe, a pretty summer peignoir, from Vanity Fair. She mentioned the kindness of that stranger to Nelle.

Unbeknownst to Alice, Nelle decided to express her own gratitude. She sent the woman a signed copy of *To Kill a Mockingbird*, with the inscription "Even though you have done it for my sister, you have done it for me."

Half the fun was picturing the woman's surprise at the mailbox. The value of an autographed copy of the novel, in dollars and in personal terms, could be a burden. Then there were times like this.

Chapter Nineteen

In the four months I had been renting the house next door, daily life had fallen into routines and rhythms as predictable as the noontime bells ringing out from the Methodist church on Pineville Road.

Sunday afternoons Alice left the front door open for me, and at the appointed time I slipped inside, locked the door behind me, and pulled the low rocking chair up to her recliner. I usually interviewed her for a few hours, tape recorder rolling. Before long, she would pause midsentence as I quickly flipped over the microcassettes, thirty minutes to a side. I'd press record, set down the little black recorder, and she'd resume her story exactly where she left off. I worried these sessions would become tiresome for her, but when I would say "I should let you get back to your afternoon," her usual reply was "Not just yet, unless you need to go." "Not just yet" often was another hour, an hour I welcomed.

On weekdays, Nelle quite often would invite me for an afternoon cup of coffee at McDonald's. We'd sit in the booth to the left of the main door or the first table over on the right-hand side. I'd ride along as she picked up Alice after work and then made the six-minute drive to the small lake down the hill from the Community House to feed the ducks and geese. As Nelle would slowly pull over and get the Cool Whip tub out of her trunk, the ducks would offer the kind of noisy welcome that only they can. They waddled excitedly over to the grass between the lake and the asphalt before Nelle had even stopped. They knew her car.

Sometimes Nelle and I went to the Laundromat. She knew I didn't have a washing machine either, and invited me to tag along.

"I'm about due for a run to the Laundromat," I would tell her when I didn't have a shred of clean clothing left and couldn't put it off any longer. I would offer to drive. Nelle had begun driving too close to the curb for comfort, once clipping a driveway mailbox with a loud crack she did not hear. But I knew better than to insist. Driving meant independence; it was a sensitive subject.

Nelle preferred the Laundromat one town over in Excel. I assumed this was because she was less likely to be spotted there than in Monroeville but I didn't ask. I just showed up with my white trash bags filled with laundry and tossed them in the trunk she would have open and waiting in her driveway.

On one such trip, we chatted about the usual news and books and friends in common—as we made our way to Excel. Her mind was as sharp as ever but her vision was growing worse. Her peripheral vision was better than what she could see straight ahead. She slid into a parking spot in front of J & E Cleaners, missing the car parked in the neighboring spot by a harrowing nine or ten inches on my side of Nelle's Buick. I sucked in my breath, held in my stomach, and tried to squeeze between the two cars.

She would be displeased if she realized she had alarmed me for a moment. We all had learned that her frustration with her vision, as well as her hearing, quickly could turn to frustration with *us*.

While our laundry tumbled in the machines, we ducked next door into the Main Street Diner and poured cream into the ceramic mugs of steaming coffee.

I told Nelle about my recent conversation with Alice about her return to Monroeville in 1945 after passing the bar exam in Birmingham. "I had two questions and we talked about it," Alice told me of consulting her father about whether she should go home to practice. "One was: Would a small town accept a female attorney? The other was: Would I be able to establish myself or would I always be known as Mr. Lee's daughter?"

Father and daughter weren't sure of the answer to either question. She wanted to try and he encouraged her.

With some trepidation, Alice set up a desk in the office next to her father's at his small law firm on the town square. She was the only woman in that profession for miles around, and as petite and polite a person as you could find.

She had her father's love of the law, his work ethic, and a ferocious attention to detail. Alice would never describe herself that way but others did.

Nelle's eyes began to dance as I recounted what they told me. "She did the work of six strapping men," Nelle told me. Alice practiced law, Nelle said, "sweetly, quietly, and lethally."

Maybe, I thought, Nelle will allow me to take notes while we spoke about this. The sisters had agreed that a book on their lives and stories was a worthwhile project for some time now. But I never knew if Nelle would be in the right mood. I was apprehensive but I set down my coffee mug and pulled the slim reporter's notebook out of my purse. I picked up a pen and tried to give her a casual "This is okay, right?" look.

"Oh, here we go," she said, making it clear this was not okay. Not today, anyway. I put the notebook away and set down my pen. Later,

I would make notes of the conversation and recent happenings. Nelle and I would discuss which comments I wanted to use, and which experiences with her I wanted to relate. Often, her directive was to use my own judgment. To her credit, much of what she wanted off the record was to spare the feelings of a relative or a friend.

Chapter Twenty

Readers have long been fascinated by Nelle's childhood friendship with Truman Capote. Rarely in literary history have two such minds met at such a tender age. Truman served as the model for Dill and Nelle was Truman's partner in his greatest success. Those facts alone have cemented their literary pairing in the minds of readers.

As a boy, Truman was left to spend time with his Monroeville aunts in the house right next door. Nelle's childhood friendship with the odd, bright little playmate turned out to be a force for good and bad. At first, what unimaginable luck it was, what fun, that they had found each other as children. The imaginations of the two precocious young readers in rural Alabama fed each other years before either went on to literary fame in New York. Truman was two years older than Nelle. For children who loved stories—reading them but also making them up—such talented company was a rare find. Truman liked to hang around the Lee home, so much so, Alice told me, that her father had a routine question at the end of the day. "Has anyone put Truman out?"

Truman and Nelle Harper wrote even then, sharing an old typewriter A. C. Lee brought home from the office. One would type part of a story, Alice recalled, and then turn the typewriter around for the other to add more.

Nelle and Alice recalled Truman not as a neglected child, suffering a miserable childhood in the care of his old-maid Monroeville aunts, as he later told it, but as the focus of their attention, a boy treated to toys and ice cream his playmates couldn't afford. He was, Alice told me on one of our Sunday afternoons, "an indulged child." She drew out the word *indulged,* like taffy being stretched to the breaking point.

Truman and Nelle went on to encourage each other as adult writers. Their time in Kansas was much more than a favor Nelle did for Truman. Nelle had told Capote biographer Gerald Clarke that she decided to accompany her old friend to Kansas because they shared a fascination with crime. It was, she said, "deep calling to deep." I later learned the phrase came from a psalm. The Lees had been so steeped in the Word, those King James phrasings just came naturally to them. She and Truman recognized in each other the allure of solving a murder mystery and exploring the darkness behind it.

Even so, the differences in their personalities and experience with fame caused a divide that only widened with time. Truman's envy of Nelle's Pulitzer Prize, something he never achieved, was the source of a poisonous resentment. She fled the spotlight; he courted it. Nelle grew disgusted with Truman's erratic behavior and the lying and mean streaks she said ran through him.

Nelle was offended by the speculation, never substantiated but persistent, that Capote might have had a hand in writing *Mockingbird.* "He absolutely was not involved," Alice declared, her voice rising, as it would when she was incensed. "That's the biggest lie ever told." Indeed, Capote's own letters to others regarding Nelle's novel indicate he had no role. By the time Capote died in 1984, after a long, drug-laden downfall, the two friends were estranged and had been for years.

In *To Kill a Mockingbird,* streaks run in families. According to Aunt Alexandra, "Everybody in Maycomb, it seemed, had a Streak: a Drinking Streak, a Gambling Streak, a Mean Streak, a Funny Streak." In Truman's family, according to Nelle, it was lying: "They fled from the truth as Dracula from the cross," she said.

Alice remembered Truman from the time he was very young.

It was a Sunday and I was in the rocker, pulled up to the foot of Alice's recliner, my hair damp with perspiration. No matter. We were in the groove.

I asked her what Truman was like as a child.

"He was a strange-lookin' little thing. He was this blond little boy with this high-pitched voice and a vivid imagination. Other than that, he could have been any child running around. Wasn't anything exceptional about him."

His imagination intrigued young Nelle. He liked how hers could take flight, too. "They used to stay up in the tree house in the big chinaberry tree right out our back door, exchanging ideas, all on a childish basis."

Truman was the only child of Lillie Mae Faulk. Lillie Mae was the oldest of five children who came to live next door when they were orphaned. She married young and had Truman when she was seventeen. She divorced and then married Joe Capote, whose name Truman took. Alice and Nelle's mother, Frances Lee, played the piano at their wedding.

"Mother was extremely fond of Lillie Mae. And Lillie Mae had more of a relationship with my mother than she had with her married cousins. I know they read books and exchanged them, you know, things like that. Mother was a paragon to Lillie Mae."

Nelle told me about the time a young Truman took off on an adventure. It was 1936. Truman was twelve and Nelle was ten. A girl named Martha was visiting the Rawls family across the street. She was from Milton, Florida, and four years older than Truman. Nelle said she noticed that the girl would sit out on the steps in her bathing costume. "I was jealous," Nelle told me, "of all the time Truman was spending with Martha—the exotic older woman."

Nelle told me to ask Alice about the details of what came next. I did.

"Truman and Martha got it in their heads that they would run away," Alice told me. "So they hitchhiked to Evergreen and created a story about why they were traveling by themselves. The clerk at the hotel realized that something was not right and called back here to have someone retrieve them. It didn't create that much attention around here. It was two little kids up to mischief. It was no big thing. The only big thing about it came later when both of 'em became well-known, but not for the same reason.

"It turns out that years later she had been corresponding through one of those lonely hearts kind of things in a magazine, and that was how she met this husband who ended up being her partner in crime."

In an uncanny twist of Nelle's and Truman's history, Martha turned out to be a murderer. She was Martha Beck, who, with her husband, lured and robbed women who had placed personal ads in newspapers. Posing as brother and sister in the late forties, they befriended the unsuspecting victims before killing them. Known as the Lonely Hearts Killers, their crimes were sensationalized in the popular detective magazines of the day—the true-crime periodicals that both A. C. Lee and his son, Ed, devoured. Alice and Nelle also were great fans of detective stories.

Articles about the Beck crime spree didn't mention her childhood escapade with Truman, perhaps because Truman's mother, Lillie Mae, pleaded with the neighbors in Monroeville not to mention it.

"She was determined that no one would connect Truman with Martha. She went around saying, 'Don't say anything about it. Don't say anything about it.' And they didn't."

Years later, Truman asked Nelle to accompany him to Kansas to research the 1959 farmhouse murders vividly recounted in *In Cold Blood*. She had turned in her manuscript for *To Kill a Mockingbird*, but it had not yet been published. He wanted to write a nonfiction narrative about the murders of the Clutter family that was so detailed and compelling it would read like a novel.

Her old friend once had seemed unstoppable as he took the New York literary world by storm. But by the late 1950s, he was floundering. Nelle took heart that the Kansas book he envisioned could be a turning point.

"I thought this could be a serious effort at a serious book and I wanted to encourage him," Nelle said.

His subject matter intrigued her as well.

Capote called Nelle his "assistant researchist," a title that did not reflect the depth of her contribution to the book. Those times in Kansas were among the last when the two old friends would enjoy a real camaraderie. In the years spent writing the book, and those that followed its 1966 publication, Capote was sinking into heavier abuse of drugs and alcohol.

"Truman was a world-class gossip and given to embellishment," Nelle told me. "If not outright lies," she added. It was one more reason the distance between them grew. He gossiped about her, same as he did with most famous people he knew, and she resented it.

What Nelle and Alice resented more than anything was Capote's claim that Frances had tried to drown Nelle. "Talk about Southern grotesque!" he had said.

The story infuriated Nelle and Alice. Even decades later, their indignation rose in their voices.

"Imagine someone saying that about your mother," Nelle said.

Alice's affable tone during one of our Sunday afternoon interviews turned to disgust when I brought up the topic. "I was upset because Mother had a very gentle nature. Nothing could have caused her to try to dispose of one of her children. Truman would say anything when he was drunk," Alice said.

After *In Cold Blood,* Capote's subsequent celebrity centered more on his society connections than on his writing. He threw the famed, masked Black and White Ball at New York's Plaza Hotel, and was a regular on the talk-show circuit. His long-awaited book became *Answered Prayers: The Unfinished Novel.* It was published in 1986, two years after his 1984 death from drugs and alcohol.

While his decline continued the Lees didn't want to have any more to do with him. Nelle attended Truman's funeral in Los Angeles, where he had been living in the guesthouse of Joanna Carson, ex-wife of Johnny Carson.

With time, Nelle's anger toward Truman was accompanied by sadness that his life turned out the way it did, that he seemed unable to put aside drugs and alcohol and whatever demons haunted him long enough to produce more of the quality writing he had in him.

She came to view his invention of his own myth, starting with his supposedly wretched childhood in Monroeville, as an inevitability, a character flaw over which he perhaps had little control.

In one of my early driving tours with Nelle and Alice, as the sisters were squabbling over Nelle's accelerating at a yellow light, the topic of Truman came up.

Nelle clarified her feelings then. As far as she was concerned, Truman lied about people and belittled them as a way of life and he didn't care whom he hurt.

"Truman was a psychopath, honey."

That stopped me short. Nelle used language precisely. She wasn't just tossing out the word like kids on a playground do, calling one another "psycho."

"You mean in the clinical sense?" I asked.

"If I understand the meaning of the term," she answered. "He thought the rules that apply to everybody else didn't apply to him."

Chapter Twenty-one

The Lees loved to explore their corner of Southern Alabama. Two of the first places Alice and Nelle took me were the nearby communities of Burnt Corn and Scratch Ankle. In 1814, local settlers fought Creek Indians in the Battle of Burnt Corn. Three years later, the town was established officially. Now all that's left is a gas station, a collection of small houses, and a shuttered general store. Not far from there is the smattering of homes, churches, and, yes, a gas station that people still call Scratch Ankle. Officially the maps designate it as "Franklin and surrounding area." The origin of the name Scratch Ankle? It's up for debate. The leading theory attributes the name to the dog-borne fleas that, back in the day, worked their way under men's socks and trousers and just below the hemline of women's long skirts, bringing on an intolerable itch.

On a shopping trip to Mobile, Nelle, Judy, Ila, and I stopped by a Barnes & Noble in a large strip mall. Nelle was muttering about the decline of civilization after the young man in the music department hadn't heard of the classical CD she was looking for: Mozart's *Magic Flute*. In the local history section, I found a slim paperback with a maroon cover titled *Place Names in Alabama*.

On the drive back to Monroeville, I found Burnt Corn in the book and read the entry aloud. Nelle had a question: "Is Smut Eye in there?"

Sure enough, on page 129 was an entry for the Bullock County community, its humorous name generally attributed to "smut from fires blackening the faces or getting in the eyes of persons working over them or passing near them . . ."

Nelle asked me to look up the town of Reform—so named, the story goes, because of a traveling preacher who refused to return to the small settlement until its wayward citizens reformed. The name game was on. Judy, Ila, and Nelle tossed out other quirky names, some official, some not. I read the entries for places closer to Monroeville: I found Pine Apple, Opp, Mexia, and the town of Brewton's Murder Creek, where in 1788, three men camping along the riverbank were robbed and killed. Once again, our drive turned to memories of old Alabama. Laughter and stories flowed as we skimmed past miles of cotton fields.

Clearly, some of the locales cited in the book were named to describe rather than to entice: Bug Tussle, Gravel Hill, Needmore, and Hell's Half Acre. Not to mention Rattlesnake Mountain, Penitentiary Mountain, Sinking Creek, Polecat Creek (polecat being slang for "skunk"), and the former Massacre Island—no relation to Murder Creek.

The nicknames that proliferated back then were as fun as the place names.

In Tom Butts's tiny community alone, he grew up with Shorty Higdon and Fatty Burt, Specs Watson and Legs Ryland. Shorty's name and Fatty's are self-explanatory. Fatty's cousins, Pig and Bear Burt—farm kids like all the rest—got their nicknames from older brothers who decided one was a stinker and the other lumbered from room to room. Or at least that's the speculation, thin on evidence.

Legs Ryland, a classmate of Tom's, was tall. As for their pal Hickory Nut Salter, Tom never knew his real name or how the young Mr. Salter came to be Hickory Nut. "He grew up to be a Holiness preacher. I don't know if he still goes by Hickory Nut or not. We could try to find out." We never did.

On a crisp, sunny October day Nelle and her friend Bill Miller, a former Vanity Fair executive, were "going to ride," taking a country drive. They invited me along. First we'd stop for breakfast at Nancy's Ranch House Café, successor to the ill-fated Wanda's Kountry Kitchen. Breakfast was eggs and grits, bacon and toast, and coffee. Lots of coffee.

Our waitress, a young woman in a black cowboy hat, stopped by our table.

"Would you like more coffee?"

"Yes," Nelle said. "Mounds of it."

At one point, Nelle held out her arm to show us a large, gold-toned wristwatch.

"Isn't this marvelous?"

She chuckled. It was from a catalog for people with low vision.

On the pearly face, the little hand and the big hand were huge. Ken Johnson, the jeweler over on the square, had replaced the already large hands with even bigger ones. She was the proud owner of a tricked-out wristwatch.

"This will see me through."

Through to the end of her life. I was growing accustomed to Nelle and Alice, Dale and Tom referring to this matter-of-factly.

We headed for nowhere in particular, passing lumber mills and cotton fields.

At the end of our expedition, we crested the small hill where Clausell Avenue meets the busier Claiborne Street and headed to West Avenue. As we passed the Hopewell CME church, Nelle had a question.

"What does Mr. Marzett have on his sign today?"

Bill slowed and I read it aloud. "EXPOSURE TO THE SON MAY PRE-VENT BURNING." Clever, but Nelle and Alice's favorite remained the one they spotted earlier. HOW DO YOU PLAN TO SPEND ETERNITY? SMOK-ING OR NON?

Language, as always, was play.

Chapter Twenty-two

In many instances, the riverhead of their language was their early training in faith. Only Alice remained as deeply involved in the affairs of the Methodist Church as their father had been, but Nelle continued to support the church, generously, and attended services, in Monroeville and Manhattan, as long as her hearing allowed.

But Nelle said if she ever wrote her memoirs, she'd want the book to be called *Where My Possessions Lie*. The phrase is from the poem and hymn by Samuel Stennett that became popular at Methodists camps.

In her novel, the African American Reverend Sykes sings and lines this with his congregation the morning that Scout and Jem accompany Calpurnia to church. There are not enough hymnbooks to go around. This is the first time they've seen a minster line, or feed lines to the congregation, who repeats them back.

In the hymn, earthly existence is one of turmoil. Not so the afterlife, the Promised Land. It begins:

On Jordan's stormy banks I stand,
And cast a wishful eye,

To Canaan's fair and happy land,
Where my possessions lie.

O'er all those wide extended plains
Shines one eternal day;
There God the Son forever reigns,
And scatters night away.

CHORUS:
I am bound for the promised land,
I am bound for the promised land;
Oh who will come and go with me?
I am bound for the promised land.

Alice offered little encouragement that any such memoir would be published, even posthumously. "There have been a number of people who have suggested she write her autobiography," Alice said. "But she has not shown any interest."

If Nelle never sat down to write her own story—and no one, not even Alice, can know for sure—she remained fascinated by the characters who populate rural Alabama. Past and present.

In fact, Nelle was so intrigued by a sequence of murders in the late 1970s in Alexander City, Alabama, that she started researching an *In Cold Blood*–style true-crime chronicle. Her research focused on a black minister who continued to collect insurance money as wives and relatives showed up dead, in succession.

After a year or so of investigation and interviews, Nelle eventually dropped the project.

Nelle told me that her research uncovered information she believed put her in personal jeopardy. She would not elaborate. She did say that she passed her notes along to a writer in residence at Auburn University, but he came to the same conclusions and also bowed out.

"Who was the writer in residence?" I asked.

"That's for me to know and you to find out," she said.

I didn't pursue it. Alice echoed Nelle's comments.

Certainly a nonfiction narrative of the case would have been fascinating. In a bizarre sequence of events, the part-time preacher, W. M. Maxwell, collected insurance money after five mysterious deaths that occurred over a few years.

In the first four cases, Maxwell was represented by attorney and former state senator Tom Radney Sr. When Maxwell requested Radney's services for the fifth case, involving the death of his teenage niece, Radney refused. During the niece's funeral, another uncle shot and killed Maxwell from the pew behind him.

At the subsequent trial, Radney defended the uncle, who was found not guilty by reason of insanity. Tom Radney Sr. died at age seventy-nine in 2011.

The defense attorney in the case, a main source for Nelle, later maintained that she struggled with the writing, and perhaps alcohol, and gave up.

Whatever the case with the Maxwell book, I had learned that alcohol could be a problem for Nelle.

That wasn't my experience. I never saw her have more than a glass or two of wine with dinner. I also never got the kind of angry late-night calls from her that Tom had warned me about early on.

"I've thought about whether to say something about this to you," he had told me. "I don't know if you'll get a call like that, but if you do, I don't want you to drop dead of a heart attack. I've gotten them.

Alice has gotten them. Other friends have gotten them. And it's really startling when it happens. And then that's it. There's no mention of it the next time she sees you."

We were quiet for a moment, as I reflected on this.

"Well, I appreciate the warning. You're right. I might have had a heart attack on the spot if I didn't know that could happen."

"She did it once to Hilda when I wasn't home and I took her to pieces over that. She never did it again, not to Hilda."

"She always speaks so sweetly about Hilda."

"And she means it. I don't know, really, what's behind it. Some paranoia that comes with being famous and being afraid people will take advantage of you for your money or whatever. She accuses people, chews them out. The alcohol fuels it. I don't know if it's some kind of release valve for pressures she feels or what. We all have our problems and doing that, well, it's one of hers."

If Capote is to be believed on the subject, the calls went back many years.

It struck me as the flip side to her lust for life. With great passion comes temptation. With extraordinary gifts come demons. As disciplined as Alice was in her personal habits and routines, Nelle was a woman of appetites. It was part of what was appealing about her; her gusto for experiences and spirited debate and food.

She was never hugely overweight but often wished she were twenty pounds lighter. She once checked herself into the local hospital ("back when you could just check yourself in") in order to subsist, with her doctor's help, on fluids for a week. She dropped weight, but quickly regained it. Many years later, when I knew her, it was still on her mind.

"I shouldn't eat this," she would say about the dessert before her, "but I'm going to." It was a point of commiseration between us, as I, too, wanted to lose a few pounds.

She could summon discipline, however. Nelle sympathized with the difficulty a friend of mine was having trying to quit smoking. We were getting back into my car after stopping at Rite Aid.

"You've never smoked, have you," Nelle said. It wasn't a question, and she was right. I hadn't. "It's terribly hard," Nelle told me. "But it can be done. I went cold turkey."

Chapter Twenty-three

I was fascinated by the Lee family history, from a slave-holding ancestor on their mother's side to the hardscrabble existence on their father's. A. C. Lee's life took him no farther than from Florida, where he grew up, to neighboring Alabama, where he raised his family. The distance was formidable nonetheless: He went from helping on his parents' modest farm to reading law and becoming the attorney upon which Atticus Finch was modeled. Alice told me that her father refused to cultivate even a garden, so strong was his aversion to working the soil given his upbringing on the farm in rural Florida. A.C. never graduated from high school, much less college or law school, but "read" the law, as was the custom in the day.

The dark brown piano against the far wall, Alice told me, was the first major purchase their parents made as a married couple. Music mattered to Frances Cunningham Finch Lee. Though some neighbors remember Mrs. Lee as a quiet woman who sat on the front porch for hours, seemingly at loose ends, Alice and Nelle described a mother whose piano playing would fill the living room, who loved to sing and read. Her more privileged background exposed her to the arts in a way she was pleased to pass on to her daughters.

The mental health of Frances Lee, and what that meant for Nelle's upbringing, has been a matter of speculation both around Monroeville and in the press. It comes up in Gerald Clarke's biography of Truman Capote, and would again in Charles Shields's 2006 biography of Harper Lee. Frances had a breakdown after her second child's failure to thrive. The ordeal with the infant Louise had not been previously reported. I wanted to know everything Alice was comfortable telling me. And she was ready to set the matter straight for the record, as this particular myth deeply bothered both sisters. In interviews before I moved to Monroeville, while I lived next door, and in the conversations that continued after, the story of Frances's ordeal emerged, along with what it meant for Alice, Nelle, and the rest of the family.

Alice was healthy as a baby; Louise was not. As she failed to thrive, A.C. and Frances grew more alarmed. They were at a loss for what to do and exhausted. "Mother collapsed," Alice said, "because Louise was not getting any nourishment and she was crying twenty-four hours a day and she was losing weight. Mother thought she was losing her baby and also did not get any rest. She could not get away from that crying child. Well, you see, what was happening, the baby was starving to death and the doctors there did not know what was wrong. They tried her on all the kinds of baby food that you had then."

Nothing worked. A.C. was working during the day. At home, he tended to his wife, five-year-old Alice, and baby Louise. "I don't know how he held up under it," Alice said, "because he couldn't rest, either, with this crying baby." In desperation, they sought out a specialist. "Well, they finally got to Selma and this famous pediatrician, Dr. William W. Harper. He diagnosed the problem," Alice said, "and put the baby on a complicated formula, which almost from the first taste,

Daddy said, she retained it and ate it and stopped crying." Frances was relieved but exhausted. She was distraught, showing signs of what the family then, and now, called "a nervous disorder."

"Well, Mother had had it," Alice said. "She just absolutely collapsed. And my grandmother in Finchburg kept us."

Again, the Lees found themselves dealing with a serious illness and sought the help of a specialist. That took gumption in an era when mental illness so often was confused with character defects. People with depression, anxiety disorders, and other conditions usually went without a diagnosis or treatment. Not Frances, who received a specialist's care in Mobile, first in the hospital and then as an outpatient.

In truth, Dr. Harper came to the rescue not only of baby Louise but of a family of four, with Frances driven to mental collapse and A.C. struggling to work, sleep-deprived, and care for his ailing wife and two small daughters. In this way, as well as others, the Lee family was quietly ahead of its time. Frances, according to Alice, was able to regain her emotional equilibrium.

Not only was A.C. ahead of his time, Frances was as well, doing what it took to recover. She lived away from the family for a year, staying with relatives near Mobile.

A.C. was living a life that resembled Atticus's in more ways than his law practice. For a time, he was a single father day to day, looking after Alice and baby Louise with the help of a black woman—like Calpurnia in the novel—and neighbors who knew one another's business, for better and for worse.

A few years later, with Frances's health long since stabilized, she and A.C. planned two more children. Louise was five when Ed was born. Five years later, the Lees had their fourth and last child, a girl.

So deep was A.C. and Frances's gratitude to Dr. Harper that when

Louise's baby sister was delivered in an upstairs bedroom on Alabama Avenue, the parents gave her the middle name Harper.

Nelle Harper Lee arrived on April 28, 1926.

All those sons and daughters named Harper, after Harper Lee, should know their name is a link not only to the author but to an otherwise-forgotten Selma pediatrician who, in 1916, saved a desperately ill infant named Louise Lee.

The Lee sisters, after all these years of staying quiet, began taking aim at the myths about their mother and other stories as well. At Nelle's request, I went on a reconnaissance mission one day to the Old Courthouse. According to the exhibit, A. C. Lee gave the young Truman a dictionary, the one displayed in a glass case. Whenever Truman heard a word he didn't know, he pulled the dictionary out of his pocket and looked it up.

It's a charming story—with one problem. "Nonsense," Nelle said when I showed her the picture I snapped of the dictionary. Her father did no such thing, she said. "That never happened."

Alice told me she was so disgusted with a book by Capote's aunt Marie Rudisill that she burned it with the autumn leaf piles in the backyard. Rudisill followed that one, *Truman Capote: The Story of His Bizarre and Exotic Boyhood by an Aunt Who Helped Raise Him,* with another, *The Southern Haunting of Truman Capote.*

Learning about the Lee family, now and going back several generations, meant learning about the black women who were part of those households.

One Sunday, Tom accompanied Alice and me on a long drive through Burnt Corn, Finchburg, Scratch Ankle, and some other communities. Alice pointed as we passed a small white church on the way to Finchburg.

"That church there was a landmark to me when I was little. That was my grandmother's cook's church. Henepin's church. I played with Henepin's daughter, named Fanny Lee, named for my mother."

Alice wanted to make sure I understood that the history of race relations in the South was not as simple as it was often portrayed. She told me, "Like with Julia. You would not have dared raise a child to be disrespectful to them. My grandmother would have chewed me out. When I grew up we always had a cook and most of the time a nurse for the little folks and my mother would have really taken us to pieces if we were rude or disrespectful to those people."

From the backseat, Tom Butts interjected his own experience. "I got a whipping once for sassing an old black man. There was respect but also strict boundaries."

Tom's later experience as a preacher near Mobile who supported integration would include finding a cross burning in his yard. That was 1957, but as late as 1984 he found a KKK card tucked in his door that read, "We are watching you and we don't like what we see."

Alice recalled the loyalty of the men and women who had worked for their family. "The morning that my father died it was an early Sunday morning on the fifteenth of April, 1962. It was a Palm Sunday that year. I had not been home an hour before the black lady who worked for me showed up in a white uniform: 'Miss Alice, I'll do anything for you I can.' You don't forget that kind of loyalty."

Chapter Twenty-four

While I was living next door, I made a decision I'd debated for years. I applied to adopt a baby from China. I thought I'd be married and raising a family by that time in my life. I'd always loved children, been good with them, and time was running out.

I had a feeling the Lees might be skeptical about the idea, and they were. "Heavens," Nelle said when I told her over coffee at my kitchen table. "How old will you be when that child graduates from high school?" I'd made the calculation a thousand times myself. If all proceeded at the usual pace for that that kind of adoption, I'd be about sixty.

I had struggled with the decision. Was it fair to a child to adopt as a single parent, and an older one with lupus? Was it realistic that I could provide the upbringing I'd want to give a child in those circumstances? But my doctors encouraged me to do so, and I knew my parents and brother, my whole close-knit extended family and friends, would wrap a child in a warm embrace.

Nelle mentioned my decision to Alice before I had a chance to tell her myself.

"I understand you have some news," Alice told me next time we were settled in her living room, a few days later.

"The adoption? Didn't I tell you about that? I thought I had."

"Nooo," she said, drawing out the word. She didn't say so but I realized she would rather have heard this directly from me. I'd learned, just intuitively, to tell them any news of interest at about the same time, if I could.

"I just don't know why you'd want to take on a baby."

I was reminded how rare it was for a single woman to do such a thing in their day, if an agency even allowed it. As it turned out, the pace of adoption in China dramatically slowed soon after. The trip I had thought I'd take in 2007, with the group I was assigned by my agency, never happened.

Melvin's barbecue is tucked away on Cherry Street, the side road that runs between Claiborne Street and Pineville Road. It's a town favorite for good reason: It is smoky, flavorful, and moist but not gloppy. Enjoying it on a regular basis, however, as we did, meant finding a way to work it off. Twice a week, Nelle and I headed for Peggy Van's exercise class. It was held in a one-story white brick building called the Community House, a seven-minute drive from downtown Monroeville, just up the hill from the duck pond. Often, we met up in the parking lot with Julia, another regular.

My first time there, I surveyed the large main room. It had hardwood floors. I saw about twenty women who looked to be in their seventies and eighties—along with one brave gentleman. Wide windows overlooked a wooded ravine. In the spring, pink and red azaleas crowded just outside the windows, as if they were trying to eavesdrop on the class.

At ten A.M. on Mondays and Wednesdays, we would start our routine under the big mirror ball. I was half the age of my classmates, but

I felt right at home; the stretching was good for my aching joints, which might be elbows one week, hips the next. Fatigue was the bigger problem. There seemed to be no way around napping a lot. On my most tired days it felt as if gravity were turned up. I wanted to build stamina, though, and hoped the exercise class would help shore up my flagging energy.

Dance bands once played here in the 1950s. Ladies in structured silk dresses the color of emeralds and sapphires twirled beneath the sparkly light of the mirror ball, under the appreciative eyes of husbands and beaus with slicked-back hair and neatly pressed suits. "They'd get has-been bands, but it didn't matter," said Dale Welch, the retired librarian. Dale went to a different senior exercise class, Silver Sneakers at the YMCA, one Nelle later attended with her. For Dale, driving by the Community House still conjured up those old dance bands.

"It was a chance to dress up and go out. People actually danced then. It was a lot of fun. It was quite elegant."

Dale missed the fun, but pointed out that those good old days weren't good for everyone. Only Monroeville's white couples got the chance to swirl around the dance floor. The black men and women present weren't dancing and enjoying themselves. They were serving refreshments.

I thought about that the day I accompanied both Nelle and Julia to class. About half of us were white, half black, and the main feeling was of camaraderie as we pushed ourselves to walk briskly in a giant circle. Peggy turned up the volume on the boom box perched on the stage where the dance bands once performed. "Remember," she told us, "heel-toe, heel-toe." A different Monroeville was moving across those same wooden floors under that same mirrored ball. I was the only one circling the room who wasn't around when half of us would not have been welcome to the dance. Or allowed, for that matter, to attend the same schools, use the same bathrooms, drink from the same water fountains.

Now the jewel tones in the room weren't the formal dresses; they were the velour sweat suits favored by many of the women. Peggy instructed us to commandeer gray metal folding chairs from one end of the room and place them in a large circle.

"Remember—sit majestically."

Peggy was in her sixties, slim and flexible. She was all energy and encouragement, and we summoned what majesty we could.

We attempted to lower ourselves—slowly, gracefully, and with straight backs—into the chairs. Sit majestically. Well, we could try; some of us were creakier than others. We sat down with varying degrees of majesty. We stretched our arms above our heads, flexed our ankles and our knees. I had one of those moments—an "Oh, my God, I'm in an exercise class with Harper Lee" moment—but the truth is, those moments came less frequently. I'd settled into a routine with Nelle and Alice. The days had a rhythm. It wasn't the rhythm of a reporter's life in Chicago, but it had its own pulse and lilt. I was getting used to it.

I asked her one day, as we headed home from Miss Peggy's valiant attempt to keep us limber, how our instructor could get by with the short Bible-based homily she appended to the end of each session.

"I don't necessarily need to take my inspiration with my exercise," Nelle said, "but Peggy's a good egg." She steered her car up Alabama Avenue.

How did she feel about the way religion is interwoven into public life? I told her I still was surprised when a public event began with a Christian prayer. "I guess I'm just so used to thinking in terms of separation of church and state," I said.

This sparked a hearty laugh. "Most people around here," Nelle said, "don't think in those terms."

That connection to the Bible, Nelle pointed out, colors the work of great Southern writers. She maintained that the King James Version of the Bible is unsurpassed in its use of language.

"How many of us," wrote Eudora Welty, "the South's writers-to-be of my generation, were blessed in one way or another, if not blessed alike, in not having been deprived of the King James Version of the Bible? Its cadence entered into our ears and our memories for good. The evidence, or the ghost of it, lingers in all our books: 'In the Beginning was the Word.'"

One day, walking out of the post office, built in 1933, complete with a WPA mural inside, I paused at the top of the steps and looked around. What would the people who populated this square in the 1930s—in *Mockingbird* days—make of it now?

Everything is oversized. Parked across the street in front of the Old Courthouse are pickup trucks and SUVs so big you don't step into them so much as climb on up; inside cup holders outnumber passenger seats and stand ready for plastic bottles of Coke that hold three times what the little glass ones did. People themselves are larger, too, wider and a bit taller. A family with an average income lives with a level of comfort and electronic convenience their '30s counterparts couldn't fathom.

Not everything has changed.

Even now, you're likely to strike up a conversation at the post office. A shopowner might call you by name at Darby's Red and White grocery.

Still, like most of the country, the town swells with stuff and selections are endless.

I told Nelle that I thought a Depression-era resident who stood where I did that day, taking in the contemporary scene, would be dazzled and appalled. Dazzled at the convenience and choice and prosperity, even in a struggling town. But also appalled by the excess, the move away from a strict moral code, the way people don't look one another in the eye as much.

"You're exactly right!" she said.

We discussed that—the way change comes at a cost. Convenience is appealing, but drive-through windows hardly foster the interaction of a general store. It was a topic we returned to often—the price we pay for convenience, appealing as it is.

The afternoon light was beginning to soften, a prelude to dusk. Alice and I had been speaking for a couple of hours, the small rocking chair pulled up to her recliner.

As if on cue, Nelle appeared from the back bedroom.

"You two about ready to go feed the ducks?"

I glanced over at Alice.

"I b'lieve so."

There always was a little something new to observe and talk over. A duck might have gone missing. Usually, the duck in question would reappear, his whereabouts the previous day a mystery. At one point, a duck was struck by a car, his feathered carcass discovered in the road. A friend told Judy, who told Nelle, who told Alice, who told me. Radio Monroeville, I called it.

"Radio Bemba" is what Cubans call word of mouth, *bemba* being slang for "lips." I mentioned the expression to Nelle one afternoon at McDonald's. We were gossiping about who gossiped the most around town, and why. It was a competitive field, that's for sure. The name of Nelle's top pick was not to go beyond our orange plastic booth. She was clear about that. "This is off the record."

She outlined the person's ample credentials for the post. One story made me laugh. She joined in, then looked stern for a moment.

"Don't put that in there," she said.

"Off the record, got it."

Later, Nelle asked, "What's that called? The radio thing?"

"Radio Bemba. It's pronounced Rah-dee-oh Baym-bah," so I quickly spelled out *B-E-M-B-A*.

Nelle nodded. "I want to remember that."

Every now and then, I'd invoke the local version when telling Nelle something that someone told someone who told me. "Rah-dee-oh Monroeville." It wasn't as much fun to say. *Bemba* bounces off the lips, playful onomatopoeia. With *onomatopoeia* having its own bouncy way about it.

Nelle was parsing language all the time.

In one brief drive along Alabama Avenue, she had the four of us in the car thinking about the origins of *grits* and *midwife*. We were headed for an early dinner at David's Catfish House. Kathryn Dawkins drove, with me beside her and Nelle and Alice in the backseat. Kathryn was a longtime good friend of the Lees, a fellow Methodist close in age to Nelle. A former Vanity Fair employee, she now was a pharmacy clerk at Food World.

"I hope this is okay, sugar," Kathryn said. She glanced over at me. "Are you getting tired of David's?" I'd been there a couple of dozen times. I imagine she and the Lees lost count of their own visits somewhere around the one hundred mark.

"No, I like David's and I like their hush puppies, too. Not so great for the diet, though."

Nelle had been watching her calories as well.

"I shouldn't have the cheese grits," she said. "But I'm going to."

"Did you know *grits is* is correct?" She recalled the British roots of the word.

On we went, past the old Vanity Fair administrative building and Central Supply, past Burger King and McDonald's, past the Winn-Dixie and the hospital. We drove by a new auto parts chain store.

Alice regarded the scene.

"Just what we need," she said drily. "Another auto parts store."

"Did you see Julia today?" Nelle asked me.

"I did," I said. "I went out to her place."

"It's really tucked back in there," Nelle said. It was easy to over-shoot Julia's home.

"Yeah, we spent some time looking at her garden and her pear tree. I wanted to ask her more about her days as a midwife."

"That's an old Middle English term, isn't it?"

"Sounds like it could be. I don't know. I'll look it up."

Nelle recalled that the word isn't at simple as it sounds. *Mid* could mean "with," not necessarily "middle" or "intermediary" back then. And *wife* simply meant "woman" at one time. A midwife worked with women, delivering babies. Or something like that.

After we finished our catfish, Alice reached into her handbag and retrieved four foil-wrapped Hershey's Kisses. With a twinkle in her eye, she gave one to each of us, "because a meal without dessert is like a sentence without a period."

Chapter Twenty-five

Dinner out meant Radley's or David's, usually, but Nelle had a suggestion for Dale and me.

"How about the Mexican place for a change of pace?"

Mexican it was. I'd passed the place a hundred times, on the way to the Excel Laundromat with Nelle or to the South Forty with Tom, but I'd never gone in. The Laredo Grill was a bit of Mexico plopped onto Highway 84, a boxy adobe structure between the log cabin ambience of David's Catfish House and the bright lights and big windows of the Waffle House, with its trademark black-on-yellow sign.

The Laredo, with its colorful sign, was meant to be festive but seemed forlorn instead. The long-established restaurants on either side were filled with regular customers enjoying familiar Southern fare.

I waited with Nelle for Dale to pick us up.

Alice and I chatted in the living room as Nelle got ready in her room.

"Can we bring you back anything?" I asked Alice.

She made a face. "No, thank you. I loathe Mexican food." She drew out the word *loathe,* so long and with such feeling I had to chuckle.

"All right. No enchiladas for you. A shake, then, from McDonald's, on our way home?"

"No, I have soup here. I don't need a thing. Just enjoy and don't worry about me. I have all this." Alice nodded at the pile of papers, magazines, and books on the table next to her recliner. She looked forward to these interludes alone, I knew. Even in her nineties, nearly deaf, and having outlived many of her clients, quiet time like this was something she prized. Even in her downtime, she was disciplined. She usually answered a letter or two—she still corresponded regularly with a number of friends and relatives—and then rewarded herself with uninterrupted reading time.

Friends were less likely to drop by after dark so she could count on a long stretch of time without distractions. Her little sister would be out and occupied for several hours, and there was no mistaking the pleasure and a tinge of relief with which she settled into her chair and bade us good night.

Nelle, on the other hand, was looking forward to a social evening.

Laredo Grill had more customers than we expected. Except for one family at a small table, all were of East Indian origin. They were seated along several tables pushed together to create a very long one.

After we ordered our enchiladas, Nelle had one other request for the waitress. Could she tell us about the long table of people near us? Was this a family reunion? One big family?

She shrugged and asked if we needed anything else. "Would you try, please?" Nelle asked me. I'd studied in Paraguay and Spain. In Spanish, I repeated her question to the waitress. She brightened and explained, while I interpreted her answer for Nelle and Dale.

This was a regular gathering, the waitress said, of families from India who owned motels in Monroe County and the next one over,

Conecuh. Some were related but not all. In their communities, including Monroeville, they were some of the only South Asians to be found. But at these meals, the camaraderie and shared experiences flowed.

Nelle was fascinated. She apologized for keeping the waitress but asked more questions. How long had most of these people lived here? How did they happen to choose this restaurant as their gathering place? The waitress wasn't sure about that.

We tried to be discreet in observing the lively table, with multiple conversations going, food being passed, and water glasses refilled. They looked to be four generations, from children to a woman in her eighties. I'm not sure they paid much attention to our table of three, the two tall white-haired women and the short blond one. After sharing so many meals with Nelle, I usually could sense when someone had recognized her and was watching, however discreetly.

So while it's possible someone recognized Nelle Harper and sent the little boy over to greet her, I doubt it. She was in a gregarious mood and that contagious laugh of hers would have floated over to the long table now and then. Maybe that's what caught the little boy's attention.

He was a striking child, four or five years old, with caramel-colored skin, black hair, and big brown eyes.

He walked over, by himself, and stood a few feet from Nelle, gazing at her intently. He didn't smile. He didn't look unhappy. He simply gazed, those big brown eyes looking at her with a calm, unapologetic curiosity.

It took Nelle a moment to notice he was there. She gave him a small nod, and continued to talking to us, but then, puzzled, returned his gaze. He just stood there.

They just looked at each other silently until Nelle laughed. She reached over to tousle his hair. He broke into a shy smile and dashed back to the long table. Nelle glanced at the woman, perhaps his mother, to whom he had returned. She gave the all-purpose, pleasant "lovely child you have" nod and returned to our conversation.

Usually, Nelle didn't welcome interruptions from children at meals. She wasn't nearly as likely as Alice to interact with a baby or young child while out to eat. But this encounter had charmed her.

Dale and I discussed it later. Ten years hence, that little boy would be reading *To Kill a Mockingbird* in his eighth- or ninth-grade English class. And he'd never know that he'd once had this encounter with the mysterious author.

It was impossible for me to watch Nelle's fascination with the sub-culture of Indian families running motels in modern-day *Mockingbird* country and not feel a pang, once again, for all the other writing she might have done. She admired their industriousness, especially at a time when she felt too many people born and raised in the area felt the world owed them a living. I couldn't help but envision a novel she could have written that included immigrants like those at the neigh-boring table, with Nelle's eye for detail and character, her empathy for outsiders, applied to the subculture of South Asians living in southern Alabama.

That evening made me a little sad, in the way that my afternoon interviewing Margaret Garrett with Nelle did. It was a reminder of how much Nelle loved something she had stopped doing, at least for book purposes, examining the way of life, the nuanced interactions in a community in the way Jane Austen did in her novels, in the way Nelle did in *To Kill a Mockingbird*.

Chapter Twenty-six

The year was off to a rough start. Just a couple of weeks into 2005, Nelle had bad news from New York. A friend had died. She told me about it as we stood in her driveway. I was tired. She was tired. Even the January sky was tired, a washed-out shade of blue tinged with gray.

Nelle had pulled into her driveway as I was backing out of mine. I'd been in bed for a couple of days with a lupus flare. I had errands that couldn't be postponed any longer.

Nelle got out of her car and gave a small wave. I stuck my arm out the car window and waved back. She began to take a few careful steps my way. I turned off the ignition and got out. The overhead light went on when the door was open; leaving it that way too long drained the battery. I left it open and ignored the insistent *ding ding ding*. I didn't want Nelle to feel crowded by this unusual proximity of ours. The open door signaled this would be a quick hello.

Nelle saw me hurry across my front lawn and waited for me by her Buick, as I hoped she would. The little side yard between her driveway and my yard was uneven in spots. Near the base of a couple of tall pines, gnarled roots with no place else to grow twisted out of the earth.

"How are you?" she asked.

Tolerable, just barely, I thought.

"I'm fine," I said. "How are you?"

Usually this was where she said "Tolerable." Instead, Nelle was silent a moment. Something was wrong.

Oh, no, I thought. Alice.

She was active. But she also was ninety-four. We all knew a bad fall or a bout of pneumonia was all it would take. One evening, the phone rang later than usual. Even half asleep I thought, Oh, no. Alice. Please, not yet. It was nothing, a wrong number. Another time, a mutual friend told me, "We've had some bad news." Oh, no. Alice. The bad news was someone else's illness. And on this day, as usual, Alice was fine. Nelle told me her friend Nell Rankin had died.

"Oh, Nelle. I'm sorry."

"Most of my friends are underground."

This wasn't the time for a quick hello. I knew Old Blue was *ding ding ding*–ing in my driveway but so be it. As we spoke, I rested the back of my hand against Nelle's still-warm car. The index finger on my left hand was swollen and throbbing. The heat felt good. Nelle was beyond tired, too, but for a different reason. She felt the weariness of loss.

Opera singer Nell Rankin was a New York friend. She was another Alabama native, another Alabama Nelle. Or, rather, Nell. The singer was eighty-one, only two years older than Nelle Harper.

A dramatic, dark-haired mezzo-soprano, Rankin was born to a Montgomery family, a musical family, in 1924. Even as a young girl, she sang beautifully and studied voice. She went on to become a star of the Metropolitan Opera in the 1950s and 1960s, known for her roles in *Aida* and *Carmen*. She died of a bone marrow disease, polycythemia vera, on January 13, a Thursday.

Nelle told me she had been on the phone nonstop. Or at least it felt like it. She was worried about Nell's husband of more than fifty years, Hugh Davidson, a physician. He was inconsolable.

Sometimes the long distance from Manhattan to Monroeville was a comfort, its own form of privacy. At times like this, though, when she had to manage from afar, it was a frustration.

Nelle brightened when she began describing her friend.

"She sang all over the world."

Her friend was larger than life, a woman who could captivate an audience with her warm, powerful voice. At one time, she had a jaguar. Not a Jaguar with wheels. An actual jaguar. With teeth.

The death wasn't reported to the press immediately. Obituaries began to appear nearly a week after she died. I looked online to see what was running where.

The *New York Times* obituary noted, "In addition to her performances at the Met, Ms. Rankin continued to sing at major houses around the world, including La Scala, where she sang Cassandra, in Berlioz's 'Troyens,' in 1960, and the Teatro San Carlo, in Naples, where she sang Adalgisa in Bellini's 'Norma,' in 1963. She also sang with companies in Chicago, Fort Worth, Buenos Aires, Havana, Mexico City and Athens."

Rankin famously brought her semidomesticated pet jaguar, King Tut, into a Metropolitan Opera contract meeting as a "negotiating tool."

I printed out several of the obituaries, put them in a Food World plastic bag with a note, and hung the bag on the Lees' doorknob. Next time I saw her, there was none of her usual teasing about what she called with slight disdain my "magic box." Just a heartfelt thank-you. Would I keep my eye out for any others? I did, and passed them along.

Inevitably, advancing age was claiming more of the Lees' friends and relatives. One of the hardest deaths to take had been Gregory Peck's, in 2003.

Peck had come up early in my first conversation with Nelle, the one begun over the noisy air conditioner in my room at the Best Western. I told her the movie would be shown in Chicago as part of the *To Kill a Mockingbird* events for One Book, One Chicago. Gregory Peck is Atticus for most *Mockingbird* fans. That was just fine with Nelle.

"Isn't he delicious?" she had said in our very first conversation. He was a dear friend who never lost that movie-star dreaminess for her.

From the start, Nelle's friendship with Gregory Peck extended to his family: his wife, Veronique, who died in 2012, and their two children, documentary filmmaker Cecilia Peck and actor/producer Anthony Peck. I was amused when Nelle suggested fixing me up with Anthony Peck. She did a quick calculation and decided the age difference was too great. Seven years didn't seem like a problem to me. I was looking to find a nice guy. When I Googled Anthony Peck, however, and saw his first wife was Cheryl Tiegs, I, too, thought better of the idea.

Before the film was made, Lee took Peck around Monroeville to help him prepare for the role. He had the chance to meet her father, who was amused at the hullabaloo created by Peck's visit.

Peck connected with Nelle on a profound level before he even met her. He fell in love with her storytelling and the opportunity to play Atticus Finch. Peck was in his midforties when he played the small-town attorney. For the rest of his life he said it was his favorite role, the one he was born to play.

"When Alan Pakula and Bob Mulligan sent me the book and said, 'I think this is something you're going to like,' well, I sat up all night reading the book. I could hardly wait until eight o'clock in the morning to call them and say, 'If you want me, I'm your boy.'

"Of course I've never had a moment's regret. On the contrary, it was a blessing and a gift from Harper Lee."

Peck told this to an audience at *A Conversation with Gregory Peck.* In 1999, the actor, then in his early eighties, traveled to regional theaters around the country. He took questions and told stories, in that sonorous voice, about making *To Kill a Mockingbird,* as well as *Roman Holiday* with newcomer Audrey Hepburn and, later, *MacArthur,* about the World War II general. His daughter and her fellow filmmaker Barbara Kopple recorded those evenings.

In the documentary, Cecilia and writer Daniel Voll are expecting their first child. It's the spring of 1998. Peck and his wife, the French-born Veronique Passani, are in Washington, D.C., for him to receive the National Medal of Arts from President Bill Clinton. Cecilia and Daniel visit their hotel room.

Peck tells his daughter about a phone conversation with Harper Lee.

"I talked to Harper yesterday for a long time."

"Where is she? In Monroeville?"

"She's in Monroeville looking after her sister. After a nice long talk—we talked about many things—I told her about you." Peck pauses. "Furthermore I told her if it had been a girl, it might well have been named Harper. She was very touched by it."

"What if I gave her name to a boy baby?"

Cecilia's mother, Veronique, knows the answer to that. "I think she'd still be happy about it. It's a great name for a boy." And indeed, their boy is named Harper Daniel Peck Voll.

Peck and Nelle had kept up a long correspondence and Nelle stayed with the Pecks in their Holmby Hills home on occasion. When Cecilia Peck lived in New York, Harper Lee would go over and read to the young Harper.

When Peck died at eighty-seven in June 2003, the family tried to reach Nelle in New York by phone but she was out that day. She learned of his death, she told me, on the evening news.

Brock Peters delivered Peck's eulogy. With more than a thousand people assembled at a cathedral in Los Angeles, Peters also sang a Duke Ellington song, "They Say." He concluded, "To my friend Gregory Peck, to my friend Atticus Finch, *vaya con Dios*."

Nelle did not attend the funeral but later visited Veronique Peck in Los Angeles.

Their grandson, Harper, was about six—Scout's age in the novel—when Nelle came over one day with a request. She wanted to buy him a kite and have it shipped to California. She wondered what we could find online. She wanted an old-fashioned kite, "plain, no writing on it, nothing fancy. Just a classic kite." She was frustrated that this was more difficult to find than ones with rainbows, gimmicks, or neon colors.

As I showed her what I was finding for kites online—nothing satisfactory that day—she glanced down at the hopeless tangle of power cords I had corralled into a basket on my floor. Cords for my laptop, my cell phone charger, my printer, and the copier all were twisted together and shoved in a basket to one side so I wouldn't trip over them. She shook her head slowly. "Mercy," was all she said.

That January 2005, Nelle also had an appearance coming up. At the end of the month, she was to attend an annual *To Kill a Mockingbird* luncheon in Tuscaloosa. No matter how relieved, and even pleased, Nelle might feel after an appearance, the days leading up to an event were fraught with anxiety.

Mystique raises expectations. Being anyone's favorite author raises expectations, much less being so many people's favorite author. Still, this was not new to Nelle. Shouldn't it get easier with time? Apparently not. As the event drew closer, a swirl of apprehension, resentment, and irritation gained momentum.

Nelle told me she continued to do the event partly because of her friendship with the event's organizers. She also liked that the focus was on students reading and writing about the novel.

Students at a predominantly black Tuscaloosa high school and at a predominantly white one write about the novel and what it means to them. Those judged to have the best essays are honored at the stately home of the president of the University of Alabama.

Nelle was modest about it, but she knew her presence was a thrill for those students. She felt like less of a commodity there. A lot of the awards offered to her, she suspected, were mostly an attempt to get Harper Lee to show up and lend cachet to an event. This was different.

When Nelle studied in Tuscaloosa in the early 1940s, it took longer to travel the 138 miles to the college town on the banks of the Black Warrior River. Now you can make the drive in two hours and forty-five minutes. It seemed farther, though, the way people in Monroeville talked about it. Tuscaloosa has ninety thousand people and all those professors and students, dreamers and gadflies, that university towns attract. Monroeville it isn't.

The event was less than a week away, and over coffee at McDonald's, in the usual booth by the window, she fretted about it: the logistics, the need to dress up, the expectations that greeted her anytime she made an appearance.

Nelle knew those sitting at her table would be repeating whatever she said as their Harper Lee anecdote, that people would want to have their picture taken with her, that accounts of the event might make it into the newspaper.

It comes in handy to have a hairdresser in your posse. For Nelle, getting ready for a public appearance held all the appeal of having a tooth pulled. The one annual event she agreed to was this one. As the event drew closer, Ila offered to trim Nelle's hair. She would trim Judy's and mine as well while she was at it.

"Oh, would you, hon?" Nelle said, relieved. "Bless you." She was uncomfortable with the fuss of primping for things like this.

Ila Jeter retired but kept her professional shears. For years, she ran a one-woman beauty shop. She shampooed and conditioned, cut and curled, teased and styled. She laughed with her customers and sympathized with their troubles. She was a natural.

For Nelle, there was reassurance in shopping for an outfit with Judy or having Ila trim her hair in the comfort and privacy of Ila's home.

And so it was that a few days before Nelle's appearance, she and Judy and I gathered at Ila's handsome one-story house at the end of the cul-de-sac in Mexia. Ila shepherded all three of us into the roomy master bathroom. It was easily five times the size of the main bathroom at the Lee house.

Ila motioned for Nelle to sit in the chair she had dragged in for this purpose. She draped a thin smock, the kind with a snap in the back, over Nelle's casual, button-down shirt. I perched on the steps to the Jacuzzi, and Judy sat on the window seat. Ila wet Nelle's hair. She went to work with an efficient snip, snip, snip.

"Are you going to make me look presentable?" Nelle asked Ila. She added wryly: "To the extent that's possible."

"More than presentable," Ila said.

"You know me," Nelle said. "It's short hair, leave it white, and be done with it."

"This is quite a bathroom," Judy said. It was gracious, spacious. In fact, Ila told us, with her husband James's cancer progressing, he had mused that perhaps they should just roll a hospital bed in here near the end and make it his room. "He said, 'Everything would be right here.'"

"Oh, bless his heart," Nelle said. It was vintage James Jeter. He was a practical man, and he didn't want to make things any harder than necessary for Ila. She lightly brushed a little wet, white hair off Nelle's smock. Ila stepped back to regard her work and returned to trimming Nelle's bangs.

"How long did you work as a hairdresser?" I asked Ila.

"Thirty years."

"So you knew all about what was happening in people's lives," I said.

"Girl, you don't know. I knew more than I wanted to know." She had a longtime customer who Ila knew was having an affair with the husband of another regular. She made sure not to book their appointments back-to-back. A last-minute change one day meant that happened, nonetheless.

So Ila worked quickly, she told us. She tried to nudge the freshly coiffed wife out the door without being obvious. She got nowhere. The woman was in a talkative mood and in no hurry. She departed, finally, right before the other woman arrived.

Ila pantomimed her relief. Nelle's laughter bubbled over. "Mercy."

Nelle had a question. Had Ila ever read "Petrified Man," the Eudora Welty short story that takes place in a beauty shop?

"I don't think so," Ila said.

"Oh, you should."

"I can make a copy for you," I told Ila.

"Oh, would you?" Nelle said.

"Great," Ila said.

Ila refused to let Nelle or Judy or me pay her. As we left her house, I told Ila I'd drop off the copy of "Petrified Man."

"I know you'll enjoy it," Nelle told her.

Welty published the story in 1939. It became a staple of high school English classes. That's when I read it, sitting in the overheated, old library of West High in Madison. All these years later, I remembered something about a human specimen preserved in a jar but not much else.

Not long after, I found "Petrified Man" in my copy of *The Collected Stories of Eudora Welty*. At my bedside printer, I lifted the lid to make the copy. Before setting the book facedown on the glass, I glanced again at the first couple of lines of the story.

"'Reach in my purse and git me a cigarette without no powder in it if you kin, Mrs. Fletcher, honey,' said Leota to her ten o'clock shampoo-and-set customer. 'I don't like no perfumed cigarettes.'"

I read on. Mrs. Fletcher marvels at the peanuts in Leota's purse. Leota tells her they came from Mrs. Pike. Who is that? Mrs. Fletcher wants to know.

I put the lid to the printer back down. I couldn't be expected to stop there, not without knowing who Mrs. Pike was or what was up with Mrs. Fletcher and Leota. The feeling I'd had reading the story twenty-five years earlier was returning to me. It was a feeling about the confining lives of the characters, more like hearing a familiar song in a distant room than recalling anything specific. I still couldn't remember the details of what happened in that Mississippi beauty shop.

I thought, I'll just read another a page or two. I climbed up on the bed and sat cross-legged with the book. Mrs. Fletcher is pregnant, married to a man she expects to reform. She has a multitude of reasons for resenting Mrs. Pike, whom she knows only through Leota's gossip. There was a "petrified man," too, a person who could stand stock-still so long he appeared to be made of stone. He turns out to be a wanted criminal, a rapist on the run. Inside the lavender walls of the beauty shop, the gossip flows. The women reveal themselves and their predicaments, more than they know.

I had errands to run, starting with getting a photocopy of the story to Ila. But there were a dozen other stories in the Welty collection.

One more and then it's back to work.

Maybe two.

Chapter Twenty-seven

In February I told Nelle that I was planning to drive to Princeton Junction, New Jersey, later that month to visit my college roommate and her family. I asked Nelle if she wanted to come along, since she was returning to New York about that same time, and flying, of course, was not an option. She could catch an easy commuter train from there. She said yes.

I began my preparations, turning to practical aspects, fighting the urge to get a window sign that said PLEASE BE CAREFUL NATIONAL TREASURE ON BOARD.

I did, however, join AAA, stock the car with water bottles, and, much to Alice's amusement, buy collapsible orange traffic cones for my trunk.

On Thursday morning, February 24, we piled our things in the car and I backed out of her driveway, dipping a back tire off the edge of the narrow cement strip, causing a noticeable bounce. "So much for getting off to a good start," Nelle told me with a wry smile.

That night I faxed Alice from Newnan, Georgia, telling her that Nelle, even with drops in her eyes, helped to get me on 85, and it was an easy drive. Nelle dashed off a note on the fax to confirm our arrival and signed off as "Dody." The nickname goes back to childhood when a young Nelle, as the family story goes, mispronounced a word as *dody* and the name stuck.

After a day of driving and several cups of coffee each, we stopped at another Hampton Inn, in Fredericksburg, Virginia. I managed to get lost trying to find the Bonefish Grill, a seafood restaurant chain. By the time I pulled into the parking lot, we were both tired and stiff from a day in the car. "My treat," Nelle said. She wanted us to enjoy a quiet dinner at a nice place.

It wasn't the subdued place we had pictured. Young men and women, still in suits after work, crowded the bar and waiting area. Waiters rushed by and people chatted loudly on cell phones. Nelle took all this in and sank onto a bench for diners waiting to be seated. "Mercy," she said.

After we sat down for dinner, our conversation turned to the grim topic people were grappling with in Monroeville. The brutal murder of a beloved local doctor and his wife the previous year had shocked everyone. Now trial preparations were under way for the couple's thirty-one-year-old adoptive son, Timothy Jason Jones, who had a history of drug addiction and anger. The prosecutor had decided this would be a death penalty case, and sentiment in town seemed to be largely in favor of that. What gave some pause was Jones's long history of addiction. The crime appeared to be related to a dispute over money he wanted for drugs.

Was someone in the grips of addiction, even someone who repeatedly had spurned his parents' efforts to help him get his life back on track, fully responsible for his actions?

I had asked Alice about the case during one of our Sunday afternoons with recliner, rocking chair, and recorder. How did she feel about the death penalty?

"No one abhors what he did more than I," Alice said. "Dr. Jones and his wife were my friends. But my faith tells me that everyone has a spark of the divine in them. I wouldn't want to serve on a jury that sent him to his death."

As I recounted this to Nelle, she leaned forward.

"That's what Alice said? That's fascinating."

"You haven't discussed the case with her?"

"Well, not in those terms. What do you think about it?"

"I understand both sides of it, I think. I do. But I don't support the death penalty. There are too many problems. Who gets executed and why. And the whole idea of executing people . . ."

Nelle nodded.

"What do you think?" I asked.

"I understand both sides of it, too," she said. She demurred on what she thought should happen in the Jones case, or in general.

If she still were writing, I wondered to myself, would a case like this be the inspiration for something she might write in a novel? The trial in *To Kill a Mockingbird* is still taught in some law schools. People are fascinated by her thoughts about social issues like that, about criminal justice. And *In Cold Blood* was about the road to the hanging of the two killers.

There was no point in wondering, though. She wasn't going to be doing that. It was another book I pictured on the shelf of those she could have written. The imaginary row of books that made me wistful when I thought about it. Wistful for what Nelle might have accomplished and taken pride in doing with her talent, with her insight. Wistful for all of us who would have loved to read them. But that decision was hers to make and she'd made it, however gradually over the years, for her host of reasons, starting with the difficulty of living up to the impossible expectations raised by *To Kill a Mockingbird*.

In my conversations with Alice and Tom, that impediment loomed large, as they saw it. Tom knew the whole question was a tiresome topic for Nelle. He let her bring it up rather than doing so himself. And she did, every now and then. As he recalled it, this was one late-night conversation over a bottle of Scotch.

"Do you ever wonder why I never wrote anything else?" Nelle asked him. She dropped it into their conversation apropos of nothing, but with a certain intensity.

Tom paused and looked at her with a hint of a smile.

"Well, along with about a million other people, yes."

He knew, Tom told her, that it would have been daunting to compete with the success of *To Kill a Mockingbird*. He began to expand on that, but she cut him off.

"Bullshit," she said. "Two reasons. First, I wouldn't go through all the pressure and publicity I went through with *Mockingbird* for any amount of money."

Tom nodded.

"Second, I have said what I wanted to say and I will not say it again."

Tom nodded again but thought to himself, he later told me, that he, personally, didn't put a lot of stock in that second reason. Only she knew, of course. It was for her to say.

But in his experience, she did have more to say. Plenty more to say. Issues of family and faith, race and religion, character and community, still animated her conversations. Someone sustained by ideas, who still was a writer to her core whether or not she had published anything in decades, had to have more to say. Didn't she?

Later on that trip, as we got closer to New Jersey, I offered again to drive Nelle into Manhattan. I knew it would be hairy but I wondered if I shouldn't deliver her to her door. "Don't even think about it. It's too difficult doing that. I want to take the train in. It's better for you and me."

Nelle and I arrived early at the Princeton Junction station, a quaint stone structure with wooden pews for waiting passengers. She had shipped all but what she needed for the car trip so her bag was easy to manage. The station wasn't crowded; most of the wooden benches were unoccupied and we found a quiet spot to sit. I sat with her bag while she went to the window and got a ticket to Penn Station.

"Thanks a bunch, hon," Nelle said. "You have a good time with your friends. And drive safely."

The train came to a stop and Nelle boarded with small clusters of others waiting on the platform. The doors closed and the train pulled out of the station. And she was gone.

I'd been close to my New Jersey friends since we'd studied together at Georgetown University. After visiting them, I decided to make the twelve-hour drive to Chicago rather than return to Monroeville. It was easier than dealing with a flight to Chicago later on, and I was overdue to make the usual round of medical appointments and to spend time with friends and family, especially my young nephews, Tommy and Andrew. At home, I received a letter from New York. Nelle thanked me for the trip and the good company.

Across the top she dashed off a line about the dark felt-tip pen I had given her, one that was supposed to be easier for people with vision problems to see. "I love this pen!"

While Nelle was in New York, Alice faxed me her phone number there so I would have it. I wrote Nelle's phone number in my little pink address book but not under Lee. Earlier, I had recorded her address under a made-up name. I was afraid if it were ever lost or stolen I would feel compelled to leap from the Sears Tower rather than owning up to the security breach.

I had thought about what name I could come up with that would fall right before Lee. Leder. I'd heard the name. I put the information under "Natalie Leder." Someone with the initials N.L. would remind me but mean nothing to any purse snatcher who, theoretically, would turn out to have a literary bent, would know Nelle Lee was Harper Lee, and would auction off the address or phone number.

While Nelle still was in New York, I returned to Monroeville with my mother. Nelle would take the train to Los Angeles for a May 19 library foundation fund-raiser planned by Veronique Peck and then another train to New Orleans for a stretch in Monroeville. She got back two weeks after my mother left. "Your mother was a big hit around here," she told me when she returned. It was true.

Having a sweet-spirited, smart momma made my stock rise a bit, I think, among my friends here. She and I were close, always, and she knew more about my experiences in Alabama than anyone else.

It was a treat to show my mother around the town she had heard so much about, to take a long country drive with Alice, see the play, and go to dinner at the Crofts' and the Butts'. With tender pride, Julia showed my mother the giant red amaryllis she had cultivated in the Lees' small flower bed. Finally, Julia had a true gardener next door, if only for a short time, someone who could talk annuals and perennials with her. My own gardening amounted to admiring the yellow lantana that grew wild by my driveway. Not that I knew it was called lantana until my mother saw it and told me.

In the Lees' front yard, Julia was telling us more about the amaryllis when a mockingbird alighted on a tree branch and offered us its song. Mockingbirds are a fairly common sight around Monroeville but to have one join us in Harper Lee's yard was a bit of magic.

My mother and I just looked at each other. We paused and listened. Julia volunteered her take on mockingbirds.

"They just sing their song and don't care what anybody say about it. It's their song and they gonna sing it."

Mockingbirds sing loudly and don't take kindly to other birds infringing on their territory. There's something strong but also vulnerable about mockingbirds; those qualities applied to the one in the tree as well as the ones living in the house.

That night, Julia finally went to see the annual play. Later, with the tape recorder rolling at my kitchen table, I asked her what she thought of it.

"It was different from what I thought it would be like. Because I had never read the book either. I have the book, but I had never read it or seen the play. Miss Alice told me. 'Julia?'

"And I said, [she speaks in a high voice] 'Yes ma'am?'

"'You ever seen that play?'

"'No ma'am.'

"She said, 'Well, Julia, when it plays again you'd better go see it.'

"So I did."

She chuckled.

What had she expected?

"I really expected that this lawyer that defend the accused, that he'd have more action than what he really did, you know. He didn't, he didn't *pound* his fist saying, "I don't *believe* he did it." Julia pounded her fist on the table to illustrate. "It was just a regular calm thing, you know. I thought—I was expecting more action on his part than there really was."

I told her there's more action in the movie, though Atticus is still pretty calm in the courtroom. She didn't like courtrooms, she told me, because they reminded her of Judgment Day in the Bible.

Chapter Twenty-eight

W eighty histories and long biographies were not the only books captivating the Lees.

That year, 2005, Gayden Metcalfe and Charlotte Hays, two Missis-sippi women, had just published *Being Dead Is No Excuse*. The slim book is, as the subtitle explains, *The Official Southern Ladies Guide to Hosting the Perfect Funeral.*

The authors had tongue-in-cheek fun with the various traditions, when it comes to funerals and receptions and all that is right and proper and reflects one's social standing, among the various denomi-nations in their town. The book made the rounds among the people I knew: Nelle and Alice, Judy and Dale, Tom and Hilda.

As a Methodist minister's wife well versed in funerals, the nor-mally soft-spoken Hilda erupted with laughter reading the book aloud one evening. I had joined her and Tom at their kitchen table for a din-ner of beef vegetable soup, salad, and her fragrant homemade sour-dough rolls, famous among their friends as devilishly impossible to resist. She made batches of them in round baking tins, used layers of plastic wrap and aluminum foil to preserve them in the freezer, and always gave me a package for the road. The only problem was the difficulty in driving while liberating the thawed rolls from those tight layers of plastic wrap.

Nelle told me her favorite passage was the one with the Episcopalian woman trying to remember the origin of her bruised knees.

"I just don't know," the woman said as she dyed Easter eggs in her kitchen, "Did I hurt my knees yesterday afternoon doing the Stations of the Cross? Or did I do it falling down drunk last night?"

In fairness, the authors, and Nelle, too, had fun at the expense of the whole array of Protestant denominations.

Not long after Nelle and I chuckled about the book over coffee, we attended a society luncheon in Monroeville.

Nelle called one afternoon and got right to the point.

"We've been invited to a to-do at Patsy's house." Patsy McCall was a shirttail relative of Nelle's who lived in a large, elegant house atop a small hill on the other side of town. Patsy married Lloyd McCall, whose sister Sara Anne married Ed Lee. Patsy was Nelle's sister-in-law's sister-in-law. No wonder people default to the all-purpose "They're kin to them."

We?

"I think they invited me so that you'd come." No, she wasn't kidding.

The occasion was an elaborate luncheon series for two dozen or so women, held September through May. Hostess duties rotated among the homes of several of the women. Nelle wanted me to see this aspect of life in Monroeville.

This was not the kind of gathering Nelle frequented.

"Well," I asked Nelle, "would you like to go?"

"I'll go if you go."

And so, on the second Friday in November, I walked next door. Nelle was still getting ready. I kept watch, just inside the front door, for our ride. Marianne Lee, the effervescent wife of her nephew Ed Lee, would be by to pick us up.

Nelle emerged from the bedroom hallway, smoothing her hair and sort of fluttering into the room. I'd never seen her quite like this. She seemed festively discombobulated, if such a thing is possible. This would be a fairly dressy gathering, she told me, and she was as dressed up as I'd seen her, save when she made one of her rare public appearances to accept an award.

She had on black pants and a pink silk shirt, and her bangs were combed straight down. On her collar was a glittery cat pin. On her feet, black loafers with a gold buckle.

She smoothed her hair again as she surveyed my outfit. I had on black slacks, low heels, and a cotton turquoise blazer. And longer earrings than usual.

"Are you dressed to the nines?" she said.

"I tried to find some nines to dress in." I smiled.

"Oh, well. I'm dressed to the sevens."

Nelle reached out and cupped her hand below the curl in my hair.

"You curled your hair."

"Trying to look respectable."

Nelle sighed. "Oh, Lord. At least my shoes will be pretty." She glanced down at her loafers, ones I hadn't seen before.

As Marianne's SUV pulled into the driveway we said good-bye to Alice, who was working at the kitchen table. It was a beautiful fall day, no jacket needed.

Our footsteps were quiet amid the clatter of women in high heels climbing the redbrick stairs to Patsy's home. It was white, two stories, with columns out front. White rocking chairs graced the wide porch.

I began to see what Nelle meant. This was an occasion, not just a get-together. It was like stepping into a photo spread in *Southern Living*.

"Welcome, welcome," Patsy greeted us as we streamed in with several others. A round table in a sizable foyer had a huge arrangement of lilies and pink roses, the size you might see in the lobby of a nice hotel. One of the three hostesses for this lunch, Mary Whetstone, circulated a silver platter with little roll-ups of salmon and cream. I'd met Mary. She was married to Dr. Jack Whetstone, now mostly retired, and went to Judy's Wednesday night bell practice at the Methodist church.

About two dozen guests, mostly older women but some in their thirties and forties, were chatting animatedly. I'd already met half of them, or more, and Patsy began introducing me to the others.

Before the meal, people stood around the table and Patsy led the grace. Then we seated ourselves at one of the tables set up throughout the house. Nelle and I chose a table for seven in the kitchen, where we sat before sparkling place settings on linen place mats: gold-rimmed white plates, weighty silverware, and crystal stemware for white wine.

Over a meal of baked chicken, vegetable casserole, rice almandine, corn salsa, and rolls, the conversation centered on the usual talk of who was doing what around town. Nelle especially enjoyed Patsy's dessert of rosettes topped with ice cream, caramel sauce, and pecans. "There go all my good intentions," she said. She noticed that some of it had dripped onto her shirt. "Never fails," Nelle said, dipping her linen napkin into her goblet to blot the stain. "Just like my grandfather."

A heavyset black woman wearing a bright raspberry velour top stood at the sink washing dishes as the conversations continued. After the meal, coffee was served in delicate cups and saucers. Nelle and I helped ourselves to cream and sugar from an elegant silver tray. McDonald's this wasn't.

Nelle once complained to me that "all anyone wants to talk about here is grandchildren and gardens." The conversation at the table, along those lines, was going on around her. She sat quietly, looking a bit ill at ease.

I asked if anyone had read *Being Dead Is No Excuse*. A few, like Nelle, had started it. She brightened recalling her favorite story. I'd heard Nelle share this with a few other people in recent weeks but that's the thing about a favorite story. It's amusing each time. And so here we were again.

"The best line in there is the Episcopalian woman with bruised knees, who said she wasn't sure if they came from doing the Stations of the Cross the day before or if she had been falling down drunk at night."

She laughed, and the others joined in.

I asked a woman in a coral suit if there was a book club in town.

"No. There are a few art clubs, a garden club, lots of bridge clubs."

Back home in the driveway I asked Nelle about the lack of a book club. I wasn't looking to join, necessarily, but I was curious about who was reading what around town. Perhaps there was one and I hadn't heard of it.

Nelle had a different explanation. "The literary capital of Alabama doesn't read." The term "Literary Capital of Alabama" had been coined in the effort to make Monroeville, home of Harper Lee, a tourist attraction.

We talked about which guests she knew; I wondered how many were from "old Monroeville." She paused. "Me and that was it."

I was struck once again at the contrast between the grand, formal house we'd just left and the modest place that houses a famous author and her attorney sister.

Later, I told Judy Croft about the lunch. "I'm so glad Nelle went," she said. "She hides her light under a bushel basket a lot of the time."

That night Judy, Dale Welch, Nelle, and I had dinner at the Main Street Diner in Excel. The talk turned to books. "These two children are too young to remember Miss Minerva," Nelle said to Dale, glancing at Judy and me, "but she was marvelous. Reynolds Price found an old one for me for ten bucks."

The Miss Minerva series followed the antics of young William Green Hill and his childhood friends in Tennessee. Miss Minerva is the genteel unmarried aunt who welcomes the orphaned, mischievous six-year-old Billy into her home. The books were first published in the early twentieth century.

She told us about a new book coming out, written by a friend of hers.

"It's delicious. If you remember the good old-fashioned novel, this is it."

In fact, she contributed a cover blurb that described it as a transcendent and enduring American novel, adding "I loved it."

Nelle was in her element now, holding court and holding forth in a way she never would in that afternoon's more formal setting. The book was *The Lightning Keeper,* she said, written by a friend of hers in New York, Star Lawrence, who was editor in chief of W. W. Norton at the time.

"*The Lightning Keeper,*" Dale repeated slowly, wondering what the title meant.

"It's about General Electric and relatives that were involved in— well, the type of people who went dove hunting in Paraguay." Nelle zeroed in on one of Lawrence's telling details. Old money with a sense of adventure went dove hunting in Paraguay.

A woman leaving the diner stopped at our table to greet Dale. Nelle asked loudly who that was. Dale replied that she was a good artist, and murmured, as precaution, "and the husband is still behind us." Nelle didn't hear the last part, I could tell, so I slipped her a piece of paper from my reporter's notebook that read, "The husband is still behind us."

I offended her. "I'm not going to say anything about someone I don't know," she said, irritated. She fidgeted with the slip of paper, folding it into a slim rectangle as she did with emptied Splenda packets.

I could feel a little pink rising in my cheeks. Usually she wanted to be alerted to such things, because she couldn't hear voices behind her very well. But not tonight.

Nelle told us she'd ordered something to help with hearing. They were earbuds with a microphone that hangs down on the chest, similar to something Alice used to have. She smiled as she tried to describe the device.

She cupped her hands behind her ears. "Artificial palms."

She also noticed that the diner's cash register was new and quieter. She could no longer rib me that I should feel right at home there with a cash register that "sounded like the St. Valentine's Day Massacre—all machine guns."

Chapter Twenty-nine

Big, fat raindrops drummed the roof of my Dodge. Kenny was running errands with me. We parked in front of the post office, waiting for a break in the downpour. Water streamed down the windows. It made the interior feel snug. I looked over at Kenny and smiled. We are buddies.

I needed a dose of that joy. As fascinated as I was by the Lees and their world, I got lonely. Kenny's enthusiasm for simple pleasures lifted my spirits. He liked to cruise around town with me in my humble Dodge Stratus. He tuned in the oldies station and turned up the volume. Anything by Elvis Presley got him singing along, making up the words here and there as needed.

With the rain still falling hard, I turned off the car and, with it, the radio. We sat quietly for a bit. I asked Kenny if he'd like to write a letter to Harper Lee, who was back in New York by that time. I had note cards in the car. I was a letter writer of long standing, a stationery freak. The sheer loveliness of Alice's regular correspondence only deepened my resolve to stay in touch with people that way.

For Nelle, inundated with letters from strangers and acquaintances, most seeking autographs, introductions, replies, book blurbs, or donations, a letter from Kenny would be a refreshing exception. He didn't want a thing from her—except her affection, which he already possessed, in abundance.

Kenny could read box scores and weather graphics in the *Mobile Register,* and write some words, but he didn't correspond. I offered to transcribe what he said. "Just like I say it," he told me. He grew quiet. A moment later, he began dictating, his enthusiasm accelerating as he went along.

Dear Harper Lee,

I am sitting in a car with Marja, my sister.

How'd it go—the New York Mets?

I want you to come over someday.

The duck sign is missing.

Miss Alice Lee is doing fine.

The ducks and geese, too.

    Love,

    Kenny Croft

I jotted down what he said in a notebook and then copied it, in neater handwriting, onto the note card. I handed the card to Kenny for him to sign his name. He did, using a notebook as a hard surface, and handed it back. He thought of one more thing to say. "P.S.," I added, and took down his postscript: "Mom and Daddy and me, Kenny, love Harper Lee so much."

I added, "MM transcribed this note—Kenny's words. Kenny signed his name."

Kenny and Nelle enjoyed a teasing camaraderie. They liked to exchange gag gifts and make faces at each other. Kenny nearly purred when Nelle would laugh and give his crew cut a playful rub.

Kenny always called his friend "Harper Lee," pronounced "Hop-palee," as if the three syllables were a first name. His parents called her Nelle. So did Ila and most of her other friends. Alice always called her "Nelle Harper." Dale also usually said "Nelle Harper." Ed and Marianne called her "Dody." Kathryn Dawkins called her "Harper." That's what Gregory Peck called her, too.

She was the author, Harper Lee, to most of the world. It wasn't a persona, exactly. Not in the way the dark-haired Norma Jeane Mortenson and the people around her created Marilyn Monroe. But it was something of a separate identity, a shield between private life and public.

She was Nelle Lee to the older people in her hometown who first knew her as Mr. Lee's youngest child. The more informal "Nelle" fit with the friends she made as an adult, too, people like Judy and Ila. At home on West Avenue, she always would be Alice's little sister, Nelle Harper.

I asked Nelle why she chose to be Harper Lee on the book cover. It was a practical decision, mostly, she said. She didn't want to be mistakenly called "Nellie." "Nelle" got mispronounced as "Nellie" or misspelled as "Nell." Even "Nelle Lee" can sound like "Nellie."

"Harper Lee" had other benefits that became clear early on. Especially in the early years, not everyone knew the author was a woman. The name could be either. Would S. E. Hinton's novel about troubled Tulsa teens have taken hold the way it did, especially with boys, if the name on the cover was Susan Eloise Hinton? Joanne Rowling published *Harry Potter and the Philosopher's Stone* under that name, but her publishers were looking at the marketplace and so her future books came out under J. K. Rowling. Nelle enjoyed the Harry Potter books, she told me, but for the most part didn't read much contemporary fiction.

She said she felt lucky *Mockingbird* was published when it was. Much later, and it might have been classified as young adult fiction and never reached the audience, and all the adults, it did.

Not long after I unpacked my suitcase back on West Avenue, after the New Jersey trip, Ila invited Judy, Nelle, and me for coffee at her house in Mexia. Judy was picking us up this time, a hot day under a light blue sky in the summer of 2005. I was keeping an eye out for her blue Buick. When I spotted it, I hurried across my front yard to the Lees' driveway. Nelle climbed into the passenger seat and I slid into the backseat. Judy drove the two and a half blocks to Claiborne Street and turned left.

This had become a familiar route. We skimmed past the armory and the Mt. Zion Baptist Church, a black congregation. It had a sign out front, the kind with movable letters that noted the title of that Sunday's sermon as well as the slogans that tickled Alice and Nelle. By the time we crossed under the railroad trestle a mile down, Monroeville was behind us and ahead was open road, slicing through rural fields and wooded areas, on the way to Ila's.

Mexia is named for a Texas town to which a local man had a connection. With no real downtown or center of gravity, and a collection of newer houses on cul-de-sacs, Mexia looks like a tiny suburban subdivision stranded in the Monroe County countryside. Surrounding it are stands of skinny pines and ravines draped in kudzu. Red dirt roads end in scruffy compounds where relatives have cobbled together a mishmash of trailer homes, clotheslines, and tire planters.

It was worth the trek to Mexia. After James retired from shift work at the pulp mill, and Ila closed the beauty parlor at the back of their house on the nearby highway, they found what they wanted here in their retirement: the close-knit Southern Baptist congregation out on Old Salem Road; a spacious, one-story house at the end of their cul-de-sac; and plenty of space. Ila grew tomatoes and cucumbers in the large garden out back. James spent long hours at the buzz saw in the big woodworking shop he built in the side yard. There he fashioned the wall of oak cabinetry that housed the Crofts' big-screen television, and the large bookcase in the Lees' entryway.

Alice and Nelle had little room or desire for new furnishings at the house, noticeably smaller than the homes of most of their friends. But a big bookshelf was a lifeline amid the rising tide of books the sisters couldn't bear to part with. James had also fashioned another gift they cherished. He made an oak dictionary stand, waist-high and strong enough to support the enormous Oxford English Dictionary opened to the latest page Alice or Nelle had consulted. They placed it to the left of their plaid living room sofa, the one with skinny wooden arms, near the small stretch of built-in white bookcases that housed copies of *To Kill a Mockingbird* in Spanish and Italian, French and German, Polish and Russian.

In Mexia, the Jeters' home looked over a ravine. Nelle suggested that perhaps she could toss all her belongings in there and burn them, preferably shortly before she died, so she wouldn't have to worry about her personal things falling into the wrong hands. She was only half kidding. I looked over at the ravine as Judy pulled into Ila's driveway.

Inside, Nelle nodded across the table at me. "You haven't said much about Chicago, child."

"It was a good trip. I got done what I needed to. And I ended up giving a party." I took a quick sip of coffee. "A friend of mine at the paper—her name is Julia—got good news. She won a Pulitzer Prize, for feature writing."

Nelle looked genuinely pleased. "Oh, that's wonderful," she said. She paused and gave me a pointed look, one that surprised me. "See?" she said. "It can happen."

The *Chicago Tribune* friend, Julia Keller, wrote a three-part series that vividly re-created the destruction of a tornado that swept through Utica, Illinois. Residents were left not only to grieve their dead and re-build the town but also to try to come to terms with the randomness of fate. When the tornado hit, what should have been decisions of no consequence instead meant the difference between life and death. Very quickly, the tornado took down buildings on one side of a street but left them intact on the other.

"Since I live so close to the paper, people could just walk over after work," I told Nelle, Judy, and Ila. "So I set a date and decided we'd make this a little bit fancy. I had some food catered, made some my-self. A couple of days before the party, I ordered a big sheet cake from this gourmet market called Fox & Obel. I told the guy at the bakery— this was over the phone—that I wanted the cake to say 'Congratula-tions, Julia. Pulitzer Prize 2005.' "

"That's sweet," Judy said.

"Well, I told the guy I wanted to be sure her name was spelled right. I told him, 'Her name is Julia, *J-U-L-I-A*, but she gets "Julie" sometimes and hates that. So I'd appreciate it if you could be sure it says "Congratulations, Julia. Pulitzer Prize 2005."'

"He said, 'Oh, that is very good. An honor. Congratulations to her.' He had a heavy accent. I couldn't quite place it.

" 'Thank you,' I said. 'I don't want to be a pain, but could I ask you to read it back to me to be sure?' He did, and spelled out *J-U-L-I-A*. 'Per-fect,' I told him.

"The day of the party, the cake arrived shortly before the guests were due to begin filtering over after work. The cake was in a white, rectangular box. I put it on my counter and hustled to set out the other food. I didn't open the lid to the box until right before people were due to arrive. My heart sank."

"They got it wrong?" Ila said.

"No," Nelle said.

"Here's what the cake said." I tore a scrap of paper out of my notebook, scribbled a few words, and passed it across the table to Nelle. She read it silently and then tilted her head back and gave one of those laughs that washed across the room. "Oh," she said. "That's marvelous."

She passed the scrap of paper to Judy so she and Ila could read the mistaken inscription on the cake.

"Congratulations, Julia. Poet Surprise, 2005."

I joined in the laughter. "It ended up being the hit of the party." Every time someone came to the door, one of us would put the lid back down on the cake box, tell the person what it was supposed to say, and then lift the lid.

"She's stuck with it," I told them. "She's the Poet Surprise now."

Nelle and Alice both were quick to draw the distinction between achievement and fame, and so Nelle's 1961 Pulitzer Prize for the novel remains a quiet source of pride. The timing of the prize was especially meaningful because the father they adored lived long enough to see Nelle's achievement.

There were moments with Nelle when we'd be reminded of her novel's extraordinary and enduring effect on the nation. One morning at Taste 2 Love, our modest breakfast place that day, Nelle sighed and confessed she had been putting off a task. Laura Bush had written Nelle a letter of appreciation, and Nelle had to figure out what to say in reply to the nation's First Lady.

One friend set down her Styrofoam coffee cup and shot Nelle a sly, sympathetic look. "I know, I know," she said. "I never know what to say when I'm writing back to the First Lady."

Nelle laughed with the rest of us.

Oprah Winfrey occasionally came up in conversation. When she had wanted to select *To Kill a Mockingbird* for her enormously popular televised book club, Oprah later disclosed that to her audience, and described, with glee, her lunch with Nelle at the Waldorf.

The author put her at ease immediately, Oprah told her audience. "I felt like we'd been girlfriends forever." But there was no budging on the book club question. Oprah recounted this to her talk show audience in an "after the show" segment, imitating Nelle's Southern accent.

"You know Boo Radley?" Nelle asked her. "Well, that's me." She didn't want the enormous attention an Oprah selection would bring to bear.

One day, Nelle told me she'd had another call from Oprah, who'd been to South Africa, where she had established a girls' school. This time she was there to celebrate Nelson Mandela's birthday.

"I asked her what she got him for his birthday," Nelle said. "She said, 'Oh, a library.' I think that was it." Nelle laughed. She shook her head from side to side in appreciation.

Over coffee at Burger King one day, Nelle asked, "What do you think of Sissy Spacek?" Was this for movie night?

"I think she's very good." I'd seen her most recently in the film adaptation of Andre Dubus's *In the Bedroom*. We discussed the movie, and Spacek's Texas accent. Then Nelle said Spacek would be narrating an audio edition of *To Kill a Mockingbird*.

Narrating Harper Lee's novel was one of the best things she got to do in her life, Spacek wrote in her autobiography, *My Extraordinary Ordinary Life*.

When you saw her every day, you could forget that Nelle's novel was something so many people had in common—not just having read it but having been taken by it. That kind of influence, of connection, is hard to grasp. How do you measure the reach of a book that goes beyond staggering sales figures and Top Ten Favorite Books of All Time lists to something more profound, to the connection of readers to the story, of readers to one another, of one generation to the next? I started to picture that influence as a silken thread, the rust color of Monroe County soil, of Maycomb County soil. Of red dirt. It was stitched through other books and movies, part of high school for many Americans, a common point of reference.

All from a first book by the woman who was feeding quarters into the washing machine at the Excel Laundromat with me on a regular basis.

Chapter Thirty

I t was time for Nelle to head back to New York. July fourth that year, 2005, was a packing day for Nelle. The following day, a friend would drive her to Birmingham and the train departing for New York.

The evening before Nelle left, I opened their screen door and hung another Winn-Dixie plastic grocery bag on their front-door handle. It was a care package for the trip, along with a letter and a book, E. B. White's 1949 *Here Is New York*.

Good thing the book is so slim. I wanted to be able to shut the screen door so the bag would be hidden from any passersby. No need to advertise that the house might be unoccupied, though in this case, both sisters were home.

I knew she liked the book as much as I did. Even more, given her deep feeling for the city White brings to life. He originally wrote the piece for *Holiday* magazine. White walked the streets of New York, observing details down to the overturned orange crates that offered an outdoor seat and relief from the heat for families suffocating in sweltering slum apartment buildings. This was during a heat wave in the summer of 1948. White typed up the piece in a terribly warm hotel room.

The cover of the 1999 edition, published on the one-hundredth anniversary of his birth, features a sepia photograph, circa 1935, of the young E. B. White walking a Manhattan street in an overcoat and a fedora. The book is less than a half inch thick and small enough that I could touch all four sides of the front cover with my outstretched hand, palming it like a basketball.

"Don't reply to this," I told Nelle in the letter. "You have enough to do before your departure. In case you're journey proud tonight and want to reread *Here Is New York,* here is my copy." I described the contents of the small care package and told her I had found the passage she had recommended from Thomas Macaulay's richly detailed history of England.

"You and Alice will make an educated woman of me yet," I wrote in the note. "I found Macaulay's description of the Hastings impeachment." The passage, about the six-year trial of Warren Hastings for corruption as a British administrator in colonial India, had come up in conversation.

Her end of the conversation, naturally. That happened a lot with Nelle. References to books and their characters, fiction and non-, laced her conversation, and Alice's, as casually as did the weather.

Nelle referred to Faulkner as much as, probably more than, any other Southern writer. One morning, over breakfast in Frisco City, she lamented the rise of what might politely be called redneck culture in the South. We saw evidence of it often. "They're the Snopes," Nelle said, referring to the family in his trilogy about a grasping, cunning clan in Mississippi, unencumbered by etiquette, scruples, or self-awareness.

She tossed out literary references as easily as some might recite their own phone numbers. In a press conference for the film *To Kill a Mockingbird,* as reported by *Rogue,* a reporter asked about her favorite writers. "Oh, mostly 19th Century, rather than 20th Century, writers. Charles Lamb, Jane Austen, Thackeray"—she laughed—"all that crowd."

Walking the short distance from their home to mine, the only sound I heard was crickets. The air was warm and still. In the odd communications routine that had developed, I then went to my bedroom and faxed a note to Nelle that I had left a bag on their door handle.

If I could avoid calling them, I did. Alice couldn't hear the phone, and Nelle often heard it only after several rings. She would hustle to get to the little phone alcove in the hallway just off the living room, only to discover the caller had hung up. It exasperated her to no end. Generally, she would rather not be interrupted. A fax was less intrusive.

Later that evening, the reply I told her not to send inched its way out of my fax machine. "Thanks!" Nelle wrote, for sending the care package and for spending time with her at home. She seemed especially touched by the E. B. White book, gently scolding me for being "a v. wicked young person" and writing that she had "peeped" into the slender book "and of course wept at the first sentence."

In 1948, when White was writing that first sentence and the long essay that followed, Nelle Harper was twenty-two and studying law in Tuscaloosa. Just a couple of years later, she would leave law school, live at home for a short time, and then wave good-bye to her father at the small Evergreen train station thirty miles from Monroeville.

The small-town woman was off to begin life as an aspiring writer in the big city. Truman already was there, publishing short stories and magazine articles and reveling in the excitement of Manhattan. The children who sparked each other's imaginations in Monroeville already had grown into adults with sharply different sensibilities. But both appreciated the escape New York offered from small-town prying eyes. "On any person who desires such queer prizes," White wrote in that first sentence that still moved Nelle, "New York will bestow the gift of loneliness and the gift of privacy."

White describes three tribes of New Yorkers: commuters, natives, and settlers. Nelle Harper belonged to the latter group. White goes on to list the different types of settlers coming to New York, including "a young girl arriving from a small town in Mississippi to escape the indignity of being observed by her neighbors."

A half century had passed since she made that first trip to New York and rented an apartment in Manhattan. At seventy-nine, Nelle once again was making the trip from Monroeville back to Manhattan.

She reminded me of American expatriates I spent time with in England and Spain, in Mexico and Paraguay. They navigate two places very well: the country where they were raised and the one in which they live. They may not be fully understood in either one, and that's fine by them. There's some privacy in that, even a bit of mystery, an unknowable quality, that follows them back and forth.

For those New Yorkers who heard her Alabama accent and inquired how long she had been in the city, Nelle had a stock answer: "Since before you were born." That settled that.

Chapter Thirty-one

O n a July morning in 2005, Tom was reading the sky. He looked up
to the heavens and knew trouble was coming. Of course, with
television weathermen talking incessantly about Doppler radar and
fronts moving in and all that, he already knew. But checking for himself, looking across Pineville Road and spotting the threat hanging low
in the sky over the Methodist church steeple, that was what quickened
his own pulse. By now, reports were clear: A hurricane was headed to
the Gulf Coast and Monroe County could be in its path.

Nelle Harper, under a peaceful New York sky, was suffering the
anxiety of being far away and worried about Alice. Everyone raised in
this poor, rural county knows how quickly a hurricane or ferocious
tropical storm can blow inland and wreak its random havoc. They've
seen it before. In one county, homes are destroyed, lives are lost. In the
neighboring county, branches blow down and that's about it. You don't
know which fate is yours until it is upon you.

Alice, always the one thinking ahead, had a plan for when the danger drew closer. Tom and Hilda planned to ride it out at their home on
Pineville Road. Alice thought it would be unwise to be in our neigh-

borhood with all the tall trees that could fall on her roof or mine. "You haven't been through this here," she told me before I left her house for mine. "You don't know what this weather can do. I don't want you to be frightened but I want you to be careful."

As she spoke, she gave me one of her looks, the appraising look. She studied faces the way Tom, and his father before him, surveyed the skies: to get a read on things. I was tempted sometimes to shield the oldest among us from the worries of the day, even as able and steady as she was. But there wasn't much point in that. She seemed to just know. She paid attention to everyone with whom she interacted.

That eye for detail made her the kind of lawyer she was, the kind of lawyer her father was, the kind of lawyer Nelle brought to life in Atticus Finch. Alice Finch Lee was as observant a person as I've ever met. She was low-key, understated, most of the time. It's worth re-membering that Atticus's stirring speech to the jury in *To Kill a Mock-ingbird* was an exception to his usual practice of law. He drafted wills, resolved disputes, handled land transactions. A careful attention to detail, far more than any courtroom drama, was at the heart of his practice.

This time I easily could pass Alice's subtle scrutiny. The Yankee wasn't freaking out. Yes, I was a midwesterner facing my first hurri-cane. But, as Alice knew, I'd been through tornado seasons in Wiscon-sin and the 1993 Los Angeles earthquake. I didn't suffer anything more than a few bruises in the earthquake, but my building was damaged, then condemned and torn down. At least with a hurricane, there was more warning. But Alice wanted to be sure Julia and I had a safe place to go. Final plans couldn't be made until we had a better idea of when the hurricane would hit.

By that Friday, Hurricane Dennis was predicted to make landfall Sunday near Pensacola. Alice was home from the office, and she faxed me the strategy. We would ride out the storm in the bank. She then had to go because her machine was lit up with faxes, especially from Nelle Harper.

The bank building, with her law office on the second floor, should be able to withstand even a hurricane. It didn't have a basement; most houses and buildings here don't. But it had a vault. Where else in town are you going to find thick walls of steel designed to be impenetrable?

And so, on Sunday, as the winds picked up and the rains began, our ragtag little group gathered at the bank, which was closed for business. Alice and Nelle Harper's nephew Ed Lee, the dentist, and his wife, Marianne, were there. So were Haniel, Judy, and Kenny, as well as several others. People brought snacks and flashlights and magazines.

We'd take refuge inside the vault only if it looked like the bank building itself could go to pieces. I wondered if the FDIC has rules about letting noncustomers like me in a bank vault. Surely this was a case where it would be better to ask forgiveness than permission. Or was Alice only kidding about taking refuge in the vault if need be?

We sprawled out in a conference room. The reports on the radio were growing more ominous. Monroeville still looked like it could be in the path of the hurricane. I peeked out a window; otherwise, we were standing and sitting clear of them. It was unsettling to see the familiar street scene transformed. No one was out. The air was taking on a sickening yellow hue. The branches and leaves on the trees were blowing straight back, like long hair in the wind.

Nelle Harper's calls to Ed's cell phone were picking up speed, just like the storm. Yes, he told her, Alice is fine. No, really. Everyone is fine. We'll keep you posted when it's over, if the power and cell phone service stay on.

Alice, as usual, was the calmest among us. I don't think it's just that she couldn't hear the howling wind or the urgent tone of the radio broadcasts. She had made her plan. It was a good one. And now her part was over.

She serenely worked her crossword puzzle while the rest of us buzzed around, trying to predict what couldn't be predicted. No doubt she had learned long ago the futility of trying to know the unknowable. Every now and then Ed passed along Nelle's admonitions to stay safe. Alice responded with an amused look, another in her now-familiar repertoire of meaningful looks and glances. This was the expression of a calm big sister dealing with her more excitable baby sister.

After a few hours, the winds let up. The power was out and we could see branches were down but the worst of the storm had skirted Monroeville. Ed and his wife had a small generator and invited Alice, Julia, and me to spend the night at their home on the other side of town. The drive there was eerie. After all the commotion leading up to this, the town was still. By the time we settled in and said our goodnights, it was late.

Alice said she would sleep better in the recliner, positioned way back. She drifted off with a throw tucked around her slight frame. I stretched out under a blanket on a sofa near Alice's chair. I was tired but not sleepy. I tiptoed over to the pullout sofa where Julia lay. I could hear the steady rise and fall of her breathing. She was asleep, too. I snuggled back under the throw on my sofa. After the thunder and lightning, the lashing rain and the howling winds, this was a quiet that filled the ears. I was reminded of the silence that enveloped my bedroom that first night next door to Alice and Nelle. I could hear Alice's soft breathing and listened for Julia's. I thought about the three very different lives that had intersected, for the time being, in this shelter from the storm.

Nelle had known that the "dry technicalities" of a legal practice were not for her. The oldest person weathering the hurricane was ninety-three but those technicalities still filled her days.

Most folks would consider the kinds of law Alice practiced to be technical stuff. Alice didn't.

"She made it seem like detective work," said Faye Dailey, who grew up the daughter of a Monroeville grocer. Dailey, now retired, did some work for Alice years ago, tracing property rights for a petroleum company. "We were trying to track down information, to piece together a puzzle. She actually made it interesting."

Alice was showing me property lines on a plat map one day, tracing them with her index finger. She was sitting at her kitchen table. Her old-fashioned adding machine, the kind that prints long slips of thin white paper with figures on them, was pushed to one side. Next to it was the banker's lamp she used those evenings she worked late on income taxes or other work she brought home. For her, those lines on the Monroe County plat map told a story about generations of a family who lived on the property. She remembered the way they fought over the land, the way some thought ahead about how to divide it to spare hard feelings among their heirs.

Generations of clients counted on Alice's discretion, whether she was preparing their income taxes, arranging a property sale, or drafting their wills. What she knew about the personal conflicts, wishes, and finances of the men and women of Monroeville could fill a library.

Right after my father graduated from law school in 1963, I told Alice, he wrote wills for servicemen stationed aboard a nuclear submarine. He always said that what you learned about all those sailors and officers in order to write their wills could inspire a lifetime of short stories.

Alice told me, "You learn a lot about people when they go to make their wills. I never shall forget all of these people involved."

People, for example, like the prosperous client whom she had known for years. He set up an appointment with her. He wanted to write his will so that he left his assets to his wife—"until such time as she might remarry." Alice shook her head ever so slightly. They had been a close couple.

"I said, 'Why on earth would you do this?' And he said, 'She might marry somebody no good. And I can't think of somebody else benefiting [from] what I've spent my life putting together.' I said—I couldn't resist it—I said, 'She married you, didn't she? What kind of judgment did she show?'"

I could see the mirth in Alice's eyes.

"That didn't change the man's mind, though. I couldn't resist his questioning her judgment. They had worked together, had a very nice, comfortable home. He just had visions of somebody coming in and occupying that home that he had worked for. To me, that's selfish."

Whether or not she agreed with the contents of a will, she wrote it to hold up to any legal challenges. Nelle wrote in *To Kill a Mockingbird* that Atticus could write a will "so airtight" nothing could slip through the cracks.

"You find a story everywhere," Alice said. "If you were a novelist, you'd get all kinds of ideas because the truth is stranger than fiction."

Stranger than fiction and, in Nelle's words, "always a better story."

Alice fixed her gaze on me. The house was as warm as ever. I could feel the usual sheen of perspiration on my face and hoped she didn't notice. There was, once again, no place I'd rather be. "So if you ever get tired of this," Alice said, referring to my book, "just pick out any dysfunctional family down here and get your plot."

Chapter Thirty-two

Three things out of Nelle's control were in the works. Not one but two movies were being filmed about Truman Capote researching his 1966 bestselling book, *In Cold Blood,* in Kansas with his friend Harper Lee. Worse still, the first major Lee biography was under way by someone she didn't know or trust. Charles Shields, the man working on the biography, had written Nelle to request her help. She wanted nothing to do with it.

"Hell, no," she wrote him. He proceeded without her. She would get word of Shields sightings. He had been spotted at the Old Courthouse, asking about her. He had contacted a longtime friend of hers in New York with questions. Tom Butts was getting e-mails from Shields, though he declined the repeated requests for interviews.

For Nelle, after years of dodging the limelight, any one of those projects would have been unnerving. Three under way at once felt like a siege. She didn't know how she would be depicted in any of the three and was trying, unsuccessfully, it seemed to me, to quell the sense of foreboding they stirred in her.

I went online one night, her bedroom light glowing across from mine, our blinds drawn. I sat cross-legged on my bed, searching

Google on my laptop for any tidbits about what she might expect from the two films. There wasn't much. *Infamous*, with Sandra Bullock as Nelle and Toby Jones as Truman, had been filming in Austin, Texas. The other movie, *Capote*, starring Philip Seymour Hoffman, was generating buzz for his ability to channel the diminutive writer. I printed out what I found to show her over coffee. She was coming over the next day.

Given Nelle's feelings about these projects, I was reminded how unusual it was for her and Alice to have encouraged me the way they had. I was a known quantity; that helped. So did the leisurely pace at which this all was unfolding, and in their hometown.

That morning, my phone rang. I was pretty sure it would be Nelle and she'd have four words by way of greeting. It was and she did.

"Hello," I said.

"Hi, hon. You pourin'?"

"I sure am," I said. "Come on over."

"You sure this is still a good time? I don't want to keep you from anything."

"No, this is a great time, Nelle. I'd love a cup of coffee with you. Come on over whenever you're ready."

"All righty. I'm on my way. Bye."

She had a playful way of saying "Bye" sometimes, exaggerating the Alabama accent. I took this as a sign she was in good spirits.

I hustled to turn the oven on and get a pot of strong coffee started. I had defrosted the round tin of Sister Schubert's rolls I got at Winn-Dixie. I was sliding the tin onto the top rack of the oven when I heard Nelle's smart rap on the kitchen door.

"Hi, there," I said. Nelle was a little out of breath. She made a bee-line for her usual spot at my kitchen table. In that chair, her back was to the wall and she was facing out to the rest of the room. "In Chicago, that would be the gangster chair, you know," I told her. She liked to tease me about being from the city of Al Capone and John Dillinger. I knew she didn't like to wait one minute for her coffee so I poured her a cup as I spoke.

I sat across the round oak table from her and handed her the print-outs with some short articles about the two Capote movies. There was no mistaking that the young Harper Lee, as played by Bullock in one and Catherine Keener in the other, would have a major role in both films. Nelle leafed through the pages I had printed out. "These are from your magic box, I assume?" Nelle said, her eyebrows arched in mock disdain once again.

"'Fraid so," I said. She didn't meet my smile. Maybe that wasn't mock disdain but the real thing. Nonetheless, she read with interest. She wanted to know about a picture a friend had spotted in *People* magazine. Bullock, as Lee, was on location. In the photo, she was crossing a street wearing white socks with black pumps. Nelle wasn't one to care about fashion but this was too much. "I never," she said.

Nelle squinted to read the printouts. She stood and held them under the windows by the table, where there was more light. "Gwyneth Paltrow," she read aloud. The actress had recently signed on to perform a song in the film starring Jones and Bullock. Nelle seemed to know very little about the plans for either film. She finished skimming the printouts in silence and returned to her coffee. I refilled her cup and she added another Splenda, folding the yellow packet over and over in the way that she did. It joined a couple of other crumpled yellow packets by her saucer. She tapped her index finger on the printouts. "May I have these?"

"Yeah, those are for you," I said.

She gave me one of those long, even looks that were hard to read.

"You don't know how Hollywood works," she told me.

"Educate me," I said.

"They do stuff and then they tell you about it later."

*C*apote hit theaters in September 2005. Judy Croft told Nelle, half in jest, that they could try to disguise her in a wig and smuggle her into a movie theater in Mobile to watch it. But with her hearing, she wouldn't be able to catch much in that setting anyway. Instead, on this November evening, Nelle had an early videotape of *Capote*, something not yet available to the public since the movie was still in some theaters. She told me Veronique Peck had sent the bootlegged copy to her from Los Angeles. Nelle already had tried viewing it once but had difficulty hearing. She hadn't caught much.

So we would make an evening of it: Her friend Kathryn would supply the VCR, Nelle the tape, and I would operate the remote control. Only among this Monroeville posse, most of them in their seventies, eighties, and nineties, would I be considered the person with technical expertise. I could rewind, fast-forward, and pause, and that was enough to earn the gratitude and relieved thanks of Nelle and Kathryn.

We'd need to fortify ourselves for this. Kathryn and I would get hamburgers to go from Radley's. Nelle requested only a salad from Burger King. She was watching her cholesterol. She was in good spirits, despite a hectic day centered on a funeral. She had jeans on and the crisp white shirt she had worn to the funeral. "It never stopped," she said. She'd had to contend with a plumber for a problem at the house while preparing to attend longtime friend Joe Watley's funeral at First Methodist. Tom Butts performed the service with another minister.

Kathryn's home, like the Lees' and mine, was a one-story redbrick ranch. After dinner, we took the two steps down from Kathryn's living room and dining area to her television room. Time for the movie. The room, once a screened porch, now was enclosed. It had bright green indoor/outdoor carpeting and white wicker furniture. On one wall hung three rural Alabama scenes painted by Kathryn's great-aunt. Those, too, held a personal story, like the painting above the Lees' fireplace, that I would learn only later. Kathryn's high-strung pug, Rocky, ran around the porch and settled in at her feet.

Nelle dragged a white wicker rocker up near the set. "Thank goodness you know how to work this . . ."

The movie opens with a moody scene of endless Kansas wheat fields under a gray sky with black, billowy clouds. We see a traditional white farmhouse at a distance, and then, inside the eerily quiet old house, is a glimpse of the aftermath of the brutal 1959 shotgun murders of Herb and Bonnie Clutter and two of their four children.

No one has spoken yet in the film. Already, though, the scene has drawn a reaction from Nelle. "Their house was nothing like that," Nelle said. "It was sort of modern."

Just a sentence into the first dialogue, Nelle was leaning forward and frowning. "What was that?" she said. I pulled my chair up near hers, remote in hand. "Tell me when the volume is right," I said, and moved it up and up and up. I rewound the tape and started it again. Nelle put her hand to her ear when the dialogue began again, and shook her head. She wasn't catching much. I paused the tape, faced her, and repeated the dialogue, enunciating the words loudly.

We proceeded that way.

After a scene of Nelle and Truman—Catherine Keener and Philip Seymour Hoffman—on the train to Kansas, we see Nelle behind the wheel of a yellow and white car, the Kansas wheat fields stretching to the horizon. Nelle glances at Truman, who is staring out the window at the rural scene.

"Does this make you miss Alabama?" she asks.

"Not even a little bit," he answers.

"You lie," Nelle shoots back. It is friendly banter between the two.

"I don't lie," Truman insists.

I paused the tape and resumed my loud enunciating, facing Nelle. "You said to Truman, 'Does this make you miss Alabama?' And he said, 'Not even a little bit.' Then you said, 'You lie.' And he said, 'I don't lie.'"

If this felt odd to me, telling the Harper Lee in the room what the Harper Lee in the car said, I could only try to imagine how it was for her.

Catherine Keener's Nelle is the modest, steady, sensible—but fun—counterpart to Hoffman's erratic, eccentric, manipulative—but funny—Truman. The dialogue might be mostly the product of a screenwriter's informed imagination, but that dynamic was true to what I had learned of Nelle and Truman's friendship back then.

We see Perry Smith, one of the two men captured and charged with the murders, walking with a halting step. "Why is that man limping?" Kathryn asked from her own white wicker chair, near the paintings.

I paused the movie. "He had," Nelle said, and paused, "leg injuries."

In one scene three-quarters of the way through the movie, Truman and Nelle are back in New York. Truman joins Nelle at a glittering reception at the Plaza Hotel following the premiere of the film starring Gregory Peck. Flashbulbs pop as photographers in fedoras snap Truman entering the hotel. At this development, Nelle—the real one in Monroeville, forty-three years after the film was released—leaned back in her wicker rocker for a moment. She took her glasses off, tipped her head back, and laughed. "If there was a premiere and a party in New York," she told us, "they didn't invite me." She laughed again and put her glasses back on.

When it was over, Nelle leaned back in her rocker again and was quiet. She seemed relieved. Kathryn and I were relieved she was relieved. Nelle liked the movie for the most part, she told us, though she pronounced it "historical fiction."

Forty-six years had passed since Nelle boarded the train to Holcomb, Kansas, to help her old friend research *In Cold Blood,* forty-six years since Nelle had submitted the manuscript for *To Kill a Mockingbird* to her publisher, J. B. Lippincott Company. She wanted, she told me, to help Capote, whose career had been "on hold." He envisioned a book that would break new ground with meticulous reporting of a true story that nonetheless would read like a novel. He had established his reputation with novels such as *Breakfast at Tiffany's* and *Other Voices, Other Rooms* but had been casting about for a different kind of project.

Now he needed Nelle, not only her writer's eye but her down-to-earth charm, her ability to fit right in around a small-town kitchen table as they made the rounds. He wouldn't inspire the same confidence, not with his floor-length camel-hair coat, flamboyant manner, and peculiar, childlike voice. Nelle and I scraped our chairs back to where they had been, away from the set, and sat facing Kathryn. "Lord, Nelle," Kathryn said. We were quiet again. "That man must have studied everything about Truman," Kathryn said of Philip Seymour Hoffman's performance.

"That was uncanny," Nelle said. "He'll get an Oscar for this." She was right. Kathryn rose from the couch. "I'm going to put that cobbler in bowls and we'll eat it out here," Kathryn said.

"I'll give you a hand," I said.

"That's okay, sugar. You keep talking."

"Was he as duplicitous as he is portrayed?" I asked Nelle.

"Oh, honey," she said. "He lied. That's what he did. I think he had to."

Kathryn brought out bowls with blueberry cobbler from Food World, topped with vanilla ice cream. "This is delicious, Kathryn," Nelle said. We all turned our attention to the cobbler, eating more than talking for a couple of minutes. Our spoons clinked against the bowls.

The only scene that unfolded as she remembered it, Nelle told us, was the perp walk up the courthouse steps one cold night.

Before long, we said our good-nights to Kathryn and made the short drive home. I pulled into Nelle's driveway to drop her off. Alice had the porch light on but Nelle lingered in the car. She wondered aloud why filmmakers make so much up in movies about real people.

"The truth," she said, "is always a better story." She was in good sprits. We had our windows down. This November weather was odd, a mix of warm and cool, often in the same day. I felt the faintest stirrings of a breeze. I turned off the ignition. I was struck by the privilege and the pleasure of the evening we had spent, the conversation we were having.

For some reason—maybe because we'd just seen a film—in my mind's eye an image flashed of the two of us in the car. Then I saw us from a greater distance, as if this were all a movie and the camera were panning back from two women sitting in a blue Dodge, porch light casting a yellow glow. At a greater distance than that, the Lees' home was one of many in Monroeville with a porch light on that evening. And from an even greater distance, Monroeville would be just one dot in the state of Alabama.

We were quiet a little while, thinking. As I spent more time with Nelle, I'd noticed, there was an ease to silences like this. They didn't feel awkward but rather companionable. Spending this much time with two women who didn't hear well changed the way I thought about silence.

I'd been in the habit, I realized, of not letting silences last too long. It was true in the car, out for coffee, or over dinner. It seemed more polite, more natural, to chat. But the opposite was true for those with difficulty hearing. When I was with Nelle or Alice, chatting just to chat made no sense. It required effort, especially in places like a car or a noisy restaurant, to catch what the other person was saying. Silence was a chance to rest.

As wonderful as they were as conversationalists, the shared, companionable silence was a pleasure of its own. It was a chance to gather one's thoughts, not to talk just for the sake of talking.

One thing I did still have to keep myself from asking them was, What are you thinking? When they volunteered, the answer was always interesting. But if they wanted to share the reason something sent them into a thoughtful silence, they would tell me. It wasn't my place to ask.

Nelle reached for the door handle.

"Thank you, hon," she said. "You are a good egg to do this."

"My pleasure," I said. A thought occurred to me again that made me smile. I don't think she'd heard when I said it before, as we walked to my car at Kathryn's. I raised my voice a little and enunciated so what I said next would be clear. We'd been talking side by side in our bucket seats but I turned to face her.

"Well," I said, "it was an interesting experience telling you what you didn't say." She laughed heartily but also shook her head. "You see?" she said.

She declined the offer to walk her to the door. I flipped on the headlights, turned the car back on—"cranked it," as they said here— and watched for her to get safely inside.

As she went, slowly, up the two steps to the landing, I rolled up the windows on the off chance of rain overnight.

Nelle opened the front door and, without turning around, raised her hand to signal "all is well." The door closed and I was quite sure she would be standing over Alice's chair soon, one hand braced against the back of it, recounting something of the evening.

That night ended in laughter but Nelle's uneasiness about the second movie would not abate until it came out the following autumn. *Infamous,* the one with Jones as Capote and Bullock as Nelle, did inspire a bit of levity as well. She liked the movie enough to overlook those white socks Bullock wore with black pumps. In a letter to director Douglas McGrath, Nelle told me, she informed him of something along the lines of this: "You have created a creature of such sweetness and light and called her Harper Lee that I forgive the socks."

Between the two movie debuts, in May 2006, the biography Nelle especially dreaded arrived. Charles J. Shields, a former English teacher who had gone on to write biographies for young people, published *Mockingbird: A Portrait of Harper Lee.* The book became a best seller and sparked a round of reviews and published reflections about Harper Lee and her novel.

Denied access to Harper Lee and her close associates, Shields pieced together his portrait with, among other things, interviews of others who once knew Harper Lee. He also drew upon correspondence he found at the New York Public Library and information in the articles about her written over the years.

One day, browsing at a Barnes & Noble with a friend, Nelle spotted the Shields book. She picked it up and observed with satisfaction that it still was in its first printing. She put it back on the shelf, way back, and slid a different book in front of it so *Mockingbird* was hidden. The defiance of that gesture stayed with me but, more so, the futility of it. The spines of thousands more copies of the book still faced outward at bookstores across the land. Nelle objected to Shields's conjecture about the nature of her family relationships and the details of her time with Capote and his Monroeville relatives, among other things.

If it's true, as novelist Carolyn See has written, that "by the time we're six or seven, we have made an agreement with the universe about the kind of people we are going to be," then perhaps young Nelle's was this: Independent, spirited, doing pretty much as she pleased, she would explore the world and express herself free of the traditional expectations assigned Southern young ladies. As a child, that meant she was labeled a tomboy; in college, a bit of a nonconformist in a culture that valued the opposite, especially in its women.

From her forties on, Harper Lee was branded a literary recluse, an imposing figure but also a curiosity. If living her life apart, and leaving unchallenged speculation about her nonconformity, was what it cost, she was willing to pay.

Not happy to pay—but willing.

After the release of the movies and the biography she dreaded, well after the perfect storm of fresh publicity was over, I reminded Nelle of what she had said about her book years before at the Excel Main Street Diner: "I wish I'd never written the damn thing." On this day, over coffee, I had my notebook out and was going over items I wanted to include in the book. "Do you still feel that way?" I asked her.

She glanced away, reflecting on the question. Then she looked at me again. "Sometimes," she said. "But then it passes."

Chapter Thirty-three

The jangle of the phone woke me one morning in early December. I was sound asleep. I rolled over and glanced at my clock radio. It was a little before eight A.M. This was Nelle, I knew, in some sleepy recess of my mind, with coffee on her mind. She never wanted to wake me; I never wanted her not to call because she was afraid she'd do so. So my reaction to the ring, even jarred from sleep, was automatic: a determinedly bright "Hello?"

"Morning, hon. Do you have time for a cup of coffee this morning?"

"You bet. I'd love one."

"Do you want breakfast?"

"You bet." I was more awake now and propped up on one elbow. Was that my second "you bet" or third?

"All right. I'll drop off Alice and come by for you."

"Sounds good. I'll keep my eye out."

"Bah-ah," she said, her playful exaggeration of a Southern, two-syllable "Bye."

"See you soon."

I'd jump up, get dressed, and look for her out the kitchen window so she wouldn't have to get out and knock. The windows were closed against the cool air now. I couldn't always hear the Buick approach in the driveway, even from the kitchen. But if I knew someone was coming for me, I could stand by the coffee machine and spot the car out that window, the one with Wes's Auburn sun catcher.

I hung up the phone and flexed stiff legs under the warmth of the covers. I hugged my spare pillow for a few luxurious moments. This wasn't the time for lollygagging. Lollygagging? When did I start saying things like that, even in my own head? In the company of these older women, I'd begun channeling some of my grandparents' sayings. I'd go to breakfast looking like a ragamuffin if I didn't hurry.

I scrambled up and half shuffled, half hobbled in bare feet across the wood floor into the bathroom off my bedroom. That new chill was in the air and underfoot as well. I could feel it in the cool bathroom tiles. Maybe that would wake me up. I was never quite ready for the pink of this bathroom first thing in the morning. Oh, well. I was glad for the cool weather, glad to be starting the day with Nelle and breakfast out.

Sometimes I missed the routine of getting ready for school or the office like everybody else. For years, I'd had energy enough to last the day and a regular place to go to, with colleagues and coffee and a workday that had a beginning and an end.

This was a more amorphous kind of work. I spent a lot more time resting, usually in bed, than I did interviewing people or even just being out and about in Monroeville. I could pass a couple of days in solitude, if I didn't see the Lees or the Crofts, the Buttses or Dale. I tried to at least get to the post office, lupus-y day or not, but my intentions outpaced my energy.

Still, it was a lifesaver to work on a project this interesting. Even at a glacial pace. The nature of the book meant that even those brief forays to the post office served a purpose beyond getting my mail. They were part of getting to know this community, the particulars of the world that the Lees and their friends inhabited in this south-central corner of Alabama. It was the kind of perspective the pace of daily journalism doesn't permit.

At breakfast at the hole-in-the-wall City Café that morning, a woman from the Finchburg area approached Nelle with her grandchildren. They spoke pleasantly for just a few moments. After they were gone, Nelle remarked, "I hope I didn't disappoint them."

What? I thought. The woman clearly had been thrilled, and Nelle had been nothing but gracious and down-to-earth, interested in finding out more about the woman and her family.

Our eggs had grown cold but the waitress came by and warmed up our coffee.

I understood, though. It was a thought she often had after encounters like these. How does anyone live up to the mystique that had grown up around her?

People introduced themselves to her in all kinds of settings as she went about her business, out to eat or running errands or at events. They were routine encounters for Nelle. But they were anecdotes that the other person would tell for years, for a lifetime, each comment dissected, each detail repeated. Even there in a down-home restaurant in small-town Alabama, that kind of fame exerts its own kind of pressure.

It was movie night. Nelle, Judy, and I were finishing dinner around my dining room table before retiring to the living room to watch the DVD Nelle had requested, Wallace and Gromit in *The Wrong Trousers*. Nelle finished her last bite of Melvin's barbecue, pushed back her chair, and made this observation about the work ahead of me.

"To understand Southerners, you need to understand their ties to their church and their property." To understand this part of Alabama, I would need to understand the ties of people here to these particular churches, this particular land.

Actually, she corrected me in a subsequent conversation, "Not land. Property. It's different."

Land is something you cultivate. Property is your home place. Often, it's your identity. It's an anchor and a refuge, a link to the past and a hope for the future. When times are hard, if nothing else it is a place to grow vegetables and keep some chickens. When times are good, it is where a person gathers friends and family to celebrate the bounty.

Really go to church, Nelle told me. Alice said the same. Go to white churches and black. Go hear Baptists and Methodists and Presbyterians. And Holy Rollers.

"You need to go to Miss Mary's church," Nelle said. Miss Mary Watford Stabler was a couple of years older than Nelle. They didn't see each other often, but they were friends of long standing. Nelle phoned Miss Mary and asked if she might take me, Judy, and Ila to Sunday services.

Miss Mary's Pentecostal church is near the tiny community of Scratch Ankle.

Miss Mary was only seventeen when she had a vision that spreading the gospel and ministering to the faithful was what she was called to do. She has been a Pentecostal preacher ever since. Her Bible is the most worn, thumbed through, underlined one you can find in Monroe County, and that is saying something.

Back when she was a girl, you didn't see many female Pentecostal preachers. You still don't. But her path began at home. Her father was a preacher. She was helping him cajole, inspire, and whip up the faithful in Monroe County revival tents before she was old enough to vote. Which, at that point, women had been allowed to do for all of nineteen years.

I wondered how her congregation compared to other Pentecostal churches in the area. There were quite a few, including a larger, breakaway congregation just down the road. The joke was, "How do you get two Baptist churches in a new community? Build one. A breakaway will form in no time." Safe to say it applied to more denominations than the Baptists.

"Don't worry," Nelle told me. "There won't be any snakes. At least I don't think so. They're the least roll-y of the Holy Rollers," Nelle said. "At least, I think that's so."

We joined a dozen others that morning for Miss Mary's rousing sermon. Several people made their way to the front to bear witness.

Afterward, one woman also made her way to our pew as we rose to leave. She had heard Harper Lee would be there. She wondered if Nelle would mind signing her name in her Bible.

Nelle signed and we were off for a picnic on the banks of the Alabama River.

We stopped at a country store for fried chicken and potato logs, the large, fried potato wedges Nelle liked.

She didn't like waiting, though.

"Finally!" she said when it was ready.

"I suppose we should wait to eat until we get there," she said in the car.

I had a feeling it was more request than statement. But we waited.

"Ila, you are a marvel," Nelle said as we sat at a picnic table, with the fried chicken and potatoes added to the bounty of foods Ila had prepared.

The morning's service energized Nelle.

"I feel like I've really been to church for the first time in a long time." Miss Mary delivered an impassioned sermon that quoted heavily from the Bible, and Nelle liked that. The "New Age stuff," as she called it, wasn't for her.

While I lived in Monroeville, many Sundays I would attend whatever church the Lees felt would contribute to my education. I went to white churches and black, tiny country gatherings and congregations large enough to need two services. I went to Baptist and Methodist churches, Pentecostal and First Assembly of God, breakaways and independents. I inquired about any Jewish or Muslim services, however small, I might visit but there was nothing in the area.

It was on that same Wallace and Gromit movie night at my house that Nelle told Judy and me about a phone call she'd made a few months before. We had lingered after watching the DVD, Nelle in my green corduroy rocker pulled up to the coffee table, Judy to her right in a floral armchair, me to her left in a wood rocker.

She told us about calling Brock Peters's home just before he died. Peters had played the falsely accused Tom Robinson in the film version of *To Kill a Mockingbird* forty-three years earlier. He had died of cancer at age seventy-eight in August 2005.

When Nelle called, the woman whom she identified as Brock Peters's lady, Marilyn, told her Brock was in his final hours and she was reading aloud to him—from the Bible and a passage from her novel that had always touched him.

Nelle had then written to Marilyn, quoting from *The Pilgrim's Progress*, the classic spiritual allegory about the search for eternal life: "So he passed over, and all the trumpets sounded for him on the other side."

Nelle had that day received a sweet letter in reply.

She was chagrined, however, that neither Judy nor I could name the source of the quote about trumpets sounding. It could be embarrassing to those called upon to identify such things, and it happened to all of us.

I n January 2006, Nelle came back from the annual Tuscaloosa luncheon exhausted and relieved.

She hadn't known a *New York Times* reporter would be there, she told me. She was quoted in a front-page story the next day.

In "Harper Lee, Gregarious for a Day," the *Times*'s Gina Bellafante reported that Nelle agreed to speak to her about the event. She wrote that Nelle was patient in posing for photographs with students, quick-witted in her comments, and appreciative of the event. Nelle got a call the following day from Howell Raines, the Alabama-born former executive editor of the *New York Times,* reporting that the story was the most e-mailed of the day. While Nelle didn't know exactly how that worked, she appreciated what it meant.

In her article, Bellafante repeated Nelle's comment that Horton Foote, the *To Kill a Mockingbird* screenwriter, remained a good friend and that as he had aged, he had come to look "like God, only clean-shaven."

Not long after the article ran, the phone rang on West Avenue. Nelle picked up the receiver to discover it was Horton Foote, Horton with the tender heart, the kind eyes, the sweet, civilized way he had about him. The Texas of his youth was still in his soothing, almost husky voice.

"God here," he said. They laughed and got caught up. He ended the call by telling Nelle, "Remember, God loves you."

She laughed again, repeating the conversation over coffee at McDonald's. She looked wistful. "He's one of the last real gentlemen," she said.

Chapter Thirty-four

I had moved into the house not knowing how long it would be avail-able. Now I'd been here going on fifteen months, which was longer than I had meant to stay, though I would end up staying another two. It was time to return to Chicago. I could gather more information in-definitely but, already, writing up what I had would be a formidable task. I had crates of files, boxes of notes, stacks of taped interviews with Alice and others to transcribe. I thought the lupus might have eased up by now but it hadn't. Nor had it gotten worse. Resting so much of the time meant work progressed at a snail's pace.

I had begun discussing with the Lees when I might move back to Chicago. I was pleased they were in no hurry to see me go but also understood.

I'd talk to Nelle about it over coffee. These daily routines, theirs and mine, these rhythms of daily life, had become second nature. Now that would be coming to an end. That Tuesday, the last day in January, I faxed Alice. As I often did, I sent it at lunchtime so she would see it before she returned to the office for the afternoon.

Alice, I spoke with Wes last night. I gave notice for March 1st. I can extend week-to-week if I want and if he hasn't found anyone by then. Just to keep you posted. I must have been prematurely Journey Proud because I didn't sleep much.

Hope you're making progress with your mounds of documents.

To a Chicago/Wisconsin girl, this feels like a sunny, crisp October day.

Marja

I was in bed when Nelle called one afternoon.

"Do you feel like a cup at McDonald's?"

I hesitated, just for a moment.

I always felt like a cup at McDonald's with Nelle, even when I wasn't feeling well. But I was back in bed, feeling worse than usual.

Nelle interjected quickly, "Not if you don't want to. That's no problem."

"No, I'd love a cup of coffee."

Maybe fresh air, as much coffee as I could manage to swallow, and the best conversationalist this side of the Mississippi would be what the doctor ordered.

"You ready now?"

"You bet."

"See you at the car."

"Sounds good. See you in a minute."

I slipped my shoes back on, grabbed my purse, and headed to her driveway. She sat behind the wheel, ready to go.

I was feeling a little shaky. The gnarled tree roots I usually stepped over with ease seemed higher.

Then I felt the earth rise up and slam me in the head.

It took a moment to realize I was on the ground. I saw my red leather purse next to me, on its side. Some of the contents—my tube of Burt's Bees rhubarb lip balm and a couple of black felt-tip pens—had spilled onto that patchy grass.

From the car, Nelle saw me go down. I was only yards away. What she saw was me heading toward the car and then dropping out of view from her perch behind the wheel. I got up but went down again right away.

Nelle recounted this to Bill Miller. "She was there and then she was down," Nelle told him. "Then she was up. Then down again."

It didn't feel like fainting or tripping or whatever it was that happened. It felt like I was minding my own business and the earth rushed up to whack me on the head a second time.

"Oh, hon," Nelle said when she reached me. "Are you all right?"

"Yes, I think so." Waves of embarrassment washed over me.

"No, you're not all right."

I was on my feet again but trembling. She helped me to my front door.

We hardly ever used this door. It was closer to their house, yes, but the kitchen door was where all the coming and going happened. The to-ing and fro-ing, in Nelle's words. I fished my house key out of my purse. My hands were shaking and I couldn't get the key into the lock. Nelle took the key and unlocked the door. She escorted me the short distance to the sofa, under the picture window.

She looked alarmed. I was mortified.

The world felt upside down. My head hurt. We were using the door we never used and I was sitting on the sofa I never sat on.

"Stay here. I'll get water. And Judy."

I just wanted to skulk off to my bedroom, recover, and know that Nelle and Judy weren't having to get involved.

I remember parts of the week that followed. People told me the rest. The Crofts had relieved Nelle and were on the phone to my parents in Madison.

I didn't know it then, but I had gotten dehydrated, seriously dehydrated, and that was descending into delirium. I was shaking and my coordination was off. I'd be lucid and then not.

This happens more commonly with old people, especially if they live alone and fall ill or lose their appetite. In my case, mouth sores, probably from lupus, had made it painful to eat and drink. The real peril of delirium is this: By the time you need medical care, and fluids, right away, you're too muddled to realize it. If you're lucky, someone recognizes you need help.

Whatever this was, a mystery at the time, the consensus was I'd be better off with my own doctors at Northwestern Hospital. In Madison, my mother booked the last available seat on the only direct flight out of Pensacola the following morning.

In my kitchen, Judy heated some of her homemade vegetable soup and placed it before me. I wanted to show I was okay but it was hard to keep the soup on the spoon.

I remember sitting at the kitchen table, mentally "running the differential," as the docs say. I felt a door was closing, a nothingness descending, and I needed to get a handle on this while I still had my wits about me. Even if half of them had jumped ship already.

I didn't tremble like this, ever. Was lupus attacking my central nervous system? Unlikely. Was I having a nervous breakdown? Doubtful, but how embarrassing would that be? An infection? Maybe.

It's an odd predicament, wanting to appear normal while you are losing your faculties.

Later, Judy and I were in my bedroom, gathering anything I'd need for my hastily arranged flight. I passed out again that evening. Judy saw it coming and leaped over to break my fall. She dived over and fell with me, protecting my head, like some kind of superhero in a sensible sweater and glasses.

An ambulance took me to the local hospital. On the mortification scale, this was getting progressively worse. I got fluids in the ER and was released to spend the night at home. Judy lay beside me on my bed that night. I slept. She didn't. So much for not wanting to put anyone out.

The next morning, the Crofts made the nearly two-hour drive to the Pensacola airport. Because this was a one-way ticket booked at the last minute, I was flagged by the TSA. Finally, after that rigmarole, Judy got permission to deliver me, a shaky, confused mess in a wheelchair, right to the gate.

I remembered her saying something to me about a friend's son. A cute, nice son who was about my age. It turned out he was at the gate as well. For Nelle and Dot and Judy, my would-be matchmakers, the dating prospects never got past the musing-aloud stage. And now here was someone else who conceivably, improbably but theoretically possibly, could be a match. If I had been coherent. Hard to make a good first impression otherwise.

My parents would meet me at the other end of the two-and-a-half-hour flight. They drove from Madison to O'Hare and bundled me off to Northwestern Hospital. Chicago made it to twenty-six degrees that day; Monroeville, seventy. It was lost on me.

I was out of it for the first couple of days in the hospital, mumbling and making no sense. The doctors diagnosed the delirium, gave me fluids, took me off any newer medications that could have interacted or made things worse.

Within days, I was well enough to write the Lees. Someone faxed the letter for me.

Dear Alice and Nelle,

I believe you owe me a cup of coffee, Nelle. As soon as possible, I'll be back to collect.

Another small herd of men and women in white coats just stopped by, poked and clucked and predicted I might be released as early as tomorrow.

"Or not," as someone else usually points out.

I'll have an EEG and MRI today. Yesterday's spinal tap and blood tests came out fine.

Hope to see you soon.

Love,

Marja

p.s. Best to Julia.

I was back, but only long enough to finish some interviews, pack up, and say my good-byes. I filled more notebooks, recorded more long afternoon interviews with Alice. I spent time with Alice and with Nelle going over anything else, besides what they had noted already, they felt should be off the record. In most cases, they again told me to use my judgment.

I was returning to Chicago with far more than I'd taken with me. I had more books and a little more clothing. Mostly, what I had accumulated resided in memory and copious notes, going back to that August day in Chicago five years earlier when my editor stopped by my cubicle.

The days became months and the months became years. The notes, the interview transcripts, the file folders captured hundreds of shared experiences. That is what I wanted to do, to preserve the stories only they and their trusted circle there could tell, those that they were willing to share. And I wanted to understand daily life in Monroeville, its routines and rhythms, past and present, in this out-of-the-way place that shaped Harper Lee and the novel beloved by three generations of readers.

I continue to visit Monroeville periodically, to correspond with my friends. I still get the *Monroe Journal* mailed to my Chicago high-rise once a week. Lupus continued to be unpredictable. I had to rest a lot; most of this book was written in bed on a laptop.

I had reams of information to organize, to research, and to shape into book chapters. Even before poring through the material again and again to glean the meaningful comments, recall the telling detail, certain memories would rise unbidden to the surface "clear as a June night," as Nelle would say. These were times I felt I was glimpsing something essential of what it meant to be Nelle, of what it meant to be Alice, in this time in their lives. They struck me immediately.

I still hear the clattering of heels up brick steps to a grand Monroeville home with white columns and a ladies' fancy luncheon, a modern-day version of something from the Maycomb of *To Kill a Mockingbird*, the Monroeville of Nelle's youth. Beside me, Nelle is wearing flats, her footsteps silent. She is out of her element but taking in every detail. We are attending the event, she says, as part of my coming to understand this part of the world that is Monroe County.

That evening, she is back on comfortable ground at the Main Street Diner in the neighboring town of Excel, where she and I drink coffee while our respective loads of laundry tumble dry in the Laundromat next door. This is the diner where, just as at other such places, she is animated, laughing, talking about books and friends and the colorful characters of her childhood. Of Aunt Alice and Cousin Louie, Aunt Kitty and the husband she herself called Mr. Nash.

She regales two friends, Dale and Judy, with tales of the luncheon and remembers another couple of people I should interview. She is a master storyteller here as well as on the page, no surprise. With one problem. She gets to laughing before she can get the story out. She tries again. Same problem. She takes her glasses off, tips back her head a bit, and lets loose with the kind of contagious laugh that washes across a room.

I see Nelle and Alice together, too, heading out to feed the ducks and geese just before dusk on a Saturday afternoon. In their living room, I am in the low, brown rocking chair pulled up to the foot of Alice's gray recliner. She can hear me better this way and she has become so accustomed to my flipping over the little cassettes in my tape recorder every thirty minutes that she automatically pauses in her stories as I do so.

Before dusk, as the light begins to soften, Nelle appears from the back bedroom, the one that used to be her father's quarters and now are hers. We are off to feed the ducks and geese. The ducks and geese know Nelle's car. Even before she has parked at the small lake, they come running, wings flapping, raising a honking, quacking ruckus. Alice counts the ducks methodically, concerned one is missing. Nelle does the same but quickly, in fits and starts, and grows exasperated. The women are taking it all in: the way the creatures interact with one another, the little power plays on webbed feet, the ducklings that follow around their momma.

And I see Alice late one evening alone at the kitchen table. Or rather, I know she is there because she has told me she will be up late working on tax returns, on Nelle's and on those of the clients she has had for fifty years. Her little sister is asleep in the back bedroom. Or it could be title work that has Alice up, or someone's will. She sits alone at the cluttered table in the 1950s kitchen, a green banker's lamp glowing at her right elbow.

She is doing the work her father, her law partner, used to do, determined that every figure add up, every rule be followed, stressed by the amount of work but buoyed by the sense of purpose. On plat maps, her bony fingers trace the property lines that etch stories for her, stories of families and businesses that go back generations, that her own family has known for generations. She is a solitary figure but doesn't seem entirely alone. Her Methodist faith, her kinship with her late father, are unseen presences in the small kitchen of the modest redbrick house under the skinny assembly of tall pines.

At that moment, with her little sister still sound asleep in the back bedroom, it seems as if this is how it always has been, always will be.

Epilogue

This memoir of my time in Monroeville with the Lees and their friends and family is a chronicle of the last chapter of life as they knew it.

Nelle suffered a serious stroke in February 2007. She underwent months of hospital treatment and rehabilitation, first in New York and then in Birmingham, and hoped to be able to walk again instead of relying on a wheelchair. That didn't happen.

She moved, permanently, into an assisted living center, a far cry from the rambling house on Alabama Avenue where Nelle was born and raised, where the weathered little Mel's Dairy Dream now dispensed hamburgers and shakes from a walk-up window.

In November, she attended the White House ceremony at which President George W. Bush presented her and seven others with the Presidential Medal of Freedom. Privately, members of the U.S. Marine Band surprised her by playing music from Elmer Bernstein's *To Kill a Mockingbird* score. It moved her to tears.

She was able, for a time, to keep up with some reading, to hold the kind of conversations she used to with friends, to get out a fair amount. She had good days and bad days.

I'd be back to Monroeville on at least annual visits over the next several years.

On one visit, as I went over shared experiences and conversations I wanted to include in the book, Nelle added comments here and there and spoke fondly, again, of Gladys Burkett.

Nelle had told me over the years that she resented any speculation that her editor, Tay Hohoff, had a larger role in shaping the manuscript than she did, as Nelle saw it. And the rumor that Capote wrote any of it was still infuriating, she made clear, and absurd. It didn't stop there.

"Rumors get started on the thinnest of evidence," Nelle said.

We were at a table in the dining area of the assisted living center. The residents' rooms were down a couple of hallways off the common area, where they could sit in sofas and chairs with visitors, and the adjacent dining area.

Nelle and I were sipping coffee from the two large cups I'd brought from McDonald's. Rather, I was sipping and scribbling away in my notes. She was draining the large cup rather quickly.

She wasn't fond of the coffee at the assisted living center.

"What they call coffee, isn't."

She discussed the rumors regarding the writing of the novel, her voice tinged with anger, then resignation.

"If all the people who said they had a hand in writing or editing it were put together, they'd fill a whole church. I'll give you an example," Nelle said.

After Nelle had finished the manuscript, she said, she gave the pages to Burkett to read. Once she had, the teacher had a student cross the school yard to return the manuscript, a stack of pages in the customary thin cardboard box, to Nelle at home across the street. It took all of a few minutes.

Burkett hadn't written many comments on the pages of the manuscript, Nelle said. The teacher did scribble a William Shakespeare quotation Nelle's novel brought to mind.

"She returned it with a quotation from *Macbeth*. Or was it *Hamlet*?"

Nelle began reciting the quotation from memory.

"'Life's but a walking shadow that struts and frets upon the stage and then is seen no more.'"

She cocked her head to one side and tried to remember again if it was from *Macbeth* or *Hamlet*.

Later, I Googled "walking shadow" to find the full quotation online. I considered copying it down by hand to give to Nelle, along with the notation that it was from *Macbeth*, as she first thought. I knew the idea of my looking that up online when it was easily findable in books ran the risk of giving Nelle indigestion. I pictured her shaking her head at me as she lamented the death of civilization.

Nelle's memory had been good, if not word for word, for the famous pronouncement in *Macbeth*.

Leaning closer to the screen of my laptop, I read the full quotation, from which Faulkner drew his title for *The Sound and the Fury*.

"Life's but a walking shadow, a poor player, that struts and frets his hour upon the stage, and then is heard no more; it is a tale told by an idiot, full of sound and fury, signifying nothing."

I wasn't sure how this pessimistic view applied to the novel, but that wasn't the issue. Earlier that day, Nelle's point was that the student's school yard errand to return the manuscript for Gladys Burkett was enough to spur speculation that she somehow had contributed to the writing or the editing of *To Kill a Mockingbird*.

I thought of all the times Nelle had, easily and unpretentiously, recited a line, or paraphrased a passage, from the literature she hadn't just read but taken into her heart and her view of the world. The times she'd refer to Faulkner or Welty or that quotation from *The Pilgrim's Progress* that Brock Peters's death brought to mind for her.

The words were a constant, a comfort, and an inspiration, when so much around her was changing. Even now—especially now, perhaps—when the stroke had left her in a wheelchair and home no longer was the familiar brick house on West Avenue but an assisted living center.

Things became increasingly difficult as Nelle's condition worsened and her memory failed, as had Louise's, who died in 2009 at age ninety-three. By the time I saw her a couple of visits later, she was not the Nelle I knew.

Nelle's decline was hard on Alice. She continued her daily work at the law office and went by to see Nelle most afternoons. On September 11, 2011, Alice turned one hundred. Family and friends held celebrations to honor her. My mother and I returned to Monroeville for the festivities. Two mornings in a row after the office celebration, Alice invited me to her home. I pulled the rocker up to her recliner, where the stories rolled once again, this time of her joy in having four generations of their family come together for the occasion.

A bout of pneumonia in December 2011 put Alice in the hospital and from there she was released into an assisted living center as well, not the same one as Nelle's. Alice grew more frail and the hope that she would be able to return to her house and routines dimmed. She had been active just a few months earlier at her centennial gatherings, but declined at the assisted living center.

I like to picture them, still, as they were all those years on West Avenue, when they would set off in Nelle's Buick for the country highways and red dirt roads they knew so well.

"We go out in every nook and cranny," Alice told me on my first visit. "We explore. If a new road opens up, we try it. We have done that all our lives."

In the time I spent with the Lees, I was in the car for many of those drives. It was a privilege and a lot of fun. I remember the drive, early on, when I was in the backseat and Nelle was behind the wheel with Alice beside her. I realized they saw a different Monroe County out the windows than I did. They saw the stories behind the houses and buildings, the characters of another era who struggled and scraped by, who gossiped and worshipped, who married one another and buried one another, and who couldn't have fathomed the changes that were to come in just a few generations.

It's the old Monroeville—the old Maycomb—that lives on in the imaginations of so many readers. It's the people and the places the Lees saw out the windows of the Buick all those years later. Nelle's portrait of that community was so richly detailed, so specific and true to the small-town South during the Depression, that something universal emerged and, with it, the remarkably enduring popularity of the novel. And *To Kill a Mockingbird* remains one of the all-time great Southern stories. In Nelle—and in Alice—this land of stories and storytellers had produced two masters of the art.

All those years later, Nelle's dark hair now white, her hands arthritic, her voice in *To Kill a Mockingbird* still could be heard on those Sunday drives, as she and Alice remembered a place that was.

Acknowledgments

To Nelle Harper Lee and Alice Finch Lee my gratitude is immeasurable. This entire book acknowledges their remarkable friendship, extraordinary generosity with their time and insights, and patient participation in a long and evolving project. To be invited into their world is to be invited behind the curtain of Nelle's beautiful and enduring novel. I am forever grateful for that privilege. Two such remarkable and different sisters would be hard to find. Despite a fifteen-year age difference, each was the expert on the other. It was fascinating to hear Nelle's perspective on Alice and Alice's on Nelle. More than that, to see how each crafted a life within certain limitations—Nelle's retreat from the spotlight and Alice's focus on their small hometown--was a lesson in living life on one's own terms.

I am eternally thankful to Virginia Smith Younce, senior editor at The Penguin Press. As an exceptionally talented editor, a native of Macon, Georgia, and the daughter of a lawyer who bears no small resemblance to Atticus Finch, Ginny was uniquely suited to help me illuminate my experience in the South. Her artful editing and endless encouragement were essential in shaping this memoir. Ginny's singular abilities were a gift to me, to readers, and, I believe, to those who live on these pages.

For all her stature in publishing, my first impression of Ann Godoff, president and editor in chief of The Penguin Press, was the mischievous glint in her eye when we discussed my book. It was intriguing and conveyed a playful appreciation of the material at the same time her broad vision for the book was clear. I am truly grateful for her belief in the book.

Publisher Scott Moyers's steadfast support was hugely helpful and much appreciated. Associate publisher Tracy Locke has been a passionate and astute advocate for the book. I am also thankful for the support and dedicated work of Karen Mayer and Veronica Windholz.

Editorial assistant Sofia Ergas Groopman is a marvel of ingenuity and efficiency, all while managing multiple projects and offering unfailing enthusiasm.

My agent, Miriam Altshuler, has my heartfelt gratitude. For any writer, much less a first-time author, it is a dream to have an agent who combines outstanding business acumen and knowledge of publishing with an engaging personality and warm encouragement. She was my teacher as well as my representative in this process and I counted on her excellent guidance. As Miriam expertly shepherded this book to publication, I was reminded why she is held in high esteem by authors, editors, and publishers. I thank John Pelosi as well for his valuable wisdom and support.

As this work began to take shape, Cathy Furlani Schmitz, then Miriam's assistant, was most helpful, as was Miriam's current assistant, Reiko Davis.

To Tom Butts, the first person Nelle and Alice wanted me to meet, I am indebted beyond belief. His skills in navigating uncharted waters were priceless, as was the genuine friendship that resulted. As a minster and trusted friend to both Alice and Nelle, Tom's frame of reference included both day-to-day interactions with them as well as a broader view of the town and the South. His early work with civil rights, his magnetism and erudition, and his guidance behind the scenes to half of Monroeville are hallmarks of his role in the lives of others. He is a book unto himself.

Tom's wife, Hilda, added authentic caring and a delightful sense of humor. Our kitchen-table chats continue to this day.

Julia Munnerlyn, the mysterious presence in the kitchen my first time in the Lee home, was endlessly generous with her time, her friendship, visits to her church, and her recollections of a remarkable life. She mused about, and was amused by, the relationship between Alice and Nelle.

As Nelle and Alice's only nephew in town, Ed Lee and his wife, Marianne, shared their unique perspective on the sisters and the extended family. Marianne's effervescence was a boost to me and, especially, to Alice and Nelle, to the three exceptional daughters she and Ed raised, and to the Methodist church.

Sara Anne Curry offered a perspective only she could. As Nelle's former classmate and the woman who married her brother, Sara Anne shared insights into her late husband, Ed, as well as his three sisters—Nelle, Alice, and Louise—and their parents, A.C. and Frances Lee.

To the Croft family, who opened their home and hearts to me, I owe a special debt of gratitude. Haniel's wise and discerning sense of the practical was invaluable to me over the years, as were Judy's unfailing kindness and welcoming presence. It is with good reason that Alice and Nelle placed special trust in their integrity, personally and professionally.

Haniel and Judy's son, Kenny, greatly enhanced my experience in Monroeville as no one else could. His unconditional and wholehearted friendship was as refreshing to me as it was to Nelle.

The late Dale Welch often compared notes with Nelle about books and their Alabama childhoods; I enjoyed long afternoons with them on Dale's back sun porch. Likewise, Kathryn Dawkins's side-porch-turned-family-room was the setting for many enjoyable hours with her and Nelle, discussing the characters of the Methodist church and a time and place long gone in Monroeville and Kathryn's native Repton.

Ila Jeter offered valuable perspective on the Poarch Native American community as well as what a person gleans about the good citizens of Monroeville and Mexia in thirty years as a hairdresser. On our outings she was a Baptist among Methodists and always ready with a quip. Bill Miller, a former *Vanity Fair* executive, explained the culture and the workings of the apparel manufacturer, a major employer for many years.

Norman Barnett shed light on the long friendship between the Barnett and Lee families. Nick Hare offered his perspective on A. C. Lee's work as an attorney. Longtime teacher Ida Guilliard shared stories of Nelle, Alice, and their two other siblings. Margaret Garrett captivated Nelle and me as she recalled stories of her girlhood. She has since died, as have Nick and Ida.

My sincere gratitude goes to my editors at the *Chicago Tribune*. As the *Tribune*'s co-managing editor, Jim Warren offered the vision and encouragement that made my long newspaper story possible. Tim Bannon, editor of the Tempo features section, placed his trust in me in assigning the story and supplied his good judgment every step of the way.

Jeff Lyon applied his considerable editing skills, and photographer Terrence James contributed stellar portraits of Nelle, Alice, and their community. My good friend and former colleague Julia Keller, author of several books, was an invaluable source of insight and help from the beginning.

The article my *Tribune* editors helped guide to publication ended up being the catalyst for this book.

The women of my writing group in Oak Park have my deepest gratitude. Each of them offered her own valuable perspective and specific suggestions for improving the book. They supplied the camaraderie that sustained me every week. I'm indebted to Elizabeth Berg, Veronica Chapa, Arlene Malinowski, Pam Todd, and Michele Weldon. I cherish their wisdom and friendship.

I'm grateful to the doctors who have seen me through this experience with unusual skill and compassion.

My mother, Carla Mills, was my partner in this book, a tireless researcher, wise sounding board, unofficial editor, and frequent fellow traveler, if one whose dubious sense of direction rivals my own. A retired editor, she blended professionalism and good sense with the natural empathy and humor that endear her to others. She has been an irreplaceable source of suggestions and solutions, solace and celebration. This was a journey we took together and I was privileged to have the finest travel companion.

My father died in 2011, knowing the book he had championed was slowly taking shape. For ten years he'd been intrigued by my good fortune in getting to know the Lees, always encouraging me to savor the friendship, to hold dear what I learned about their town, and to cherish a novel that epitomized everything he valued as an attorney.

We had celebrated the Penguin Press's acquisition of the manuscript just a few months before his unexpected passing. All his life, he had that "spark of fresh adventure" in his eyes—as Scout says of Jem in the novel—and it remains a source of joy and inspiration, as are the nearly fifty years of my parents' marriage.

My frame of reference in understanding Monroeville was my father's hometown of Black River Falls, Wisconsin. It was as if my grandfather, Tom Mills, had slipped a key into my pocket that opened the door to quick rapport with Alice and Nelle. He and Alice were born a year apart and shared a strikingly similar sensibility. He died in 1999, but his spirit and values infuse this book and my time with the Lees.

My appreciation of small town life, in all its humanity and humor, began in Black River Falls and extended to Monroeville, also a county seat in a lower-income area. I extend my thanks for the insight and understanding of my relatives and friends: Gene and Janet Krohn, Gil and the late Alice Homstad, Ann and Waldo Peterson, and Tom and Sally Lister.

For their patience and support, I send affectionate thanks as well to my brother, Mark John, and his sons, Thomas and Andrew, in Minnesota.